London Babylon

The Beatles and The Stones

In the Swinging 60s

By Steve Overbury

To Bruce
from
Steve
July 2010

ISBN 978-0-9564084-0-2

Published by Stephen Overbury

Each noble reader, whether they have bought this book or not, is entitled to a pdf of the two 'missing' chapters. The first concerns 'Professor' Bruce Lacey - robot builder and possibly the model for Doctor Who; and the second is about Pauline Boty, the only contemporary female British practitioner of Pop art.

Email Steve@londonbabylon.co.uk

About the Author

Now a writer, Steve has also been a record company staffer, a recording engineer, a band manager, a graphic designer, a pig farmer, a fishmonger and Joan Collins' chauffeur.

He lives in South London with his wife Jane and two daughters Lucy and Jess.

Steve's first book Guns, Cash and Rock 'n' Roll: The Managers was published in 2007.
www.gunscashandrocknroll.co.uk

Acknowledgements

Thanks to the first draft readers Mark, Andy, Doog and Tony.
Also to Tom Pollock

CONTENTS

"Right now, London has something that New York used to have: everybody wants to be there. There's no place else. Paris is calcified. There's an indefinable thing about London that makes people want to go there".

Robert Fraser - Art dealer to the stars

London was always a dark place often full of foreign tribes. During the second war, it had been an interzone where off duty squaddies whored, drank and scrapped with the flash GI's, the Canadians, the free French, Poles, Czechs, exiled Italians and, when the obvious enemies ran out, each other; the Military Police patrolling Soho happily cracked heads alongside the Soho bobbies, the bleeding soldiers carted off in ambulance, jeep or Black Maria. When the troops caught their trains home waving goodbye to sobbing girls clutching buns in the oven, the city night time was given over to the gangsters, spivs, queers, Teddy boys, Maltese pimps and prostitutes, who conspired in the jazz clubs, coffee bars, street corners and pubs and got on with business: trading pills, cigarettes, petrol and teenagers.

In the Notting Hill ghettos, the blacks moved in next door to the Irish; the Irish laid the tarmac and dug the tubes; the blacks drove the red buses and the silver tube trains.

Just the other side of Hyde Park, in the Royal Borough of Kensington and Chelsea, the upper classes as ever grappled with the weighty business of running other countries, finding an abortionist for the up-the-duff au pair and searching out a decent claret to go with the

Chateaubriand. For their sons and daughters there were the usual dull distractions - deb's balls, house parties and messing about with horses. They thought they were having fun.

Then came pop.

The capital's stately radiograms and tinny transistors began crackling with vulgar clarion calls from the country's distant northern provinces, and from as close as the capital city's own wild borders. If Londoners had put their ears to the ground and listened they might have heard the gathering sound of the footloose heading to town, an itinerant influx that would soon turn the old order on its head.

With the Beatles and the Stones there came light. Along for the ride came fandom and fashion, hair and rebellion. The city began to glow, the big magnet turned on and anyone who could walk went downtown.

Prior to the invasion of the pop groups, their groupies and minions, the rich kids of London 'scene' was a small set of buttoned up junior aristocrats, old Etonians and debutantes, all well bred, well fed, rich, refined and beautiful; they flitted between each other's mews flats and crumbling country piles. They dressed like their mums and dads; they voted Conservative and listened to big bands and jazz.

The early 60s British bands came to London in order to conquer the UK before taking a crack at the USA, but first they had to conquer London itself. They needed what only the big city could give them - record deals, money, clothes and all that goes with it, glory, glamour and girls. They marched in, plugged in their amps, made a load of noise and took control. It was a bloodless coup, more a conversion than a battle and the masses dutifully fell in adoration. Even the spawn of the grandees of Kensington and Chelsea prostrated themselves before the noisy horde of arrivistes who became the new lords of a city that was beginning to swing. The blue bloods had unwittingly opened the door to a rag tag pack of ruffians that had crashed the party without an invitation, pulled all the birds and showed no sign of leaving.

Pop stars.

Feted by labourers and Ladies, debutantes, and dope dealers alike, these self appointed aristocrats had the keys to the city and their Bentleys parked outside. They dominated London's clubs and its haunts and when they returned from their tours at home or abroad it was to new homes in London; the provinces were only for visiting now; they had lost their allure. They'd come to London to seek their fortunes and now those with fortunes sought them. They were cheeky, charismatic, sexy, rich and irresistible. They were the flames to which the moths of Kensington and Chelsea were drawn; and at the centre of them all, where the fires burned brightest, were Mick, Keith and Brian, Paul, John and George. If you added special guests Jimi Hendrix, Eric Burdon and Keith Moon to this heady mix then turned up the heat to 11, you had the nucleus of Swinging London.

Rock's Rat Pack.

And like Sinatra's Rat Pack they amassed 'friends', the bit part players and hangers on, sniffing for flash and cash, the pilot fish that pick the bits from the skins of sharks: car dealers, dope dealers and thieves, madmen, wastrels and scoundrels, losers, romantic fools, sex kittens and killers, torturers, millionaires and bum boys.

There is a theory that the phenomenon known as Swinging London was basically a tight group of about a hundred people radiating around the same two bands, the same few clubs, some choice restaurants and each other's beds, with perhaps occasional trips to the Kings Road to pick up more drugs, a couple of bottles of Mateus Rose and some fags. The bands had money, style and pretension in abundance. They were anti establishment and yet at the same time they were soon buying up all the mansions in the establishment's heartland. Chelsea's Cheyne Walk began to resemble Stella Street with Mick living at one end and Keith at the other and assorted exotic riff raff in between, oh and Pink Floyd recording just around the corner.

There was a long tradition of exotics graduating toward the area: Oscar Wilde had lived in Tite Street; Dante Gabriel Rossetti had once lived at 16 Cheyne Walk, near to Keith's six story townhouse and the same house where friend to the Stones, Paul Getty later lived. Rossetti suffered sharing the capacious mansion with a suicidal sado masochistic poet, some armadillos, a couple of kangaroos, two barn owls and a wombat named "Top", which was often allowed to sleep in the middle of the dinner table during meals, and was said to be the inspiration for the dormouse in *Alice's Adventures in Wonderland.*
Paul Getty, once one of the golden ones, just suffered 15 years of panic and lonely, suicidal gloom.

Liverpool, Manchester, Newcastle, Birmingham and the Dartford Delta. In the 60s, these great cities (and Dartford) produced some world-class musical talent, The Beatles, The Bee Gees, The Hollies, Herman and the Hermits, The Animals, half of Led Zeppelin and The Move, were all from the northern provinces. Jeff Beck, Jimi Page, Pink Floyd and Clapton sprung from the southern shires. The Rolling Stones, Rod Stewart, Bowie and the Who drew from the city's edge; Jimi Hendrix came from the skies. But from whatever point of the compass, they all headed for town, the Smoke; they'd seen it in the movies.

The record companies and agents were there; it was where the recording studios and producers were based, the TV and radio stations, the PR men and pluggers: London was where the movers and shakers hung out in the hip new clubs, where all the rock and roll roads, rails and airways led. The musical talent of the nation had no choice; sooner or later it found its way to the city, from whence it could take on fresh supplies before sallying forth to spread the word

to a fevered world, that its rock and pop capital was now London.

This is the 60s: London's Belle Epoch.

Two hundred years earlier, the Industrial Revolution had happened first in Britain, its effects rippling out across the world, and there are a thousand theories about why that should have been so, why it happened here and nowhere else. It led to Empire then war and austerity. But you couldn't keep the old bulldog down and as soon as the rationing ended, the party began. The Rock Revolution made its thunderous impression first in London, a corner of the planet where life was changing faster, more radically, more brutally even, than anywhere else. It accompanied a social revolution, which was anti authority in its nature. Army conscription had just finished; teenagers had money, leisure time, transport and big new hedonistic ideas. Like the opening sequence of Cliff Richard's *Summer Holiday*, the world turned from monochrome to Technicolor.

Way back in the twelfth century, a section of London Wall was known as *Babeylone* but it was in the nineteenth century that Prime Minster Disraeli dubbed London 'a modern Babylon' and Henry James called it 'this murky Babylon', all long before Kenneth Anger appropriated Babylon for the title of his scandal-packed book about Hollywood. Indeed the 1860s have a familair ring of hedonism about them; it was a decade of bare fist fighting, wars over opium, the first package holidays, colour photographs, music hall, football and cross class debauchery.

The past ran into the future: in 1868 the last public execution took place at Newgate gaol; however the first London Underground trains had started rolling five years earlier in 1863 and were routinely hauling huge numbers of Londoners to work; the first mass commuters. To witness the hanging - this special event, the public snapping of a neck - clerks and tailors, drunks, thieves and children alighted the tube trains at the new Farringdon station, walked down Chancery Lane to Newgate, and crowded the prison yard, to sing *Rule Brittania* and *Champagne Charlie* as the body of Michael Barrett, an alleged Irish Republican bomber dropped, before resuming their rowdy journeys home. Barrett was likely innocent.

A century later, everything yet nothing had changed and the mansions of London still creaked with unusual sex, drug-taking, drinking, gambling and all the other earthly delights, sins that as ever were shadowed by abortion, addiction, the clap, debt, destitution and death.

While Kenneth Anger's *Hollywood Babylon* had the great movie studios of West Hollywood as its backdrop, *London Babylon* has the great music studios and Tin Pan Alley dives of West London. Where Hollywood erected great edifices and facades under the Californian sun, the British music business built invisible soundscapes under London's leaden skies.

Away from the studios, the real action in both these famous pleasure towns took place in the cafes and pubs of Chelsea and Soho or the back rooms of the London clubs; across the pond it was in the cocktail bars of Sunset Strip, the houses in the hills or sleazy LA motels. Peel back the front walls of the drawing rooms and bedrooms of the mansions of the capital and it was like *Hollywood Babylon* but with a soundtrack. A trip round London's rock spots is the British equivalent of the Hollywood homes of the stars tour. McCartney was married here; Jimi choked there.

In *London Babylon* there was sex, lots of sex, there were drugs, lorry loads of drugs but there was also the best rock music the world has ever known.

With the death of the stocking the hemlines got shocking. Flash back to 1965, a mythic time of mini skirts, Mini Mokes and marijuana. Was it real? Or was it all just a rag-trade con? Whatever it was, from across the Atlantic the Americans were watching. The expression 'Swinging London' first appeared in an article in Time magazine.

"Ancient elegance and a new opulence are all tangled up in a dazzling blur of op and pop".

Time magazine April 15th 1966.

While the British bands went west, many excited American kids came east. The word was out on the international grapevine. Some said go to London, take drugs and get laid; others heard that as well as pills, pop music and dolly birds there was something astonishing going on.

And it wasn't just incoming Yanks; there were Australian smart arses, Italian film directors and Japanese performance artists clogging up the airport lounges.

Was Swinging London real? Perhaps it's only outsiders who believed it existed or wanted it to exist or who willed it into existence, that where Londoners saw only drudge and dirt in the gutters, others were dazzled by streets paved with gold and the whiff of love in the air.

Oz magazine writer David Widgery frequently used to argue that Swinging London was all a hoax but the Oz artist Martin Sharp who created some of that magazine's most memorable and psychedelic covers (as well as sleeves for Cream) was outraged and threatened to resign "because he thought Swinging London was so wonderful."

Perhaps it takes outsiders to see what the cynical British hacks couldn't, that London in the 60s, full of musicians, actors, artists, dancers and style tribes, was crackling with ideas and ideals. Not since the Romans had it seen such incandescence - a shimmering city of dreams next to the dirty old river.

Camelot-on-Thames.

Whether it existed then or not, Swinging London does now. It has entered the popular mythology and for years to come, perhaps hundreds of years to come, outsiders will flock to the capital city's stately streets and dark alleyways in search of a half remembered time, a dream world, some golden youth; beautiful history.

London Babylon

1

Edith Grove

JAGGER stood on the foot-high stage at the Ricky Tick singing and shaking his head to the music because there wasn't enough room to dance. He looked around the room at the sweating audience in front of him trying to pick out a girl to take him home while ignoring his mini-skirt-and-mascara girlfriend Chrissie Shrimpton. Then he started wondering, 'Who are these people?'.

Over there were the earnest rhythm and blues fans - nutters – short hair, white shirts, narrow ties and mad eyes, a few in daringly new black crew necks. This tribe had started calling themselves Mods. They dug Ray Charles and Long John Baldrey but they also liked Chuck Berry who was sort of more rock 'n' roll. Mick and Keith loved Chuck almost as much as Chuck did. Their girls were doing a new dance they called 'the Shake'.

The Mods always looked like they were about to start trouble but they hadn't so far. "Maybe that's because they're enjoying our music too much", mused Jagger, "or maybe it's because they're all scared of Stu". Stu was Ian Stewart, the Stones hulking piano player who stood head and shoulders above Jagger and looked like he could throw his piano across the room, although he wasn't as big as Mr.

Hammersmith (later known as Andy from the Sixties) who really could.

It was rumoured that Andy from the Sixties could squat press a grand piano even when he was fifty-six years old. But he was no ordinary muscle man having read the works of Wittgenstein and other philosophers when he had been doing an eight-year stretch in Maidstone prison. His favourite story was about how he used to get amphetamines and rent boys for Brian Epstein. He would encourage the boys to steal things from Epstein's beautiful Georgian house at 24 Chapel Street, Belgravia, which is in the exclusive embassy district of London, and there were many desirable things to steal. Brian's guests would eat from ceremonial silver tableware glittering with white gold.

There were subtly exquisite pictures on the walls including two life-size photo portraits of him taken by David Bailey. He maintained a staff befitting a junior royal and his dinner parties became legend. For example, he would pay scrupulous attention to his guest's likes and dislikes, observing what brand of cigarettes they smoked, and ensuring that that particular brand was by the side of their plate at dinner. When George Martin was married to Julia Lockhart-Smith; to mark the celebrations, Brian arranged to have silver monogrammed napkin rings by each guest's plate, carrying the letter 'M'.

But Andy from the Sixties wasn't a Fagin, his boys would steal the stuff while the poor troubled Epstein was in the same room hiding behind the sofa, watching the crime go down live and getting off on it. Later the boys were apprehended on the stairs by Brian's manservant Antonio and would have to sheepishly hand their spoils back to their owner; however one of them got away with a test pressing of *Penny Lane/Strawberry Fields*. Shortly afterwards 'Brian Epstein is a queer' was scrawled on the garage door in lipstick.

Excerpt from Old and New London Chapter 5 by Edward Walford 1878 which describes the Belgravia area and some of its characters in the period just before it was developed:

"Through a cabbage-plot to a tavern known by the agreeable name of 'The Monster.' Beyond this came an embankment called the Willow Walk (a convenient place for quiet murder); and at one end of this lived that eminent public character, Mr. William Aberfield, generally known to the sporting peers, thieves, and dog-fanciers of the Regency as 'Slender Billy.' Mr. Grantley Berkeley once had the honour of making this gentleman's acquaintance, and visited his house to see the great Spanish monkey 'Mukako' ('Muchacho') fight Tom Cribb's dogs, and cut their throats one after the other—apparently, at least—for the 'gentleman' who really bled the dogs and the peers was Mr. Cribb himself, who had a lancet hidden in his hand, with which, under the pretence of rendering the bitten and bruised dogs help, he contrived, in a frank and friendly way, to open the jugular vein. A good many of the Prince Regent's friends were Slender Billy's also. Mr. Slender Billy died, however, much more regretted than the Regent, being a most useful and trusty member of a gang of forgers."

Jagger spotted Andrew Oldham's rusty hair and dark glasses in the crowd; here for the second time and tonight he's bought that head-case pill-popper friend of his Peter Meaden. They were both Mods as well, but edgier than the others, more stylish, first division. The other Mods looked up to them. Meaden and Oldham would call people 'baby' like they were black hep-cats in a 40s big band. Oldham wanted to manage the Stones but he was younger than they were and it would mean the band would have to kick out Giorgio Gomelsky who thought he was their manager. Mick didn't mind ousting Giorgio; it was just that Giorgio ran the club and they might lose this gig if they sacked him, and it was a good scene here if a bit small.

And what could a kid like Oldham do for them anyway? They needed a record deal and Oldham wasn't even old enough to sign a contract. Mind you, Keith liked him, he reckoned Andrew was a supersonic bullshitter and should be given a go. He'd have to ask Brian Jones what he thought after the gig. But to do that he'd have to try and avoid the inevitable row with Chrissie who was staring daggers at him because he was eyeing up the girls again.

Andrew smiled at Mick who smiled tenderly back but then Mick started scanning the room again as did Andrew. They were *both* wondering who the Stones audience were. Stage right stood a bunch of blues fans – hardcore purists who could just about tolerate mingling with the old-style jazz fans with their scraggly beards wet with Watneys Pale Ale and who at the end of the evening obediently put their pint pots back on the bar and collected their duffel coats from the cloakroom. Both these tribes were only grudgingly enjoying themselves, where they considered anything written since the war non-authentic. Both these tribes wished that they were black, poor and oppressed.

Over there were some Trad Jazz types who, looking a little embarrassed and not quite sure what they were doing here, had impeded Chrissie's view of the stage. They'd *really* transcended the rigid rules of modern musical taste and its complex mores because most of London was Trad Jazz at that time, all *Stranger on the Shore* and stripy waistcoats. *Their* usual fare was highly rehearsed Dixieland numbers involving clarinets and tubas, but they definitely liked what they were hearing tonight in the Crawdaddy; they just couldn't help themselves. This blues, rhythm and blues or rock and roll, whatever it's damn well called is just great. These Rollin' Stones are just great.

Chrissie Shrimpton wasn't tall but she made her presence felt all right. She barged right through the self-conscious boys and regained her vantage point. One time at the Ricky Tick, she'd climbed up on to a table and then clambered up into a load of fishnets that hung over the room and crawled her way towards the stage above the crowd, some of whom helped her by pushing her up and paddling her along with their hands – crowd surfing. 'Stupid girl,' thought Jagger.

And so the music listening tribes of London gathered to hear this big new thing. There was even a rocker or two keeping a low profile, leather jackets hidden in the hedge outside, bikes parked round the corner, marked out by their gum chewing girlfriends, since girls were, so far at least, thin on the ground in this club. Chicks like that didn't interest Mick.

He liked them posh.

Teddy boys had been rock 'n' roll fans too but there weren't any of them here tonight, not unless they'd dumped their uniform drape coats and combed down their bobbing quiffs which is quite possible because Teds had become a dying species. The times, they-were-a-changing. The original 50s Teds wouldn't have ever quite got the Rollin' Stones. Brian Jones's leering stare and fuck-me-fringe would have enraged them. They might have got lairy and busted the place up a bit, like in the glory days when *Rock Around the Clock* was in the charts and *Jailhouse Rock* was in the cinema.

'ROCK 'N' ROLL, 400 RIOT IN CINEMA yelped the headline of the Daily Sketch in 1956. Ringo had been a Ted, John even, however despite determinedly hanging on to their quiffs for a short while when they first went to Hamburg, in their second fashion phase, they'd enthusiastically jumped at the chance to don leathers and drag on a pair of drainpipes before they changed again when they became moptops.

And among the jazzers, bluesers and proto Mods, keeping an even lower profile than the rockers was a smattering of genuine all-English, old Etonians and Harrovians, aspirant bohemians who found that their blue blood had been boiled by the rhythm and blues grind. Was that really the Marquis of Londonderry shyly lurking over near the bar all sweaty under that chunky roll neck sweater?

A few months later Mick looked around the room again, Andrew was at the helm and the Beatles were in the room. The world changed.

War babies, full of great expectations, packed with potential and all sexed up. Young dumb and full of cum, except they weren't so dumb, at least half the room had been to a university and it looked like the rest were art students; they were full of big ideas. This was the first generation in nearly forty years that hadn't been scared of the future. It was like the London fog had lifted. It was the 60s but it could have been Year Zero.

Back from the gig, the sweat barely dry on his skin, the libido pumped, steaming from the girl action, the ego hyped by all the back stage flummery and … the chicks man, the chicks! Of course Brian thinks he's the stud of the band, prancing like some Palamino stallion on heat. And all those bastard kids he's got, all those unmarried mums. Brian's impish grin with its sardonic twist, Brian's leering eyes, his way with words, his musicianship. He reckoned he could have any girl he liked and play any instrument he liked and dammit most of the time he could. Mick had plenty to say about the band, life in the mid 60s and the youth of today, but Brian's pronouncements were off pat, slick, easy, and more often than not, the reporters' microphones were held under his nose rather than Jagger's. Brian seemed like the man with the plan and as he so elegantly espoused, the plan was to play music, get famous and have huge amounts of sex. Mick naturally approved but he wasn't gonna show it and he wasn't gonna be outclassed; he had to get his schtick together.

102 Edith Grove – what a dump. It was right down the wrong end of the King's Road and round the corner. OK, it was a place to lay his head, preferably next to someone else's; it was a place for Keith and Brian to work up the act and there was enough space for Mick to practice his dance steps, experiment with his make-up and try on some of Chrissie's clothes much to John Lennon's horror who, when he popped round the other night, witnessed some strutting and swirling skirts and became all hoity toity. Lennon asked if Mick was wearing her pants man, acting all worldly, acting like he wouldn't have wanted to put her pants on. Although you have to give Lennon some respect, after all he had worked Hamburg's sleazy strip clubs and drag bars and he'd definitely seen some sights, but even so he acted as shocked as some old matron - dead straight really.

Edith Grove: this end of the street just wasn't trendy despite Chelsea's glamorous restaurants being just a short walk up the road, so close in fact, you could almost smell the foie gras, hear the chinking glasses and the tinkling laughter; but they may as well have been on the moon. Instead of foie gras, what you *could* smell was the stinking gasworks down the road, rotting food in the kitchen bin, dirty clothes and the bucket-full of cigarette ends that sat in the middle of the room. Mick couldn't wait to get on and get out. Him and Keith had only moved in with Brian to help him out with the rent and avoid having to drive all the way back to Dartford in his dad's car every night knackered from the gig. And he couldn't take birds back to Dartford… not that any of them would want to go anyway.

You needed money to live in Chelsea, even down in Edith Grove but he was skint all the time and that was because him, Keith and Brian were all pretty much living on his student grant, which meant constant starvation, apart from those times when they received an occasional food parcel from either Keith's mum or Bill's mum. Brian seemed to live on sandwich-spread and steak and kidney pies. Mick used to turn up with a Vesta Chow Mein packet meal now and again; a taste of the east, and he'd be lucky to get a mouthful. The flat was unbelievably squalid – all boys together, no one cooking, no one cleaning, having to lug your stage clothes up the road to a laundromat. There was never any money. Where was all the money?

You had to remember to come home with a pocket-full of shillings to keep the meter fed otherwise none of the amps would work, the heaters would go off and you'd be freezing. Chrissie hated the place too and who could blame her? But Keith was in paradise; he had everything he needed and was quite happy sitting in the cold playing guitar with Brian all day long, stealing milk from the neighbour's doorstep for his cups of tea and living on chips and pickled eggs from Johnny's Fish Bar around the corner; that is when he wasn't having it off with the Sheffield chicks who lived downstairs.

Oh how Jagger yearned to be up the other end of the King's Road or in the middle at least, amongst the mink and the Rolls Royces. He'd felt ridiculous, like a little boy with his face up against the sweet shop window when he'd looked into Alvaro's restaurant the other night and seen Bridget Bardot on one table and Princess Margaret on another.

Alvaro's, outside which John Barry, who while he was working on the music for *Thunderball*, sat in his E-type Jag fiddling with the gear stick transfixed by the antics of his future wife, the elfin Jane Birkin,  who sprawled across the car's long bonnet and cooed sweet nothings at him through the windscreen; Jane Birkin who played one of the models in *Blow Up* and who would provide orgasmic vocals for *Je t'aime... moi non plus.*

Andrew Oldham and his co-manager partner Eric Easton had taken the band to some groovy places in Soho, like the Trattoria Terrazza which had garlic in the food, plastic grapes hanging overhead and candles in the Chianti bottles, but it was demeaning having Eric always pay the bill at the end of the evening and Mick having to ask him if he could have another glass of wine please like he was your dad or something. And it was the band's money; Eric was buying the brandies and the cigars with the band's money! Mick hadn't needed to be an economics student to figure out that an advance was something you had to pay back. Eric should have been asking *them* if *he* could have a drink.

Keith just laughed at Mick's petit bourgeois aspirations, the tidiness of his room, the neatly folded clothes and the way he would hide his food from the others. Of course Keith wanted money too but every time he got hold of some he'd just catch the bus up to Denmark Street and buy another guitar.

Where is all the money?

Earlier, there had been the usual row with the Shrimp's sister. She wanted to go on to the Scene tonight with all her girrrlfriends. She knew he had a show to do tomorrow but still she'd gone and left him in the Edith Grove dump.

And he's all hot; he's on fire.

He wants… he needs her home right now and he gets angry but then he gives in and telephones the club; he tells her he'll pick up the bill for the champagne providing she's home by 3am. That's a good tactic, that's neat. He smiled. 'Then it's down to me' he thought watching the clock.

Sometimes Chrissie would fly into a rage and then she'd lash out, fists flying. He wanted to hit her back but he never did. You can't hit women even if they hit you first. Well there was that time when he'd had a few too may whiskies, when she *says* he hit her. He thinks he just punched the wall and hurt his hand but even if he had hit her, then man she definitely deserved it.

Do you ever feel like you're on camera; every move being watched by an invisible film crew? Well he did all the time. That's why he decided to treat his life like a movie – a movie starring him. He could have had ten different girls back here tonight. Brian's got two in there now; Mick knew he had, he could hear the dirty bastard, hear him him mumbling, hear them giggling. Couldn't Brian spare just one of them or maybe even better share both of them? Should he go in there? Get in bed with Brian and the girls? Naaah just wait for Chrissie. Mix a Scotch and Coke. No ice, cos there's no fridge. Fuck

Lennon offering us fifty quid to buy a fridge. He never carries any money anyway; he acts like he's the Queen or something.

Chrissie and Mick had met when she'd put an ad in the newspaper for a cleaner and up turned Mick applying for the job. He'd been

cleaning flats for pocket money when he was at the LSE, and then when he'd become her maid she'd fallen in love with him. Well that's the story told by Andy Warhol's friend Nicky Haslam the old Etonian interior designer. Nicky's textile merchant father had been the mayor of Bolton and his mother was Queen Victoria's goddaughter. Nicky, dubbed 'Ponsonby Hasbeen' in Ossie Clark's diaries, was just the type to fit in with the network of friends Warhol was amassing; he was gay, urbane and a wicked gossip-monger. He claims he'd kept telling Chrissie that Mick was awful looking and that she should raise her sights but then she'd just reply, "Not really".

And even now that Mick had stopped doing her cleaning and was a bona fide rock star she still thought she was in the driving seat. Well, not for much longer. Model. He could get any model anytime; he could get himself a countess to do a private fashion show if he wanted to. He could probably get his hands on her super model sister Jean if he really tried: steal her away from David Bailey.

Sexy; sexy and posh; he liked 'em posh all right. Why was that? Was it climbing the social ladder by sexual conquest – another high-class notch on the bedpost, another rung on the ladder? Was it that having got the knickers off one of *Debrett's* debutantes, nothing else would do? It was like he was doing it for a bet, like when they'd been young boys back home in the wrong part of Kent, born on the wrong side of the tracks, like something from a Thomas Hardy novel. 'Bet you can't lay the squire's daughter'. 'Bet you I can'. And in time he did bag himself an aristocrat of course, when Marianne Faithfull, the daughter of the Austrian Baroness Erisso fluttered her eye lashes at him.

Soon they were all at it: Peter Sellers married Lord Mancroft's stepdaughter Miranda Quarry (after a fling with Princess Margaret); Eric Clapton lived with Lord Harlech's daughter, Alice Ormsby-Gore (they both got massive heroin habits and she overdosed and died in the 90s); Georgie Fame met Nicolette Powell, who'd left her husband, the 9th Marquess of Londonderry for Georgie, (she committed suicide by jumping off Clifton Suspension Bridge in the 90s). And, although he had bedded plenty of blue bloods, Bill Wyman didn't marry one; he'd had to content himself with becoming one when he acquired Gedding Hall in Suffolk and with it the title Lord of the Manor of Gedding and Thormwood.

McCartney, the one who everyone watched, fell for Jane Asher who, though she lacked a title was definitely a toff; she had an aunt

with a house in Westminster who had a uniformed maid who served afternoon tea and cucumber sandwiches. Another aunt had a manor in the country with dogs, horses and a wood-panelled library although Asher, the daughter of a doctor and a professor of music, lived in London's Wimpole Street W1 right near the exclusive Harley Street. McCartney hadn't been slow to realise you didn't find many pale-skinned goddesses like Asher around the Liverpool Pier Head.

Sexual intercourse began
In nineteen sixty-three
(Which was rather late for me)
Between the end of the Chatterley ban
And the Beatles' first LP.
Philip Larkin, 'Annus Mirabilis'

Nineteen sixty-three was the year the Beatles moved to London. They, at first, resisted moving to 'the Smoke', they thought they could make it up north or in northern Germany but resistance was useless and the old Commer van was soon heading south loaded up with fab gear.

They did the sights and the guitar shops and as soon as they had a spare evening, dressed up in matching long black suede coats and caps and went to Richmond to see the Stones. That was the night that a starstruck Jagger decided to abandon the blues and take up rock 'n'roll; it was the night he started calling the Beatles, 'the four headed monster'.

The 'monster' was instantly the toast of the town; not only with their fans and other bands, but with photographers, writers, gangsters, satirists, artists, theatricals - McCartney talks about going to parties with Harold Pinter, Kenneth Williams, Ken Tynan, Jill Bennett, John and Penelope Mortimer, John Schlesinger, Ned Sherrin and Maggie Smith, the crème de la crème of theatre and film plus some royalty.

A favoured Beatle restaurant was Parkes on Beauchamp Place where the Liverpudlian owner first introduced the band to exotica like oysters, avacados and bamboo shoots, but as swinging as London was becoming, there were as yet still no all-night restaurants, so when the band was hungry after a concert in the wee small hours, they would drive out to Heathrow airport where they would meet up with other bands in the airport café.

However there were a very few exclusive clubs which were good for a late night meal, if you could afford it: the Blue Angel in Berkeley Street, the Hawaiian bar at the Mayfair Hotel, Annabel's in Berkeley Square. McCartney was doing the whole man-about-town routine, phoning ahead to make sure the lackeys were at the door ready, awaiting his arrival, vibed up. In the small hours it would be the casinos: the Cromwellian in Kensington and the Curzon House, where he might run into Brian Epstein running out of cash and trading his Dunhill lighter, his Rolex or his cufflinks for a bet. Paul was having a ball as he told the writer Barry Miles: "I could get into these clubs with my fame. I could afford them and I could give good tips. What more do you want man?"

Then the Ad Lib opened at 7 Leicester Place and everyone turned up - the Beatles and the Stones, the Hollies and the Moody Blues. Is that London's most eligible bachelor Paul McCartney over there in the shadows listening to grande dame gender bender April Ashley telling him tall tales?

A couple of miles west of the bright lights, Jagger and Chrissie were moving into their flat at 13a Bryanston Mews East; it was Mick's flat really but Chrissie never went back to her own if she could help it, a change from the Edith Grove days. It stood behind a big stucco-fronted house with Ionic columns in Bryanston Square and the flat was small and inauspicious by comparison but it was in a mews and that was definitely groovy.

London's mews houses, originally stable buildings converted into bijou little apartments after the advent of the motorcar, stood at the rear of London's great houses either side of narrow cobble-stoned streets, and had become synonymous with jet-setting bachelors, bohemians and celebrities. Michael Caine, Agatha Christie, James Hunt, Jacqueline du Pré, Peter Cook, Mandy Rice Davis, Jacob Epstein and Christine Keeler had all been mews dwellers at some time or other. Keeler's friend Stephen Ward, the socialite who introduced her to John Profumo, the Secretary of State for War, thus causing a national scandal, had a flat in Wimpole Mews equipped with two way mirrors to facilitate lubricity. A mews was a place to see a Morgan sports car full of rugby kit outside a young doctor's house and to catch leggy models tip toeing home in the early morning mist with smeared make up and messed up coiffures, carrying their shoes. The mews cottage is much beloved by American fim makers for whom it defines elegant London living.

Brian Jones was a frequent visitor to the Jagger's mews back in the days before he became persona non-gratis. Once, he'd bought a guy called Spike with him who was a big time Stones fan and a friend of the velvet trouser-splitting P.J. Proby (There's a place for us/Some-uh-where/A place for us). According to Kim Fowley, the eccentric music producer who alleges he was involved in managing Proby at the time (as had drug smuggler Howard Marks at some point… well, according to Howard that is), Mick and Keith had been indulging in a bit of horseplay and had shaved Spike's head, an act which for some reason enraged Proby to the extent that he sent word that he was going to get Chrissie into his bed as revenge. Fowley further alleges that Proby successfully pulled off the dirty deed which, if true, undoubtedly made Proby and Jagger's already troubled relationship just a little more strained, especially when Proby put the word out that Jagger wasn't too well endowed. However there is a legendary clip from the film *Performance* that was left on the cutting room floor showing Mick letting it all hang out which is clear evidence to the contrary.

A legendary insomniac, P. J. Proby often threw wild sixteen-hour parties in his Chelsea home where any night of the week you might see a smashed John Lennon throwing up in the toilet while a clutch of pilled up, half dressed aristos writhed on the bed in the next room.

P.J. would be slinging back Jack Daniels and firing his .45 revolver into a wildebeest head that hung above him on the wall, egged on by the crazies with whom he shared the house. The merry bunch of pranksters included Kim Fowley and Proby's best friend Bongo Wolf, the disabled son of a dentist who would frequently wear porcelain werewolf fangs. Bongo, who can be seen lugging a virgin upstairs in *The Body Beneath*, a hippie horror exploitation movie made in 1972, accompanied PJ on the road and apparently inspired much of PJ's madness, that is before he was kidnapped by his own drug dealer and carted off to America - last heard of somewhere in Louisiana.

It seems Proby may have talked up his sexual prowess, or so suggested his long-term lover Billie Davis who, when she eventually abandoned Proby, choked to the press. The very attractive Davis had been only 18 when she had a top ten hit with *Tell Him* and had been swept off on a tour with the Beatles; the red blooded Beatles had taken bets about who would get to have her first; it isn't recorded which, if any of them won.

About Proby, she told the salivating newspapermen "In the time that we dated he had one erection. It lasted three hours. He was so pleased that he spent the whole night smiling at it. I didn't get a look in". Proby often claimed that he could never be the father of all the kids that he was so often accused of siring because he had become sterile at the age of seven. Perhaps this could be attributed to the fact that as a child he used to play in a prison electric chair that his grandfather, the prison governor, used to strap him into. "A shame they didn't turn it on", said another ex-wife.

After his Chelsea period, P.J. went to live in Hollywood for a while and was one night drinking in a bar when someone informed him his house had just exploded (the reasons for the explosion are unclear). "I took the pay phone and called my neighbour, Bobby Darin. I said: 'Robert, will you look out and see if my house is still there, please?' He said: 'No, it sure isn't, Jim. Lots of fire engines, but no house.'"

In the crazy stakes, PJ definitely blazed a trail. He had been variously deported, attacked his secretary with an axe, had been accused of shooting his wife, was regularly declared bankrupt, became a shepherd in the Pennines, died of alcoholic shock (and was resuscitated) and now makes a living performing in clubs around the country whilst he resides on a roundabout near Evesham in Worcestershire. At a historic gig at Fagin's in Manchester in the late 80s he had left the stage after half an hour telling the audience "I'm sorry. I cannot go on. I am suffering from gonorrhoea".

Despite Chrissie and Mick's stormy relationship, the interference of P.J. Proby and Mick's embarrassment that she had taken a job writing a column called *From London With Love* for the American teen magazine *Tiger Beat*, Mick had been happy enough to give Chrissie a little white Austin Mini as a coming-back-from-tour present. Later in the year Brian Jones bought a Rolls Royce with its dancing-with-the-devil number plate DD 666.

Mick had thrown a party just after Christmas and John, George and Ringo had come round which had certainly impressed the other guests especially Robert Fraser the art gallery owner with whom Mick had become friends. Having one Beatle at your party was truly special, a mark that you were really at the centre of something - one of the in-crowd - but having three of the four of them there was exceptional. It put Jagger into the epicentre. He wasn't just one of the in-crowd now, he was one of the leaders of the pack.

To get to Mick's party, Ringo hadn't had to travel far because he and his 19 year old girlfriend Maureen Cox, (they had been together since the Cavern days), had just moved in around the corner at 34 Montagu Square right by a bright red post box. (Later in the year he would be photographed on the doorstep with his newborn son Zak). Ringo and Maureen could have easily walked back home from the party in three minutes but instead the Starrs drove there in Ringo's exotic new Italian Facel Vega; it was his first car, he'd only just passed his test at the age of 25. Ringo acknowledged to the press that although he could afford the car he couldn't spell it.

The other Beatles and their manager were also acquiring or had acquired new cars partly because Brian Eptein had gone into partnership with a car dealers out in Hounslow, which he used as a cheap way of keeping his fleet up to date and as a source of cash at a time when his gambling debts were running at £5,000 a week and he was too embarrassed to admit the losses to his own office. Epstein acquired a silver Bentley convertible and a black Mini Cooper to go with his red Rolls Royce. George had changed his E-Type Jaguar for a white Maserati, which he quickly became bored with and returned to the garage with only 4,000 miles on the clock. He drove home in an Aston Martin like Paul's. John who had great difficulty learning to drive acquired a Rolls Royce, a Ferrari and a Mini Minor; the Ferrari was returned with only 1,000 miles on it.

When he saw McCartney's beautiful Aston, Mick immediately extracted some money from Eric Easton and went round to the Aston Martin showroom. The salesman looked shocked at the longhaired louche young man examining his classic cars. It finally clicked with him who Mick was after a couple of double takes, which was OK because then he became suitably obsequious and started laying on the royal tour, lathering on the soft soap.

Would Mr. Jagger like a cup of tea? Look at this fine walnut dashboard, all hand-made you know and how about a cigarette? But all the time Mick could see him thinking, 'has this Rolling Stone really got enough money for this expensive machine?' When

McCartney bought his Aston, the salesman had probably let Paul pay with a cheque, smiling and wringing his hands like Uriah Heep, almost bowing as he accepted it and blowing the ink dry saying, 'Although we usually insist on a banker's draft sir, it won't be necessary in your case'. But you could tell he didn't really want to take any cheques from Mr. Jagger… not yet, not until Mr. Jagger had safely had another couple of hits under his belt. Oh no, being a

Rolling Stone isn't the same as being a *Beatle* after all. Mick gritted his teeth and selected a £25,000 midnight blue Aston Martin DB6 with electric windows, a radio and even a record player, spending more than he meant to.

That'll show the bastard. A few months later he crashed it with Chrissie in it. He hit a Ford Anglia belonging to the Countess of Carlisle down the road from his new flat in the Marylebone Road (which says something about the way the roles were reversing in 60s Britain; the arriviste pop star had a fabulous blue Aston while the blueblood could only manage a little Ford). It was only a scrape that would cost Jagger £121 and no one was hurt but there was still a row about it.

Peter Whitehead's in town and is talking to Andrew about filming the band on tour in Ireland. They all liked the way he'd filmed that big poetry thing at the Albert Hall – *Wholly Communion*. Mick had thought the poetry evening looked like a load of old crap but went anyway, just to be seen - Allen Ginsberg, Lawrence Ferlinghetti and all the other so-called 'Beat Poets', taking themselves too seriously and spouting on for hours, although Ginsberg's *Howl* with all its allusions to the degradation of alcohol and drug taking was seriously not before bedtime stuff. But just because a bloke writes a poem, that doesn't mean to say he's the best person to recite it does it? Stones songs exempted of course.

He thought the best bit of the poetry evening had been when those Germans did a poem that consisted entirely of sneezing. That really was hilarious but the other stuff? You could keep it. Yet Whitehead had made a good job of the film, using portable cameras, keeping on the move, making it lively.

 Andrew had been agonising about the problem of making a Stones film. The Beatles' *Hard Days Night* had been a tour de force but how to follow a film like that? How could he beat them at their own game? The thing about the Beatles is that they were naturally funny. All you had to do was stick them in front of a camera and say be funny and they would. The Stones just weren't funny. Bill and Charlie were taciturn to the point of being mute – which was a blessing really, and certainly the glory-seeker Brian couldn't be trusted to start spouting off to the cameras. He'd start thinking he was the spokesman for the band again. Jagger and Keith spoke very little to each other for long periods unless they were trying to write something. It was one of the mechanisms they used to avoid arguing with each other; don't speak at all. They maintained their

relationship this way, by not talking about it. Anyway they had Andrew as a go-between in their great, unrequited love affair. That aside, zany, droll, dry, acerbic, fast-paced badinage just wasn't their bag, man, and Andrew knew it.

Mick didn't know what Andrew was after when he hired Peter Whitehead to follow them around on tour. The gigs were OK but off stage there was little conversation. In fact there were excruciatingly long silences between the band members. It was all a bit boring. And then there was the marijuana smoking and girl chasing. You couldn't show any of that – especially to their wives and girlfriends. The film would be instantly banned, their relationships ruined and their reputations, already blackened by the press, could be utterly destroyed.

2

The Extraordinary Story of Peter Whitehead

UNDERGROUND filmmaker, crystallographer, friend of the stars, falconer to the Saudi royal family, mystical Egyptologist, Howard (Mr. Nice) Marks's partner, novelist, the originator of the pop video; an alleged MI6 agent.

Described by Jenny Fabian (who co wrote the notorious 60s sexed up page turner *Groupie*) as "like a Nordic god, with wild blond hair, and an intense charm", Whitehead had a laid-back demeanour and spoke fluent cool cat with a cultured accent. He'd studied physics and crystallography at Cambridge University where he worked for Crick and Watson, the discoverers of DNA; there he came to know the future British poet laureate Ted Hughes as well as Ian McKellen and Peter Cook. Later he attended the Slade school of Art studying cinematography, all top notch achievements but he was nevertheless a working class boy made good – a mere Scouser plumber's son. He'd only used the faux cut glass accent to get by at university, to merge into his top-drawer surroundings.

When Whitehead made the film, *Wholly Communion* about the 1965 poetry readings in the Albert Hall which featured American beat poets Allen Ginsberg, Lawrence Ferlinghetti and Gregory Corso as well as home grown talent like Michael Horovitz and the Scottish junkie writer Alex Trocchi, Whitehead established himself as the counter culture's favourite filmmaker by helping to nurture the very counter culture itself into existence. When the 8,000 strong audience looked around the Albert Hall auditorium, they were stunned to see others blinking back at them, others who looked just like them. All of a sudden there was the mass realisation that they were not alone. There were other freaks everywhere. It was the first great hippie happening.

Wholly Communion gave Whitehead the leg up he needed. All of a sudden, the phone never stopped ringing; among the callers, Andrew Loog Oldham, the Rolling Stones' dynamic young manager who wanted him to film the Stones on tour in Ireland. Oldham was apparently miffed that Whitehead didn't know who he was when he called, but Whitehead definitely knew who the Stones were and told the Guardian he was "envious of the erotic, pagan power they had over their nubile audience". The resultant footage entitled, *Charlie is my Darling* (cocaine was occasionally called charlie back then so perhaps the pun was unintended), like their later on-the-road documentary *Cocksucker Blues* was considered too wild and incriminating to be seen and on Mick's orders languishes somewhere on a dusty shelf, bootleg copies available only.

Undeterred, Whitehead followed the band to New York and shot the classic promo for *Have You Seen Your Mother Baby*. He also shot *We Love You*, the day before Jagger and Richards went to court for marijuana possession. The film depicts Jagger as Oscar Wilde in the dock; Richards was dressed as a High Court Judge and Marianne Faithfull camped it up as Bosie. The BBC promptly banned it.

His third film effort *Tonite Let's All Make Love in London* consisted of collages of interviews with the beautiful people of the age, including Jagger, Michael Caine, a craggy Lee Marvin, David Hockney and Julie Christie. 'How does it feel to be one of the beautiful people?' When Whitehead needed accompanying music, he put Pink Floyd in the studio to make their very first recording, *Interstellar Overdrive*. It has been said that the only reason he financed their recording was because he had been having a fling with Jenny Spires, Syd Barrett's then girlfriend and when she had

developed a guilty conscience about the affair she had convinced Whitehead to finance the band's session by way of recompense.

Footage of the Floyd and others, including John Lennon attending the first great psychedelic event, the *14-Hour Technicolour Dream* at Alexander Palace was included in the film. Organised by Barry Miles and John 'Hoppy' Hopkins, it was a fund-raiser for the *International Times,* which along with *Oz* and to a lesser extent *Gandalf's Garden* was the backbone of London's freak press. The mere names of the artists that appeared are almost enough to get you high: the Tribe of the Sacred Mushroom, David Medalla and the

Exploding Galaxye, the Social Deviants, Suzy Creamcheese who had been dispensing banana skin joints to new arrivals, the Utterly Incredible Too Long Ago to Remember Sometimes Shouting at People, Alexis Korner, Champion Jack Dupree, Graham Bond, Ginger Johnson and his African conga drummers, Savoy Brown, the Pretty Things, the Purple Gang, the Crazy World Of Arthur Brown, Soft Machine and top of the bill Pink Floyd who took to the stage just as the sun rose.

It was one of those events that every old hippie in town says they attended but didn't really. Whitehead was not only there; he filmed it, and it was quite a show: Afghan coated hippies cranked up on acid (one of whom was John Lennon in his little round glasses period, strolling around with John Dunbar), the vaulted ceilings, the huge windows, flower children with petals stuck on their cheeks, girls who looked as if they modelled for Arthur Rackham illustrations, tripping girls playing with dolls, the smell of patchouli and sandlewood, barefoot girls with painted faces in granny nightdresses, sex in the bushes, the OM signs, the tinkling of bells, photographers, film crews, all set against the panorama of London viewed from the hill. Yoko Ono arranged for a model to be seated and then encouraged members of the audience to cut off pieces of her clothes with scissors, until she was left sitting naked. John Peel later commented: "It was like paradise. It was wonderful. You spent a lot of time rushing around saying, 'Brian Jones is here, Hendrix is here, where, where?'" But the bands offering a soundtrack to the extravaganza were really just bit part players until Floyd took to the stage, made the building shudder and became the main event.

The list of Peter's friends lengthened as he became close to Jagger and the Jagger set. Indeed both Nico and Anita Pallenberg had been between his sheets, and when Mick and Bianca broke up much later in 1979, Peter was at hand to provide solace, a shoulder to cry on and then eventually two strong arms to hold the Nicaraguan beauty close. This was the disco decade and the beautiful couple would flit around London's clubs together where Whitehead might be seen in earnest conversation with a party of well heeled Arabs, sometimes going off in limousines with them on mysterious assignations, exchanging suitcases in underground car parks. These assignations led some to speculate that Peter was a secret agent.

Bianca foolishly kept telling him about her beautiful friend Dido Goldsmith, the niece of business tycoon Sir James Goldsmith and how he really ought to meet her. When he did he was stricken, and presumably she was too because the couple were married within weeks. Somehow he convinced the jilted Bianca to be the maid of honour at the marriage ceremony and the best man was no less than Howard Marks - Mr. Nice himself, the notorious big time dope dealer who, it transpires, had been laundering some drug cash by staking Peter's films.

Of his filmmaker friend Howard said, "Peter was very quick to tell me he was working-class - otherwise I'd never have guessed; very trustworthy, a man of broad vision. He broadened my mind". Later, Howard, who at that time was estimated to be smuggling a sixth of the marijuana in the world, remarked, "A lot of my money went into Peter's films. That's all part of what was going on. I had money. He had other things."

Among the things Peter had were enormous cages-full of falcons by his house in the little hamlet of Pytchley near Kettering. When he had proudly showed Howard his birds, Howard stared over his shoulder and right past the fabulous creatures; he was looking into the darkness of their cavernous cages. Could there be a better place to store bales of marijuana! Who would ever think of looking for dope in Pytchley in the first place let alone in the back of falcon cages with the gimlet-eyed birds of prey acting as custodians?

Another thing Peter had was a legitimate film business which was in the business of hiring locations for shoots – locations like a Scottish stately home with lawns running down to the sea – just the kind of place to make a moonless landing of a boatload of dope; Conaglen House was rented for £1,000 a week, the agents only too glad to get some income on the empty baronial mansion just by the Caledonian Ship Canal at Fort William.

Marks chartered the *Karob*, a deep-sea salvage tug that bristled with loading equipment. It picked up fifteen tons of Colombian marijuana and headed for the Irish Sea where it disgorged its cargo on to two 40-foot yachts. One boat went to the sparsely populated island of Kerrera close to the town of Oban and the other went to the rented Scottish castle. Of the stash landed at Conaglen House, five tons went down to a lock up in Essex and another five tons went into the depths of the falcons' cages. In 1980, the fifteen tons hit the street and

Howard broke a record; it was the largest amount of marijuana ever to have been imported into Europe. He estimates that the haul was "enough for every inhabitant of the British Isles to get simultaneously stoned".

The cargo started selling at the rate of a ton a week and the money poured in. Howard moved into a £500 a week flat in Hans Court, Knightsbridge directly opposite Harrods.

Things got a bit iffy when a customs officer ferreted out the Scottish connection and went after the drug smuggling gang but Marks' antennae twitched and in the nick of time he jettisoned a few tons of the merchandise into the sea, whereupon it floated down the coast a way and started washing up on nearby beaches to be picked up by lucky local pot heads and grazed on by a few curious sheep and deer.

And there was another Whitehead asset that Howard could utilise; Peter's fuck pad at 18 Carlisle Street in Soho had become surplus to requirements so he passed it on to Marks who used it as the headquarters for *Worldwide Entertainments*, Mr. Nice's front company for many future nefarious dealings.

Back in the 60s, Whitehead's next film effort was *The Fall*, about the American student uprising, actually filmed from the inside of the Columbia university building as the police beat their way in. The sit-in students got whacked with flashlights and then dragged out to the police vans down the stairs floor-by-floor with their heads bouncing.

The Fall included interviews with Bobbie Kennedy; the underground film director and the U.S. Attorney General photographed chatting together.

The Fall is commonly regarded as Whitehead's most important film but it almost bankrupted him. During its editing, feeling that he was having a mental breakdown, he would wander around Manhattan where, on one occasion, he found himself in a tree-lined square.

"I suddenly heard a noise behind me, a twittering and flutterin", he told *Sight and Sound* magazine in 2007. "It was like a Hitchcock film: hundreds of birds were flying behind me. Then I heard a strange shuffling sound, and around the corner walks a little old man. He stops about three yards from me, pulls something from his pocket and shouts: 'Charlie! Where are you?' Then I see a bird fly down, and the man takes his hand away, saying, 'Not you! You wait. Charlie!' Charlie comes down, sits on his finger and eats. 'Now you, Rose. Where are you?' And Rose flies down. He was there for half an hour, feeding all the birds, one by one, by name. At that moment I realised I would sooner have this old man's talent than the talent to make *The Fall*, so I quit film-making, bought my first falcon for £8 and spent 20 years living in some of the most remote and beautiful places on earth".

But before he did, he created some of the first pop promos for *Top of the Pops*: short films of The Rolling Stones, the Dubliners, Eric Burdon and the Animals, The Shadows and Jimmy James and the Vagabonds, as well as Jimi Hendrix and Nico. In 1970 he photographed and edited Led Zeppelin's *Live at the Albert Hall* film.

During this most fecund period he was living in the super-central Soho bachelor pad, which as well as a having a busy double bed, was stuffed with objects from Ancient Egypt, heads, sculptures and pictures by Max Ernst; carved falcons stared down from the ceilings; it was so handy for the restaurants, the clubs and the girls.

Whitehead was a red blooded boy alright: in the early 70s he was shacked up in a house in the south of France with a young actress Mia Martin who had once starred alongside Joanna Lumley in a Hammer horror effort, *The Satanic Rites of Dracula* and had been one of Hill's Angels in the *Benny Hill Show*. He took on holiday with him a huge stash of psychedelic drugs, a camera and a crate of film. The black and white erotic/surreal shots with a doll parts theme are gathered together in a photo album *Baby Doll*. It's steamy stuff; such was the heat of the project, it took him 25 years to get it published.

When the law finally caught up with Howard Marks, it was Whitehead who was coerced into being chief prosecution witness at the trial. He'd had little choice in the matter; it was a question of testifying against his friend or going down himself. Marks recognised that his former partner was being coerced and exonerated him for testifying, saying, "His [Peter's] ethics were such that he would not wish to be responsible for putting anyone in prison. But he didn't want to end up in nick himself. He saw a way out without directly incriminating me and he took it. The price he paid was to be a prosecution witness". Marks' incredible defence which included claims that at various times he had been either working for MI6 in an attempt to infiltrate the IRA, or Mexican Intelligence investigating drug gangs, somehow convinced a jury and they acquitted him; however Howard would go down for other offences shortly after.

Whitehead ducked out of sight only to pop up in Pakistan and Afghanistan, coincidentally political hotspots. However, he says, he was not an agent for MI5 or MI6; his expeditions to the wild border areas that have become war zones, he explained were merely to investigate falcon-nesting sites.

On one genuine falcon-hunting expedition in Baluchistan, Peter was stricken with black cholera, in a village 50 miles from the nearest road. "I was saved by a witch doctor". He recalled in an interview with Jennie Fabian. "They tied me up with ropes to stop the blood flowing into my arms and legs, and then they stood on me and paralysed me, so that finally the stomach was unable to vomit. They broke two of my ribs, but saved my life".

In another tale of derring-do, he found himself on an egg-hunting expedition in Morocco hanging from a cliff face. When the ropes

seized, Whitehead was forced to cut one of them and slide down the other, badly burning his hands in the process, before falling 45 feet into the sea. He still bears the scars.

Some time later Whitehead surfaced in Saudi Arabia where he was training falcons for Prince Faisal in a dramatically positioned cliff-face breeding centre in the clouds 3,000 metres above sea level, near the peak of Jebel Soodah, the highest mountain in Saudi Arabia. This was no small enterprise; the Al Faisal Falcon Centre remains the largest private falcon breeding facility in the world.

Jenny Fabian's vision of Whitehead as a blonde-haired Nordic God could now be enhanced by the addition of a falcon gripping his gauntleted wrist. However after some years living on a cliffside as the Saudi royal family's chief falconer, the 1991 Gulf War brought another phase of his extraordinary career to an end.

Since then Whitehead has been writing books: Syd Barrett, his old friend inspired his first, *The Risen*. They'd bumped into each other in Cambridge and reunited in London at the UFO Club. Aptly its lead character John takes a drug and disappears. It may make a decent movie some day; it's thought that the actor Gabriel Byrne owns the film rights to the book.

Now in his seventies, Whitehead still lives in the tiny hamlet of Pytchley near Kettering. Books and falcons remain his twin passions although nowadays the cages contain only birds of prey. He is frequently called upon to curate retrospectives and maintains an interesting web site, PeterWhitehead.net. Described as a fabulous character, it might however be him who did the describing since he is often accused of being a self-mythologyser.

The Swinging London phenomenon is given a fantastic slant in his book of the film *Tonite Let's All Make Love in London*. In it he postulates that maybe, just maybe the CIA had inspired the Swinging London *Time* magazine piece in an effort to trivialise, to make a tourist attraction and a commodity out of what was essentially a left wing counter-culture movement in the UK. Unable to stop themselves meddling in the affairs of others, the CIA was, in his treatise, as determined to stamp on any perceived buds of revolution in the capital city of America's oldest ally, as they were to bomb it out of Vietnam.

In a 2006 film *In the Beginning was the Image*, Whitehead summed up the period that everyone always asks him about – the 60s, presumably because in some ways he was such an archetypal figure of the period; working class boy made good, handsome, sexually charged, friend of the stars and ultimately a dropout: "Everyone thought it was a wonderful time. I didn't actually think it was a particularly wonderful time at all. For me the 60s was the Aldermaston march (a CND rally in protest at the British Atomic Research facility in Aldermaston), the war in Vietnam, bomb culture... the *Dialectics of Liberation* at the Roundhouse with Stokely Carmichael, Allen Ginsberg and a load of other people describing what was going wrong", (this event held in 1967 brought together a cast of Marxist intellectuals, psychiatrists, including the celebrity shrink R. D. Laing, anarchists and political leaders to discuss social issues and the future. Stokely Carmichael was a black activist who headed the Black Panthers and is credited with originating the expression 'institutional racism').

"The only miracle about the 60s," he continued, "was that it was a moment of extreme change that managed to get through without savage violence. It was a revolution".

3

London's Ultimate Rock Pads

BACK IN Montagu Square, Marylebone, Ringo had a new baby and a bank full of money. He decided to move out to the stockbroker belt, to Weybridge close by where John had already been living for a year. The West End flat was too small for a young family and the address had soon come to be known by Beatles fans who camped out on the pavement day and night, making it difficult to leave the house without climbing over a sink and then squeezing through a tiny window into the mews behind. The original plan was for all four Beatles to buy adjoining properties that backed on to a fifth property where Brian Epstein would live – at the centre of a mock Tudor hub where he could literally keep an eye on all 'his boys', particularly his beloved John. The Beatles had only once all lived together and never in four knocked-through terraced houses as depicted in *Help!* When they first moved to London they'd all lived at apartment L, 57 Green Street, Mayfair where the nearest shop to get your fags was Selfridges.

George derailed the Weybridge plan by buying a country house elsewhere – nearby but not as part of the compound. Then McCartney decided not to move to the country at all, but he did move his father out to the country, outside Liverpool; he bought him a place on the Cheshire Wirral that boasted its own wine cellar. As a bonus the old man was given a racehorse to play with.

Despite the big wage packets Ringo was more down-to-earth. Although he was a rich young man he wasn't in Paul's league. It had been their accountant who'd recommended that they invest in freehold properties rather than renting or leasing, but despite the fact it was a bit costly and Maureen told him she thought it was a daft idea, he figured he'd keep the Montagu Square apartment on for a while. It was nice to have as a London base and friends could use it. It certainly looked the part, having been decorated by Brian Epstein's interior designer, Ken Partridge, in green watermarked silk wallpaper with silk curtains and lead-streaked mirrors.

Paul McCartney had been living at 57 Wimpole Street, the medical district of the west end of London, with his girlfriend Jane Asher – well not exactly with her. It was her parents' house; her father was a doctor, an endocronologist who had discovered Munchausen's syndrome, and her mother a professor of music specialising in the oboe. Margaret Asher had once taught George Martin at the Guildhall School of Music and also taught McCartney the recorder, which he played on *Fool on the Hill*. She was descended from the Saint Germans family of Port Eliot (coincidentally, the then Lord Eliot later became one of the shareholders in Seltaeb, a company that would merchandise Beatles related products. Lord Peregrine Eliot was heir to the 6,000 acre Cornish estate and paid a mere £1,000 cash for twenty per cent of the multi-million pound company. The lord thought that flogging plastic Beatle wigs and other Fabs tat would be a good way to raise a bit of money to re-carpet the ancestral home. However, with Seltaeb garnering 90% of the merchandising spoils while the Beatles earned only 10%, Lord Eliot could well, if he'd wished, have carpeted the whole of Cornwall with his profits).

McCartney lived in the attic on the top floor across the corridor from Jane's brother Peter, sharing a landing with a Beatle who suggested to him, 'Why don't you sing?' and then gave him a song. The hastily formed duo Peter and Gordon had a huge hit with Lennon and McCartney's *World Without Love*, however after a great career kick start, McCartney preoccupied elsewhere, Peter and Gordon withered. Peter Asher went on to manage Linda Ronstadt, James Taylor and Cher as well as briefly, talent scouting for Apple.

Jane's bedroom was on the floor below Paul's. Dr. Asher used the ground floor as his consulting room (one of his techniques for dealing with psychotic patients was to enter the room and lie on the floor, on the basis that even violent deranged people won't hit an old man lying on the ground) and her mother gave music lessons in a small studio in the basement. It was here that John and Paul wrote *Eleanor Rigby* and *I Want to Hold Your Hand*, their first US number ones. McCartney wrote *Yesterday* in the attic on a small cabaret piano, which stood next to his bed. The room was full of interesting objets d'arts, some original Jean Cocteau drawings entitled *Opium*, rare books including some first editions and bundles of teen fan's correspondence. Under his bed were a number of gold records and his framed MBE. One day when Paul was out, Peter Asher had needed a pair of clean socks and rummaging around in Paul's sock drawer found bundles of thousands of dollars which were obviously his cut from the band's last American tour and which McCartney had clearly forgotten, Some time later when McCartney was living in St. John's Wood, one night his friend Tony Bramwell was deputised to go and get some Indian food. When Bramwell asked Paul for some money, he was shown a drawer in an unlocked safe that contained hundreds of little unopened paypackets, each containing fifty or so pounds, a few coins and a payslip, weekly wages from the Beatles office that he had never needed and which he kept as petty cash.

Because Paul's room was too small, he parked his two large Brenell tape recorders in Peter's room. On these machines, he had recorded many of the backwards effects and tape loops that appeared on later Beatles recordings.

On the stairs stood a Bakelite telephone with an electric bell next to it with a straggle of wires looped around the banister, some sort of Heath Robinson device rigged up by Dr. Asher. There were similar set-ups on the various landings. Whichever of the house's occupants answered the 'phone would ring the bell a preset number of times for whoever the call was intended.

The eccentric doctor demonstrated to McCartney how he could sign his name upside down, a skill he had learned when working in hospitals when nurses proffered him things to sign. Another party trick he displayed related to an ailment he had which necessitated regular injections; these he performed on himself and he would often save the treatment until meal times when he would horrify dinner guests by reaching behind his head and plunging the syringe into the back of the neck while sitting at the table.

Fans regularly staked this house out and when the Beatles were filming *Help*, it became a particular problem. Doctor Asher devised an escape route for Paul which required him to climb out of a back window and cross a roof into the flat of an old army colonel who lived at number 56; from there Paul could take a lift down to the basement flat, 10 Browning Mews and get away in a waiting car. In thanks for the use of their flat McCartney bought the couple that lived in the mews flat a fridge.

Arthur Conan Doyle was one of the first notable residents of Wimpole Street when he opened his ophthalmic practice there in 1891. At 50 Wimpole Street, Elizabeth Barrett was kept a virtual prisoner by her tyrannical father (played by John Gielgud in the 1957 film *The Barretts of Wimpole Street*), before she escaped by eloping to Italy with fellow poet Robert Browning in 1846. When they married, she became Elizabeth Barrett Browning. Her father disinherited her.

Jane Asher had her first film role at the age of five playing a deaf girl. She read out the letters on *Children's Hour* and had played Wendy in *Peter Pan* when she was 14. She left school at the age of 17 and met McCartney a little later after becoming a regular on *Juke Box Jury* and running into all the Beatles on an assignment from *Radio Times*. She was a strawberry blonde Swinging 60s chick. When she met Paul again at a party; McCartney remembers that he and Jane spent part of the evening talking about gravy. She has said that the

Beatles couldn't believe she was a virgin. Apparently Irish whiskey played its part in the encounter; McCartney assessing that George was also after the girl moved in fast and won. It seems he was very proud of his English rose conquest commenting, "We all said, 'Will you marry me?' which is what we said to every girl at the time. (Jane was) a rare London bird, the sort we'd always heard about"

She was the envy of every female in Beatleland.

One night when McCartney missed his train back to Liverpool, she asked him if he wanted to stay over for the night and he didn't really leave for three years. As he would later with Linda, Paul sought a rural retreat for him and his new girlfriend, somewhere to escape the constant pestering of fans. He bought a farm in Campbeltown, Argyllshire and he and Jane were regularly seen wandering around the town where the locals studiously ignored them. It seems the local bobby was in the habit of checking on the farm when the couple were away and took it upon him self to water the tomato plants there. It was only when a new constable arrived from Glasgow and spotted that the plants were not of the tomato genus but were in fact of the Cannabis sativa variety, that McCartney was rumbled. It led to an appearance at Campbeltown Court. (It's worth looking up the You Tube clip of the court appearance – more Mullet Kintyre than Mull).

But their relationship came to an end after they had moved to 7 Cavendish Avenue, St. John's Wood, the £40,000 house he bought because it was near the 'office'. He could walk from it to Abbey Road Studios. The first home McCartney ever owned, it is a beautiful regency mansion, far larger than the Ashers' with substantial gardens and an orchard that made visitors believe they were in the country. Years later Paul and Linda would keep chickens and a horse in the garden and the neighbours would complain about the cock crowing. Paul told his architect (John Dunbar's elder sister Marina. Dunbar was Marianne Faithfull's husband) that he wanted the smell of cabbage coming up from the basement just like in the Wimpole Street house. McCartney wanted all the latest new fangled gadgets and set about installing eye level cookers, spit roasts, tape decks, record players and a built in movie screen in the living room. Over the years he accumulated art including Aubrey Beardsley and Magritte

originals. He also owns Magritte's easel and his spectacles.

Penny Lane, Getting Better and *Hey Jude* were all written in the first floor music room, which had a small upright piano painted in psychedelic patterns. It is said that Mick Jagger smoked his first joint in the room. Down the garden was a meditation 'chapel', which featured a circular bed, given to the Beatle by Alice Cooper who was in turn given it by Groucho Marx.

Jagger and Marianne Faithfull were regular visitors. In his book *Paul McCartney: Many Years From Now*, Faithfull told Barry Miles: "We would go and see them a lot, but I don't remember him coming to see us. Mick always had to come to his house, because he was Paul

McCartney and you went to him. Paul never came to us. I was always curious about how Mick saw him, how Mick felt about him. It was always fun to watch. There was always rivalry there. Not from Paul, none at all. Paul was oblivious, but there was something from Mick. It was good fun. It was like watching a game on television".

McCartney's relationship with Asher went bad when she was playing in theatre out of town and Paul was, in her absence, touring the clubs playing the Beatle about town. One night he foolishly took that night's dance partner back to the house, passing through the cordon of 'Apple Scruffs' as the Beatles most devout fans were called, to get in the gate. The 'Apple Scruffs' more or less lived on the pavement; that's when they weren't clambering over the wall and burgling the house when he was out when they would head straight for his bedroom and its wardrobe from which they frequently stole his clothes; taking turns in wearing them out on the pavement. When Paul complained about the burglaries, abashed, they had a whip round and bought him a monkey.

After a while, one of the Scruffs, Margo Stevens who had been standing outside the Cavendish Avenue address on and off for over a year, aware that her beloved Paul had a girl upstairs, spotted Jane Asher driving towards the house. Margo rang the buzzer to warn Paul that trouble was about to arrive but he assumed it was yet another prank and resumed his wooing. Jane caught the two in flagrante delicto and stormed off. Her mother Margaret arrived later to collect Asher's daughter's possessions. Despite attempts at reconciliation one of London's most golden couples parted.

Lots of people used to ring McCartney's doorbell and for a long while he made a point of always answering it. On one occasion a visitor announced that he was Jesus Christ and McCartney invited him in because he figured that if the guy really was Jesus then he shouldn't really refuse him entry. That night McCartney took the young man to a recording session with the other Beatlles where he sat quietly in the corner. When the others asked McCartney who he was, he said, "Him? Oh that's Jesus Christ".

Now Jane Asher is married to Britain's greatest caricaturist, Gerald Scarfe who designed all the visuals for the Pink Floyd film *The Wall*. They live on Cheyne Walk, London's avenue of the stars. Interestingly Scarfe was doing drawing work for *Time* magazine in New York at the time it ran the *Swinging London* cover although he didn't design it. Perhaps employing this dashing Londoner with the savage pencil helped inspire the London vibe that was going on at that time in New York; that is if it weren't the creation of the CIA as Peter Whitehead had once suggested.

Asher now directs several catering companies and writes novels, some of which have dark edges that seem at odds with her projected fresh-as-a-daisy persona, a moodiness that may hark back to the anguished period of her life when her father committed suicide. She is a shareholder in *Private Eye* magazine.

After Asher left the Cavendish Avenue house Paul became the definitive batchelor boy; the house became a mess of records, tapes and pots of dope; at any one time there might be three or more semi clad beauties wafted room-to-room trying to attract his attention.

Ringo's flat was empty now bar for the occasions when it was being used as a London stop over for friends or as a knocking shop by members of the Beatles entourage. It gained a new (non live-in) tenant when McCartney was looking for somewhere to put his tape recorders and do a bit of recording both of himself and other passing people and projects that took his fancy. One of those projects was to record some experimental music since he had recently, tentatively started dipping his toe into the dark waters of the avant-garde.

The Beat Poets, Allen Ginsberg, William S. Burroughs and the others were certainly considered avant-garde; when Allen Ginsberg had come over from the USA to perform at the Albert Hall poetry concert that became Peter Whitehead's *Wholly Communion* film, instead of wanting to meet British poets, Ginsberg had insisted that he be introduced to the Beatles. Barry Miles, known only as 'Miles' steps into the tale now. A poet, a writer, and a friend of Peter Asher, Miles had come to town from Cheltenham intent on getting involved in the nascent London underground poetry and literature scene. He had been instrumental in getting Ginsberg to come over to Britain and was helping to arrange a birthday party for him on his arrival. In an effort to fulfil the expectations of his important visitor, he sent amusing hand drawn invitations around to Beatles HQ and hoped for the best. At the party, Ginsberg became very drunk, took off all his clothes and hung a 'Do not disturb' sign on his manhood. It was at this moment that John Lennon and his wife Cynthia walked in with George and his girlfriend Patti Boyd. John left rather abruptly, seemingly because he was aghast at this drunk, nude poet. He hissed indignantly to Miles on the way out of the door, "You don't do that in front of birds".

A few years later John had obviously changed his mind about 'doing that in front of birds" when he and Yoko, who were at the time living in Ringo's apartment in Montagu Square had a photographer pop by to take full frontal shots of themselves naked for the cover of the *Two Virgins* album (Lennon resisted suspending a sign from his manhood). The cover described by Lennon as a picture of "two slightly overweight ex-junkies", outraged much of America; some of the states shrouded it in brown paper bags and others impounded it.

But before John and Yoko moved into 34 Montagu Square, McCartney's tape recorders were dominating the rooms. William Burrough's ex-boyfriend, Cambridge maths graduate, Ian Somerville had some knowledge of the recording process so he was given a bundle of money and told to build an avant-garde studio (Burroughs had been a regular visitor to the book shop where Miles had been working). Miles and John Dunbar, his partner in a new venture, the Indica Gallery used the studio to record them selves bashing up some percussion instruments and various kitchen utensils. Robert Fraser, who also liked to smoke loads of dope and pretend he was being avant-garde, came by on occasions to rattle a tambourine. Burroughs though, used the studio extensively and recorded hours of material there, sometimes with Brion Gysin, pioneer of the cut-up technique, of whom more later.

But despite the arty experimentation, it was in Montagu Square that McCartney recorded most of the early demos of *Eleanor Rigby*, surely one of the Beatles' most commercial songs, although at the time, with its pounding cello rhythms and poignant storyline, it was in pop terms, very different.

When Paul had no further use of the Montagu Square flat it fell vacant again. Ringo, still not keen to part with his west end bolthole, sublet it to Chas Chandler the gentle giant Geordie manager of Jimi Hendrix in December 1966. Chas moved in with his girlfriend and in so far as Jimi lived anywhere during his extraordinary time in London it was either there or at 23 Brook Street, Mayfair with his girlfriend Kathy Etchingham. The loose limbed Hendrix was, needless to say, enormously attractive to a large number of long-haired, wide-eyed London girls, hippie chicks who hauled him off to a variety of west end flats in the late evenings, so it couldn't be said that Hendrix slept

there often in the conventional sense – crashed might be a better term for those moments when his eyes eventually closed. However his guitars, his songbooks and the pile of silks, tunics and velvet that constituted his wardrobe resided at Montagu Square where Chas and he had looked at the green shot silk wallpaper and painted it black.

It was a busy time for the manager and his protégée, recruiting band members, setting up and playing gigs, making recordings, arranging record company meetings, interviews with journalists and photo shoots: in the evenings while Jimi was out jamming with some band at the Speakeasy or trying out a new girl and another new drug, Chas would kick off his Cuban heels, snuggle his feet into the Persian rug and relax in his armchair at his new home with a cup of tea and his collection of sci-fi literature. When Jimi crawled home at four in the morning or maybe three in the afternoon, eyes red from all-night girl action and leapers, he'd strum his omnipresent guitar for a spell then take down a book and examine it, hoping it might help get him off to sleep. One of these was Chas's *Earth Abides* by George R. Stewart from which he gleaned ideas for his first album, particularly the deeply psychedelic *Third Stone From the Sun* that might rate as one of the first acid trip tracks ever written.

Peter Asher was enlisted as a partner in the new gallery/bookshop and they set up a company MAD (Miles, Asher, Dunbar) Ltd. John Dunbar provided a venue for early business meetings, the living room of his girlfriend, Marianne Faithfull's flat at 29 Lennox Gardens off Pont Street SW1, acquired with the money she made from *As Tears*

Go By, the first song Jagger and Richards had written when Andrew Loog Oldham demanded they write their own material. He'd told them to come up with something that would conjure up "brick walls, high windows and no sex".

Marianne had met John Dunbar when she'd gone to a Cambridge ball when she was 17. He was, she says, "my catalyst, my Virgil… different from any boy I had ever met". She'd seen the Leonardo Da Vinci *Vitruvian Man* drawing on his bedroom door and was intgrigued: who lived within? On meeting him, she knew instantly he was the one, "the very model of hipness, circa 1963" she said. Naturally he had an exotic background – nothing else would do for Marianne – boasting a Russian mother called Tatiana and a Scottish filmmaker father, who during the war was the British Embassy's cultural attaché in Russia. John had been born in Mexico and was brought up in Russia. A nihilist, he talked of John Coltrane, Beethoven and suicide. He attended fashionable parties when his parents had moved to Mayfair, just down the road from the Asher house in Marylebone, where he bumped into Peter.

It was at these parties in Hampstead or Belgravia where lords and ladies, "Lord thingummybob… oh you know, that whole posh crowd", rubbed shoulders with the new bohemians. Princess Margaret had once stuck her finger through a hole in his jeans. It was at such a party that Andrew Loog Oldham had spotted Marianne and asked if she could sing, It was quite a weekend for Marianne; she met a Beatle - McCartney, a couple of Rolling Stones – Mick and Keith; lost her virginity to Dunbar, and was discovered by Andrew; all in 48 hours). Little realising that his response would change the course of both their lives, Dunbar replied by asking her, "You sing a bit don't you?" It was at this party, hosted by aspiring singer and actress Adrienne Posta that Marianne first came across Mick. "As for Mick Jagger", she said. "I wouldn't have known he was there if he hadn't had a flaming row with his girlfriend Chrissie Shrimpton. She was crying and shouting at him, and in the heat of the argument her false eyelashes were peeling off".

Marianne claims that the idea of Swinging London was more or less contrived over a table in a Chelsea coffee bar when Dunbar, Miles and a beatnik called Paolo Leone – intellectuals all – "more or less invented the scene in London, so I guess I was present at the Creation". She goes on to characterise the oncoming revolution as, "Free love, psychedelic drugs, fashion, Zen, Nietzsche, tribal trinkets, customised Existentialism, hedonism and rock 'n' roll". Well she certainly had her share of all that.

When, one day, Dunbar and Marianne had a row, he went off to Greece in a huff and when he got back she was a pop star. She went on tour with the Hollies and started having it off with Allan Clarke the lead singer, so perhaps her earlier statement that Dunbar was her perfect partner now needed revision. Indeed on the next tour it was Gene Pitney who got her undivided attention. An abortion later (ah, the rigours of the road), she went back to her fiancée and started making plans to marry him; soon she was pregnant.

Then the Bob Dylan caravan arrived in town and camped at the Savoy hotel for weeks holding court with Joan Baez and humiliating Donovan, while D.A. Pennebaker's cameras whirred, collecting footage for the *Don't Look Back* film. Marianne was drawn like a moth and sat at the feet of the great man day after day. At first he ignored her, then he began to pay her a little attention and then he seemed to fall as so many had done before for that virginal/sensual look. Dylan became aware that John Dunbar was a rival and like a petulant jealous kid, he began to ridicule him. On one occasion Faithfull even allowed him to deride Dunbar's poetic aspirations while Dunbar himself stood outside in the rain waiting for her. "You can't marry someone who wears glasses, said jealous Bob. "He's the eternal student". Dylan threatened to drop things from the window on to Dunbar's head as John loitered miserably, collars turned up, waiting dutifully for his miscreant wife-to-be.

When Dunbar told a local newspaper that Marianne would be continuing with her singing career despite the marriage and a forthcoming baby, Faithfull saw that as a declaration of his idleness which is perhaps a tad rich considering. "He'd got the goose that laid the golden egg and he knew it", she said. "Never have to work again. Well it's the ambition of every bohemian isn't it?"

To say he didn't work isn't entirely accurate because over at his flat at 11 Bentinck Mansions in Bentinck Street with Barry Miles and

Peter Asher, he was putting together plans for the Indica Gallery and bookshop, soon to become a unique focal point of the 'counterculture'.

In the Spring of 1966, just a few months after their son Nicholas was born, Faithfull and Dunbar were at the opening of the gallery at 6 Mason's Yard, which shared the same courtyard as the Scotch of St James club (13 Mason's Yard, SW1 now the Directors Lodge Club where table dancing rather than rhythm and blues is the Saturday night speciality). The 'Scotch' was the late night hip hangout of the pretty young things, where you might see Paul McCartney chatting with Stevie Wonder; Stevie Winwood or Sonny and Cher. *Ready Steady Go!* Producer Vicki Wickham would pop in after the show wrapped with that night's guests in her trail: James Brown, the Supremes, Rod Stewart, the Ronettes, Stevie Marriott, Tom Jones. Perched on a stool at the end of the bar was the club's most regular regular, Eric Burdon, who lived only staggering distance away, around the corner at 11 Dalmeney Court, 8 Duke Street.

John Lennon went to an orgy after a night on the scotch in the Scotch around the corner from the club, where he watched Eric crack amyl nitrate capsules under the noses of some semi-clad girls and then when they ran out cracking raw eggs over them. Lennon whooped Burdon along, shouting, "You're the egg man; go on egg man". So even if the walrus was Paul, one thing is certain about the crazy lyric of *I Am the Walrus*; the egg man was Eric.

A curious McCartney was involved in the new gallery before it even opened. He would sit in the basement sifting through the boxes of radical texts, reading and removing those he fancied and leaving a note for the shop owners listing what he'd taken and telling them to send him a bill. And his assistance to the project wasn't just that of a well-heeled customer; when they needed wood for shelving they used McCartney's Aston Martin DB4 to collect it from the wood yard. McCartney didn't pick up the stuff himself; instead he let a friend

Taff, who used to claim that his previous job was getaway driver, use his treasured car. Taff called the sportster "the D-B-Far-Out" and had once taken it out to the airport at 120 mph and brought it back at 130 mph. He was chased by the police on both occasions but couldn't be caught.

When they needed a till, it was the old Victorian till that Jane Asher played with as a child that was utilised. McCartney hand drew the first flyers and the shop's wrapping paper. Dunbar carved an elaborate banister for the stairs. Jane's mother arranged a bank account at Coutts and Co., the Queen's bank where a footman dressed in a frock coat would bring you your chequebook on a silver platter.

The opening party bought many exotic creatures out of their lairs: the party animal Eric Burdon, esteemed rock photographer Gered Mankowitz, producer Michael White who (with Ken Tynan) made *Oh Calcutta!* and the *Rocky Horror Picture Show* (he also produced *Monty Python and the Holy Grail* and went on to produce the TV series *The Comic Strip Presents* with Peter Richardson). Other attendees were John Pearse, the Saville Row tailor who was a partner in the King's Road clothes shop *Granny Takes a Trip* and a corkscrew-haired boy called Mark Feld who was on the brink of becoming Marc Bolan, the leader of Tyrannosaurus Rex; elsewhere were beat poets, art critics and glittering young aristos from the in-crowd.

William Burroughs, the poet, girlfriend killer and junkie who wrote *Naked Lunch* briefly sidled in looking weird and freaked everybody out. The flamboyant art dealer Robert Fraser in his tight pink suit who ran his contemporary art gallery at 69 Duke St, Mayfair chatted with a range of Ormesby Gores, the daughters of Lord Harlech, one-time British Ambassador to Washington. Later, Roman Polanski and Sharon Tate dropped by.

A few months later a Mini driven by his chauffeur dropped John Lennon off so that John, at Dunbar's suggestion, could meet a strange performance artist called Yoko something-or-other.

Jonathan Aitken (who in 1966 took LSD and then tried to write down his impressions for an *Evening Standard* feature) met Dunbar when he was assembling interviews for his 1967 book, *The Young Meteors* in which he views the burgeoning scene with a mixture of fascination, envy and lofty disdain. Aitken wrote scornfully of the exhibits at the Indica Gallery, "Handbags, lumps of cement, pieces of machinery and odd scraps of miscellaneous bric-a-brac all glued together on a canvas and priced at £200", before turning his attentions to the shop's proprietor John Dunbar: "Dickensian gold-rimmed glasses perched precariously on the end of his nose, his face covered by enough spare long hair to weave a carpet". Presumably the Scrooge glasses prompted Aitken to inflict on Dunbar the arcane, patronising and syntax-lite mode of speech that he is supposed to have used in the subsequent interview, "Sure it's amateur. Didn't have anything else to do so I started this gallery. Hadn't run anything before in my life. I'm a writer really. I write films. Whatcha mean—where did I learn about modern art—got eyes, haven't I?… Whatcha mean—have we sold any of the paintings? Sure I've sold one or two—Paul McCartney bought the Takis aeroplane dials.

Haven't had any wages for the last sixteen weeks… It's nothing spectacular, sure. I don't have some kind of generator to blow a different air around. London's so slow man. It's up to me to do something about it… I'm way ahead. Where else can you see things like this? Don't have any rules—that's what I'm trying to get away from".

4

The Richardsons and The Birds

THE 30th July 1966 was no ordinary day for Charlie Richardson. Instead of the usual visit to his scrap yard in Camberwell south east London to supervise the breaking up of some old Ford Cortinas, or perhaps a rival's knee caps, or cutting off the toes of some fellow villains with some bolt croppers, Charlie was looking forward to meeting up with some of the chaps, having a few beers and watching England do the Germans in the final of the football World Cup. However, at 5am on that famous day, he and 10 associates were arrested by 60 police officers and charged with grievous bodily harm; the arresting officers no doubt taking great pleasure not telling Charlie the score as he sat waiting for his interrogation while the match played in the station office next door.

Eddie Richardson, Charlie's brother and the twin ruler of the Richardson's gang which dominated south London through the 60s, was already in prison along with 'Mad' Frankie Fraser having been convicted a month earlier of causing an affray at Mr. Smith's club in Catford. The ruck in the plush casino, which had been opened a few weeks earlier by Diana Dors, was in fact a showdown between the Krays and the Richardsons, London's principle crime families (although the Kray twins weren't actually present at the time), and was subsequently described as a 'wild west shoot out'. When the police arrived to pick up the pieces, they found six men wounded by either bullets or shotgun pellets and one man dead; the dead man had had his jacket pulled down over his shoulders so that he wouldn't have been able to move his arms; he'd been savagely beaten and then shot in the back at point blank range. Among the wounded were Frankie Fraser and Eddie.

Eddie Richardson and Fraser escaped murder convictions because nobody would testify against them; they were sentenced to five years each for affray. The police, smarting that the two villains had escaped life sentences and annoyed that they hadn't been able to nail Eddie's big brother Charlie in the affair were delighted when one of Charlie's 'colleagues' came forward to explain that on a completely separate occasion, Charlie had tortured him.

Charlie was no common criminal, in fact it's been said that the Richardsons were businessmen who turned to violent crime while the Krays had been violent men who had turned to business. The Richardsons had used the money from the scrap yard to go into business; selling and maintaining fruit machines and juke boxes before, to great effect, developing the 'long-firm' fraud technique (Read Jake Arnott's splendid book *The Long Firm*).

What they would do is take on premises (in a third party's name) and start some kind of legitimate business, establishing lines of credit with wholesalers and scupulously paying their bills on the dot. Then, having established trust, they would place large orders with numerous suppliers and when the goods arrived, shut the building down and run off with the stock.

An even more profitable scam they found was starting up business, insuring it heavily and then simply burning it down. Another fine fraud was the discovery that the car park attendants at Heathrow were fiddling the time clocks on the gate and pocketing thousands from unsuspecting motorists; the car park attendants soon found out that they had to share a large percentage of their haul with 'Mad' Frank and the Richardsons or get their heads kicked in.

By now Charlie had a whole pile of money and started looking around for more grandiose investments, utilising one Major Herbert Nicolson, who was well connected with the Conservative government, as a front. Together they invested Richardson family money in mining schemes in South Africa and smuggling diamonds packed inside frozen fish. This bought Charlie into contact with the South African secret police (BOSS), which turned a blind eye to his activities in return for using the Richardsons' gang to burgle anti-apartheid offices in London.

Suddenly, the scrap yard owner had an investment portfolio that included a small bank that operated from London's Park Lane and he began rubbing shoulders with the great and the good as well as the shady. The problem was the violence, more specifically his alleged penchant for torture. If you transgressed, you would be hauled before a 'court' that usually consisted of Charlie, Frankie Fraser and wild-eyed others, then the sentence would be passed; this would consist of any combination of beatings, whippings, cigarette burning, having your teeth pulled out with pliers (Frankie's speciality), being nailed to the floor or having your toes cut off with bolt cutters. The legend continues that sometimes the victim would have his genitals and/or nipples connected to an old army field telephone generator, be placed in a cold-water bath and then electrocuted into unconsciousness, although Charlie denies this vehemently. If the victim had been too badly injured to 'take a new shirt' and go (it was Charlie's habit to award victims clean shirts to go home in) then a struck off doctor in the pay of the brothers would fix him up first. One victim was nailed to the floor for several days; each time a member of the gang passed, they would urinate on him. Another spoke of being beaten and then being made to mop up his own blood.

Perhaps then, a band called The Birds, featuring Ronnie Wood, a rhythm and blues outfit that served as one of Ronnie's stepping stones on the way to joining the Jeff Beck Group, then The Faces and then ultimately legend status with The Rolling Stones, should have been a little more cautious when in March that year they were approached in a Catford club by a couple of heavy looking characters who liked the band so much they wanted to manage them.

And indeed, at the time the band were having management difficulties, what band isn't? The manager was taking all the dough, they complained; he would send them to a gig at one end of the country and then the following night they would have to be down at the other end, and also the van was shit; it was the usual refrain. Their new friends told them that this was a terrible situation that couldn't be tolerated, that they would supply the band with a plush Ford Transit if only they would sign themselves over; that they had connections in clubs, good clubs, and that the band would get nice gigs if they would just sign over; that they had offices in Mayfair and a heavyweight solicitor and all this and much more would be theirs if only they would just sign over.

The thought of a new van alone could probably have swung them over but that and the prospect of more wages utterly seduced them; their new managers announced that the band would start using the Roy Tempest Agency of 13-14 Dean Street a firm that considered itself 'Europe's Largest Band Agency', and which would require them to break their exisiting deal with the Harold Davison Agency. Of course they would have to break their contract with their existing manager; if the band didn't break the contracts then, it was made clear, they would be broken on their behalf.

The band's old manager Leo de Klerk was no slouch himself; he was a large body builder who with two equally muscled partners ran clubs and had a sideline appearing in TV shows as a heavy. However, he wasn't prepared for the Richardsons and their even heavier lawyer when they eventually met up at the brothers' Park Lane headquarters. Leo, his partners and his solicitor sat at one end of the vast polished table; the Richardsons and their lawyer sat at the other and a very nervous band sat on either side in the court-like surroundings; this, of course, was the very room where the brothers would pass sentence on their 'business colleagues'.

The Richardson's solicitor cut to the chase; any contract that Leo held was null and void because all the band were too young to sign legal documents. Leo thought he had that one covered and explained that all the band member's parents had been present at the signing and had affixed their own signatures, so get stuffed. The Richardson's solicitor then asked what provision Leo had made for the continuing education of the band; contract law dictated at the time that those signing minors were obliged to provide them with daily tuition; if Leo hadn't done that then the contract was null and void. Indeed, he suggested, there might even be problems with the authorities.

De Klerk looked at the unsmiling, silent men at the other end of the table and realised that the game was up. He stood, called his own solicitor a c*** and left the room, copies of his contract strewn across the boardroom table, so much waste paper.

That night the wide-eyed Birds went to a celebration party at a large house in Bromley where peroxide-haired women bristling with jewellery gave them fine foods and wines and lit their cigarettes with solid gold lighters. It was announced that a new company was to be set up unsubtely called Popgressive with the Richardson's solicitor as the chairman. Press releases were sent out, the new van appeared and grand plans for record releases were made. However, within weeks, their new management wasn't answering the telephone; then stories started emerging about police informants being nailed to floors and about a Mayfair boardroom, which was used as a kangaroo court.

The directionless band began to splinter; Ronnie was joining Jeff Beck and the band realised they were running around in a borrowed van for which they owed money to a crime syndicate. They sold the van to the Bee Gees who would ever remain oblivious of its previous owners.

In the so-called 'Torture Trial', Charlie Richardson was sentenced to 25 years for grievous bodily harm, the longest sentence ever passed down for that particular crime; that was why he wasn't answering the phone. So long was the arm of the Richardsons considered to be, that during the trial, each of the jurors was given a personal bodyguard.

For mysterious reasons, possibly because of the large number of high-ranking police officers that had been in his employ, the full details of this case are still unavailable to the public. Charlie was finally released in 1984, however he had a spell of freedom when he escaped and went on the run for a year in 1980; he didn't run far, frequently to be seen buying drinks for friends (including police officers) in bars up and down the Old Kent Road and even dressing as Santa to give presents away at a children's party whilst he campaigned to be released. He eventually gave himself up and was eventually released a few years later. After prison Richardson worked in the city, a place he has described as being considerably more corrupt than gangland.

Charlie's photo is on display in the National Portrait Gallery and in 2004 a film *Charlie* went on release. Richardson had the dubious honour of seeing himself on the silver screen depicted by Luke Goss (from Bros) with Steven Berkoff and Ania Dobson playing his parents.

In 1990, Charlie's brother Eddie Richardson was sentenced to 25 years for conspiracy to smuggle 153 kilos of cocaine into the country from Ecuador.

There was undoubtedly a lot going on in London; the provinces too but London was crackling with creative sparks. It was a fertile time, possibly Europe's most fertile period culturally speaking, since the time of the Impressionists, certainly more so than the bohemian period of 50s Paris. And as the creativity in 60s London was largely music driven or music inspired it was a terribly exciting period too – much more so than those previous belle époques, thrilling though they must have been - because great pop music has a quality completely absent from great writing or art; its rhythm makes the pulse race, the heart speeds up, the body warms and excitement comes in a rush. You didn't need Jagger to demonstrate that you wanted to grind your hips, or shake your head or wave your arms around to *Not Fade Away*. It was in the fabric. You felt compelled to dance to great pop music. The works of Picasso and Hemingway could excite the mind, enrich the soul and inflame the emotions but no matter how hard you listen you won't get a beat out of art; it can't make you dance.

The Stones dared you not to.

Fertility – human fertility in its purest sense was of course at the heart of this and was perhaps the reason why this golden period had sprung to life in the first place. The baby boomers were conceived in a fecund climate of hope and idealism, they were the progeny of peace, of war-battered young parents who yearned for political and social reconstruction and a bit of fun. The unnatural selection of war had left its survivors intent on change, a new deal, a modern world, a just and fair place fit for heroes. The sap had risen and many healthy babies were the consequence. Those drawn to London in the early 60's were ambitious alpha teens, male or female, strong and determined, all things bright and beautiful; the pick of the crop. If love was in the air in the 60s it was because love had been in the air in the mid to late 40s. As Jagger put it, "the 60s of course didn't come out of nowhere".

These young giants hustled and bustled, made plans, had sex and played with outrageous vigour and not a little abandon. Nothing, it seems, could stand in their way and it should have been more than obvious that there would sooner or later be a backlash; there were dark mutterings and a growing realisation that this youthful energetic freedom had an anarchistic streak that threatened the status quo and shouldn't be allowed to take hold. The erstwhile glacial progression of society, politics and culture shot through as it was with prejudice, petty rules and convention was about to become an iconoclastic fast track of change; but the Telegraph-reading fuddie-duddies, the old boys' network, the dinosaurs of empire, even the boomers' own parents weren't going to give up the keys to the kingdom without a fight. When the two protagonists of the Rolling Stones bought homes in the very centre of the Establishment it was like a stake had been driven into its heart.

It wouldn't be long before the whip came down.

But before Mick and Keith bought their Cheyne Walk pleasure palaces, in the remaining days prior to the big royalty cheques plopping onto their mats, Jagger had briefly stayed with Chrissie in the basement of a house in Berkeley Square with most of the Mamas and the Papas lodging upstairs. It must have been a short let or belonged to a friend because shortly after he moved to a flat in humble Harley House at 52 Marylebone Road – nowhere near as glamorous as the Berkeley Square address, unremarkable but semi-central. Chrissie Shrimpton traipsed along but was shortly afterwards elbowed by Mick at the twenty-first birthday celebrations of Tara Browne (the young aristo who a short while later would blow his mind out in a car) in Ireland. She took some acid, had a breakdown of some sort, attempted suicide and had to be admitted to hospital.

The bewitching but unfaithful Faithfull hove into view and sparks flew. Mick and Marianne stole a week together on a boat in the Mediterranean off Cannes. He wanted her to move in with him in Harley House.

"It had been Mick and Chrissie's place", she said, "and, although Chrissie had moved out, all her stuff was still there. Rummaging through her belongings, I found some charming things: a rocking horse, a Victorian birdcage with a brass bird in it that sang, hoop earrings. I remember she used Givenchy perfume". Chrissie also left her big brass bed.

Marianne observed, "I was always amazed at how vicious their relationship was... At the beginning, Chrissie seems to have had the upper hand; she was at least as strong as he was. But in the end he had completely worn her down and she was, as in the infamous song he wrote about her, under his thumb.

"Chrissie was from the old scene, the Swinging London of dollies and pop stars. It was a very put together look. The wig, false eyelashes and thick make up. It took her simply ages to get ready. She could never spend the night anywhere because she'd just fall apart; the times were changing and Chrissie wasn't".

People identify with songs. They'll detect a message in some song that relates to their lives, that strikes a chord. Even a misheard lyric can send shivers down the spine. How many Stones fans have listened to *Wild Horses* with a tear in their eye and thoughts of the one they love or the one they left behind? In that moment, *Wild Horses* becomes deeply personal; it becomes their song. Marianne thought it was hers and she can certainly stake some claim to it, yet it can't be entirely her song or their song or our song because *Wild Horses* is actually coveted by millions across the world who all think the same thing. They all think it's their song; they fantasise that Mick has somehow tuned into their heads and hearts and of course he has but they are universal emotions and despite its personal message, no individual or couple can actually possess it; it can never be their own.

But what about if the Stones actually wrote a song *for* you, or better still wrote a song *about* you? In fact how would you feel if they'd written five songs about you (*19th Nervous Breakdown, Stupid Girl,*

Under My Thumb, Yesterday's Papers, Out of Time) – or more specifically Jagger had allegedly written the lyrics about you? That would be great right? An honour? *That* would be personal.

Er no. That wouldn't be great. Not if all the lyrics tell you your stupid and out of time and yesterdays news, that you're having a breakdown, or that you're under his thumb. That unique distinction, five songs, or even more if you believe some accounts, belongs to Chrissie Shrimpton the stupid girl who fell in love with Jagger, who at first had him just where she wanted him, under *her* thumb in fact. But then the tables turned and it was her turn to cry and it was all over and you have a breakdown and try and commit suicide. You leave the flat you share to go to hospital. You leave all your possessions behind, your rocking horse, your brass bird in a cage and even your big brass bed. You leave it all for a bed in a hospital and the next thing you know Marianne Faithfull is climbing in under the still warm sheets and looking over your possessions as she boxes them up to make room for her own.

And it's your bed.

It's a tragic tale but Chrissie's loss is our gain since the tracks inspired by her miserable breakdown and suicide attempt are some of the best the band ever did.

She said "Mick doesn't like women; he never has".

When she was back on her feet, The Small Faces singer Steve Marriott took Jagger's place as her beau. They made the cover of *Rave* magazine, Chrissie planting a smacker on Steve's cheeky chops but a short while later, they were being busted for drug possession and that romance was off too.

Brian Jones and Anita Pallenberg had a new flat in the appropriately named Courtfield Road, a second floor artist's studio with high ceilings, massive windows, skylights, secret rooms and a minstrel's gallery situated just off Gloucester Place SW1, overlooking the tube station. It was appropriately named since it was the new hangout, a place to go and groove with your contemporaries after the club's had shut. Courtfield Road had become the glamorous couple's 'royal court' - Rat Pack central.

On any given night you might meet a drunk Eric Burdon chatting to McCartney both wearing Afghan coats, Donald Cammell licking a Rizla who could talk only about this film he was going to make, a luminous Tara Browne, the doomed heir to the Guinness brewing fortune, Robert Fraser sprawling in an armchair beneath giant sunflowers, a lamp covered in chiffon by his side (his Moroccan chauffeur, house servant and bed companion, Mohammed Chtaibi aka Mohammed Jajaj would be waiting obediently outside in the Rolls). Keith, who'd more or less moved in since he'd stopped going out with Linda Keith (the beautiful lynchpin figure who had persuaded Chas Chandler to manage Jimi Hendrix), was practicing being elegantly wasted. He'd stashed his guitars, apart from the one he was playing, in a backroom with a couple of bags full of his trademark street cowboy clothes and looked like he was going nowhere. The Queen's page Sir Mark Palmer, who later went off in a gipsy caravan to find the Holy Grail and was gone for 22 years, was pouring another drink and trying not to stagger while Brian lisped on about druids and aliens.

The exquisitely decadent Christopher Gibbs, antique dealer, doyen of Cheyne Walk, the nephew of a former British Governor of Rhodesia and voted one of the best dressed men in the world by *Vogue* magazine in 1965 was laying stoned on the Moroccan rug with joint ash all down his suit. Marianne Faithfull in brocade velvet lay next to him watching it all; well, she was watching Anita mainly but occasionally darting glances at an ostentatiously unimpressed Keith, which was funny because Keith was darting glances at Anita as well.

Byronic Brian and Anita quivered like ethereal self obsessed spiders in the middle of their web, like those around them, determined to change the world by dressing up in vivid hand-made duds, listening to the best music, taking the best drugs and above all staying young forever.

The rays of starlight emanated from the flat like some midnight Versailles. For a short time, it was here that all the multi-coloured butterflies alighted, but it was rare that any of the richly dressed party were more dazzling than Anita and Brian. By comparison, Mick and Chrissie might have appeared positively plain. Were Brian and Anita attracted to each other because they looked the same or did they grow to look like each other? The way they swapped clothes, adopted the same hairstyles, wore similar make up, smoked their cigarettes the same way; if you saw one from the corner of your eye, you'd have to double check which of them it was before you spoke: the more stoned you got, the more interchangeable they became. Was he having an affair with his own sister? These were the appetites of a Caligula; it was horrible yet fascinating.

Over in the corner under a stack of coats Jimi Hendrix was snoring off a four-day Black Bomber binge.

Apart from the wardrobes, suitcases and boxes spilling feathers, velvets and silks, the flat bristled with hi-fi and Brian's fabulous array of musical instruments, the stuff he used to co-create songs like *Lady Jane, I Am Waiting, Under My Thumb, Ruby Tuesday* and *Paint It Black*: some marimbas, a mellotron and his trademark Vox teardrop guitar. A true innovator, when Brian went into the studio with a sitar, a tamboura or a dulcimer, it was often the first time that instrument have ever been recorded in Britain.

Mick only ever dropped by occasionally. He disliked the grubbiness, the overflowing ashtrays, the dirty plates piled high in the sink and some of the peculiar, usually stoned strangers that would stumble around after accepting a lift back from the Speakeasy in Brian's Rolls Royce. He'd smoke a joint and make his excuses, unless there was a Beatle there of course and that didn't mean Ringo.

It was funny how the members of the band had a preferred restaurant or watering hole; for Mick it was The Casserole in the Kings Road, for Bill it was the Scotch of St. James; Keith favoured the Terrazza in Romilly Street, Soho; Brian would eat at Alvaro's and then go on to Blaises depending who was playing but then in truth, when he hit the bottle and the pills, he might visit all of them. Charlie didn't go out much unless there was some jazz going on. Mick usually avoided the Speakeasy because they'd overcharged him a couple of times.

Lennon, the Nowhere Man marooned out in Surrey, had found a new hangout, somewhere to drop off on the way home from the Scotch or the Ad Lib Club and then sometimes not go home at all, leaving the chauffeur slumped in the Rolls out in the street. Courtfield Road was the place to get stoned with your peers, drink a whisky or take a trip and talk bollocks about music, stardom, rip off managers, boutiques, the latest dealer in town and be surrounded by any number of adoring girls. It was an excuse to avoid going back to the stockbroker belt and Cynthia. Sometimes he'd just stay in the clubs rabbiting to yawning friends a mile-a-minute while the staff respectfully swept around him; sometimes he'd sleep in the Rolls Royce, him in the back and one of his despairing chauffeurs, Bill or Anthony in the front. What the hell was he doing out in stockbroker land? Why was he still with Cynth? Why had he got married in the first place? Why hadn't he waited and had a chance to play the field like McCartney? Why did he have Julian so young? The kid was great but John wasn't ready for children, he was still a kid himself and he wasn't happy in snooty suburbia.

The London scene was unfolding like a flower, evolving fast. It was getting damned exciting here and he was stuck out in the sticks; he was missing out; he wasn't meeting *the* people. Paul was getting off on introducing him to crazies like Robert Fraser and his sidekick drug dealer Spanish Tony, acting the man-about-town, coming on like Mr. Super Hip and he hadn't even taken an acid tab yet. McCartney made Lennon feel like a tourist - a day-tripper for chrissake, like it was *his* city. Lennon chatted with Tara Browne who would be dead soon and Lennon would write a song about him.

"Oh, that was a great period," Lennon said. "We were like kings of the jungle then, and were very close to the Stones. I spent a lot of time with Brian and Mick, and I admired them. I dug them the first time I saw them in whatever that place is they came from - the Crawdaddy in Richmond.

"We were all just at the prime, and we all used to just go around London in our cars and meet each other and talk about music with the Animals and Eric and all that. It was a really good time. That was the best period, fame-wise; we didn't get mobbed so much. I don't know; it was like a men's smoking club, just a very good scene.

"We created something, Mick and us, we didn't know what we were doing, but we were all talking, blabbing over coffee, like they must have done in Paris, talking about paintings . . . me, Burdon and Brian Jones would be up night and day talking about music, playing records and blabbing and arguing and getting drunk. It's beautiful history".

Another mini galaxy was 11 Gunterstone Road, West Kensington. Andy Summers later of the Police was in the basement with 700 records and a load of macrobiotic food. Zoot Money was on the ground floor with his girlfriend; the Moody Blues were upstairs. Hendrix's girlfriend Kathy Etchingham and Eric Burdon's girlfriend Angie King shared one of the flats. George Harrison was going out with another resident Marie, before she married Justin Hayward. Billie Davis lived next door in a house that was briefly occupied by Brian Jones. There were other young beauties distributed through the premises, most of whom worked in the clubs in the evenings - the Speakeasy or the Bag o' Nails - while they took stabs at making it as models or actresses during the daytime. These young ladies held a magnetic attraction for Lennon and Ringo at a time when their respective partners were tucked away and hushed up back in Liverpool. Hendrix, eager for any new scene involving bright-eyed girls was also soon on the scent.

It was a non-stop party; lights blazed and a knife was jammed into the gas meter to keep the place hot – as if it needed help.

The Bag o' Nails started life a hundred years before as a place where gentlemen could meet ladies who charged by the hour. These days it is the Miranda Club - a private members club where hostesses are available for dining and dancing, so not much has changed – except for a spell in the 60s when Chris Farlowe and the Thunderbirds or Georgie Fame might be the cabaret. Hendrix did a showcase there and the rock cognoscenti stood among the hookers who stared up at wild thing Jimi from under their false eyelashes.

It's hard to know how much time was being devoted to the big world issues in these late-night raps in clubs and flats, how much talk of peace movements and revolution; very little probably, in those early days anyway. McCartney was showing some awareness, some appreciation of the arts and politics, courtesy of Robert Fraser and the Ashers. Brian Jones could be as pseudo-intellectual as the best of them but it is odds on that the real awakening of political awareness only occurred at the cusp of the 60s and the 70s despite the student sit-ins and peace marches. Back in those joyous days of naiveté, the message was the music, best heard stoned, and the place to be was here with all these colourful, beautiful people, these chosen few who were also passengers on the crazy train. This was the centre of the world man, selfish and sure of itself and although the first tender shoots of political understanding were emerging, you wouldn't have ever dreamt that somewhere out there the Vietnam War was raging.

 It's said that the Beatles song, *Day in the Life* is about Tara Browne, the charming young Guinness heir although McCartney says, "In my head I was imagining a politician bombed out on drugs, who'd stopped at some traffic lights and he didn't notice that the lights had changed. The 'blew his mind' was purely a drug reference, nothing to do with a car crash".

The story goes that in the early hours of December 18, 1966, Browne was driving with his girl friend the model Suki Potier, (who would later go out with Brian Jones) in a Lotus Elan through South Kensington at over 100 mph. There is no evidence that he was under the influence of booze or drugs but he was a regular visitor to Courtfield Road and frequently stayed up all night taking acid. For whatever reason, he jumped the traffic lights at the junction of Redcliffe Square and Redcliffe Gardens, smashed into a parked lorry and was killed instantly. Potier was not injured. Another account of the accident says that Tara was on his way to visit David Vaughan who was painting a design on the front of Tara's Kings Road shop *Dandy Fashions*. He smashed his Lotus Elan (the same model that Emma Peel drove in The Avengers) into the back of a parked van while swerving to avoid a Volkswagen that had pulled out in front of him.

David Vaughan, the father of actress/model Sadie Frost was a highly eccentric psychedelic traveller and anarchist artist. With partners Douglas Binder and Dudley Edwards, he had painted another of Browne's cars, a Cadillac that became impressively psychedelic in the process. Paul McCartney saw it and got the team to paint his favourite piano and asked Vaughan to paint a mural at his St. John's Wood home. It was in the post-Jane Asher days and in truth McCartney really wanted a bit of company more than a mural and so Vaughan moved in for six months. He recalled watching Paul sitting in a big sofa in front of a huge open fire in the dark playing music at top volume for hours on end. Vaughan laboured with his paints while

McCartney took young Sadie to London Zoo.

An uncompromising artist, Vaughan, when constructing a living tableau, had once put four year-old Sadie on a crucifix outside the Royal College of Art dressed only in her knickers. The painting of the event was entitled *The Crucifixion of Sadie*; another was called *Sadie in a Mental Prison.* He left Frost's mother and his younger daughter Sunshine Tara Purple Velvet shortly after. Vaughan's later works depicting harrowing scenes of war and famine have been compared with those of a 21st century Goya, but his 60s murals were optimistic splashes of colour and were highly prized by the likes of Eric Clapton and Princess Margaret. Other customers included Lord Snowdon, the Admiralty, Henry Moore and Paul McCartney. David Bailey made a series of posters with him. Of his later work, one critic pointed out that Vaughan's subjects were, "the victims of our time, victims of poverty and famine in the third world, or victims of isolation in the rich industrialised countries, not reached by general prosperity: unemployed youths at the edge of town, who, wearing masks, are waiting for something to blow up. People somewhere between desperation and crime."

Sadie, who clearly adored her largely absent and volatile father and who was inconsolable when he died in 2003, had become accustomed to a household where drugs and alcohol were in the kitchen cupboards and commented that she had become clean living as a consequence: "I've kind of gone the other way. I don't drink much. I don't smoke and I'm scared of drugs".

Her father returned her love by trying to make amends for not being around at those times when she might have needed him. When her marriage to Jude Law was breaking down, he had discharged himself from Manchester Royal Infirmary where he had been being treated for hepatitis C, and arrived at the Frost household threatening to shoot Law. He freely admitted that he might have made the threat but claimed to police that he was on medication and was feeling "stressed". He later expressed frustration that Frost had abandoned her acting career when she'd married Law, disparaging his son-in-Law saying: "She was the star and he was in some bloody soap or something or other when they first met".

Despite on one occasion being put into an asylum after a bad acid trip and spending three years as a down and out after the experience, Vaughan had a large body of work to his name; he decorated a burns unit in a hospital, an adventure playground, numerous projects for youth groups, has exhibited at the ICA and the National Portrait Gallery and had his own gallery.

Lennon had been reading the Daily Mail report of the accident that killed Tara Browne, and the words for the start of *Day in the Life* started appearing in his head. McCartney knew Browne a lot better than John and had in fact introduced the pair to each other. They'd once gone to Liverpool together and Browne was with Paul when he had an accident and split his lip (there is a lot of mad internet speculation that McCartney died in this accident and that Browne was employed to become McCartney because of the slight resemblance they bore to one another).

An old Etonian, Tara was the son of Lord and Lady Oranmore, otherwise known as Dominick Browne and Oonagh Guinness, he famous for sitting silently in the House of Lords for 72 years without ever speaking in any debate; and she an heiress to the Guinness fortune and the youngest of the three Golden Guinness Girls. Had he lived, he would have inherited £1 million on his 25th birthday. One of his older brothers was the Hon. Garech Browne, of Luggala, County Wicklow in Ireland, an enthusiast of traditional Irish music who encouraged the set up of The Chieftains, Ireland's famous group of traditional musicians and founded Claddagh Records which was Clannad's record label.

It's said that you couldn't fail to like Tara who had a beaming smile and brushed his hair forward so he looked like a Beatle. In the book *Blinds and Shutters* by Michael Cooper, Anita Pallenberg described taking a trip with him: "I remember being with Tara Browne on one of the first acid trips. He had a Lotus sports car and suddenly near Sloane Square everything went red. The lights went red, the trees were flaming and we just jumped out of the car and left it there".

His death shook Brian rigid. It drew a pall over Courtfield Road and brought to an end those innocent days of hedonism. The court moved on; a lot of them found a new rendezvous in Mount Street - the lavish apartment belonging to Robert Fraser.

5

Robert Fraser

CATALYST, GALLERY owner, art director of the *Sergeant Pepper* sleeve, the man who inspired the Apple Records logo and the song *Gimme Shelter*, supplier of exotica to the stars, one of the first men to die of AIDS in the UK. He went from being perhaps the pivotal 60s figure to a squalid existence preying on young boys in Leicester Square amusement arcades. It was Robert who was handcuffed to Jagger in the back of the car in the famous Redlands drug bust.

Robert hated the soubriquet *Groovy Bob* and would have detested  the idea that anyone thought he was a drug dealer because he would never sell you any drugs; he'd just have a whole range of them in a box that you could dip in to. "Try one of these dear boy; they're simply splendid". He wouldn't take any money, although God knows he always seemed short of it but then he would occasionally try and sell you a Magritte. Ask McCartney who bought several from him. Even when he was flogging you a painting, he did it with incredible old Etonian panache. After talking with McCartney about a logo for the Beatles' new Apple Records label, he'd visited McCartney's big house in Cavendish Avenue and discreetly left a small, framed picture of an apple by Magritte on McCartney's table. Paul commented, "I thought that was the coolest thing anyone's ever done with me. When I saw it,

I just thought 'Robert'. Nobody else could have done that'.

Robert was *so* cool, he was quoted in the 1965 Swinging London article in *Time Magazine*: "Right now, London has something that New York used to have: everybody wants to be there. There's no place else. Paris is calcified. There's an indefinable thing about London that makes people want to go there".

His gallery was a rainbow flash in a then drab Duke Street, one of the only sources of contemporary art - Andy Warhol, Jim Dine and the like - in a West End packed with galleries knocking out fox hunting scenes. The Robert Fraser gallery was the White Cube of its day. In fact, Lord Snowdon took a photograph of Robert Fraser in which it is hard to tell that he is not White Cube's Jay Jopling - another Old Etonian with a glamorous celebrity client list and a very small discreet nameplate on the door of his gallery.

The appearance of the gallery was sensational; one day there would be a conventional window display, the next, the window had been taken out and an AC Cobra sports car painted in psychedelic colours would be nosing out onto the street.

Fraser was the son of a Scottish merchant banker, who was in turn the son of the butler to Gordon Selfridge the department store magnate and he was thus identified at Eton as being nouveau riche and developed that unique kind of snobbery the newly moneyed oft acquire. He coupled this with outrageous social climbing and an utter disregard for the rules. He liked the company of toffs and yobs in equal measure. He loathed sport but loved sportsmen.

Robert was of course gay, it was almost compulsory at Eton as fellow old Etonian, the writer Derek Raymond commented: "It was an absolute hotbed of buggery and an excellent preparation for vice of any kind". It was also where you went to get that tremendous self-assurance with which its old boys are shot through. Eton "formed him to a great extent", added Paul Getty. "Formed his style, his personality. It's still one of the best places to learn arrogance".

Flung out of Eton for smoking cigarettes, he was conscripted into the army and joined the Kings African Rifles stationed in Uganda, in charge of a regiment of black soldiers. Here a young boxing champion caught his eye, a 6 feet 4 inch sergeant major in the army and a fine physical specimen. Robert and the junior officer Idi Amin, later to be the President of Uganda (and the last king of Scotland), became friends and made rather strange bedfellows - there is speculation that that is exactly what they became. It was the last days of Empire and the east coast of Africa was alive with goings on – white mischief. Later, when Amin had seized power and was threatening Britain, Robert would get hot with pride whenever he saw the strutting figure on the television.

After the army, Fraser went to New York and immediately fell into an artsy set in Manhattan, working in galleries and setting up exhibitions. Here he started to foster the healthy contempt for money that only those who can write home for a few quid whenever necessary can have. His parents seem to have coughed up every time this happened right until the end although his relationship with his father must have been a strain on him since he would become almost overwhelmed by stuttering whenever they spoke together. School friend Christopher Gibbs reasons that perhaps Fraser felt over indulged and to some extent it annoyed him. "I think it was a little bit of a disappointment to him that his father was so understanding, he said. "I think it deprived him a little of the agonies of being misunderstood".

Having networked the art scene of NYC, Robert became convinced that taking modern American art to London was a potential money-spinner. He acquired the investment to open his Duke Street gallery from his parents and returned to England in the early 60's with big plans and a bulging address book. The artist Jim Dine commented, "Robert knew everyone in the world at one point". He'd made the acquaintance of all the movers and shakers in the New York art scene and he already knew all the West End's well heeled. Soon he would be able to add the rising new wealthy of pop to his client list.

Fraser's promiscuity was a constant undercurrent. He would apparently discuss the manhood of a Puerto Rican boy with the same gusto with which he might describe a fine wine. In London, he haunted sleazy clubs with Christopher Gibbs. He had a regular boyfriend but it was the bits of rough that interested him, rent boys and louts. On one occasion they swayed into Muriel Belcher's Colony Room in Soho and Francis Bacon remarked, "Here come the Belgravia pansies", although he and Robert were great friends; Bacon even wanted to paint him. Fraser had high artistic standards but low morals and he could be incredibly snobbish; sometimes he wouldn't sell someone a painting merely because he didn't like his or her look or thought the person was vulgar.

Of course the libertines of the pop world didn't mind all the bright coloured suits, buggery and hep cat talk. McCartney said of him: "For me and many others, Robert Fraser was one of the most influential

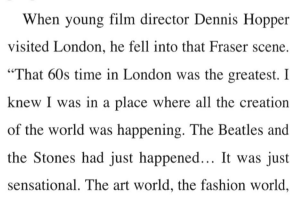

people of the London 60s scene".

When young film director Dennis Hopper visited London, he fell into that Fraser scene. "That 60s time in London was the greatest. I knew I was in a place where all the creation of the world was happening. The Beatles and the Stones had just happened… It was just sensational. The art world, the fashion world, they were exploding. It was the most creative place I've ever seen. I said all this to Billy Wilder and he said, 'It sounds like you're describing Berlin just before the Second World War'".

Later, Fraser and Hopper would tour Mexico together looking at art hoovering up all the cocaine the country could offer.

Fraser's flat at 23 Mount Street (only a few yards from the gallery but Robert would only ever go to work in the Rolls Royce – and was frequently late) was for many years the hub of the 60s, the place to be if you weren't in Courtfield Road before its demise. In fact if Brian Jones wasn't on the road with the Stones or at home then he was invariably in Mount Street. Michael Cooper who photographed the *Sergeant Pepper* sleeve was always at hand with his camera to record the comings and goings. Terry Southern (who wrote *Candy* in which Ringo Starr had a small part, and the screenplay for *Barbarella*) would be arguing with Brian Jones drinking Turkish coffee and smoking a pipe of Moroccan. The Bonham Carters would be talking to Robert who was trying to sell Mick Jagger a Magritte but Jagger was still not yet in the art-buying league although McCartney was, and so was J. P. Getty Jnr., son of the richest man in the world. Getty liked art and hash and coke and heroin and whisky and beautiful women and anything else he could get his hands on.

Peter Blake, the artist who actually put the *Sergeant Pepper* sleeve together with his then wife Jann Haworth (Haworth waits in vain for her equal share of the acclaim for the project), watched the way that the riff raff of rock radiated around the Fraser apartment. As much as the pop stars were adored and feted and mobbed in the street, conversely bohemians like Fraser had pop stars sitting at his feet.

"You could just as well say that Mick Jagger and the others were interested in hanging around Robert", said Blake. "Mick at the time was still a ruffian, although famous. In a way he got more from Robert than Robert got from him. He learned a certain sophistication from those people. The rock people were glamorous too, but Robert was very glamorous. He was handsome, incredibly well dressed. He kind of tutored them". And he did it in an incredibly plummy Richard Burton kind of way.

One of the things Fraser undoubtedly taught them was how to acquire premier grade drugs. 'Spanish' Tony Sanchez appeared on the scene, nobody knows quite from where save that Christopher Gibbs thinks Fraser might have found him in an amusement arcade and taken him home for hanky panky. Sanchez makes no mention of being gay in his own book *Up and Down with the Rolling Stones*, indeed he himself had an up and down relationship with Marianne Faithfull at some point but a little bit of bi-sexuality was de rigueur in those days.

A visitor with a stash from Italy introduced Fraser to cocaine and clearly Fraser introduced it to everyone else, starting with McCartney. When that ran out, Spanish Tony found a local supplier and was from then on in high demand; so impressed was Keith Richards with Tony's resourcefulness that he was taken on as a personal assistant/driver just so Keith would have him on tap.

Prone to flying off to Los Angeles at the drop of a hat, Fraser was also instrumental in introducing the drug there. It's a dubious claim to fame but now every dollar bill in the town is impregnated with the stuff.

Robert had his first acid trip one night in Rome and was found hours later, collapsed under a tree in a square with no idea where he was or indeed who he was. Undeterred by the traumatic trip, Fraser the sensualist somehow sniffed out the drug in London and shared it around his friends. Anita Pallenberg says he was the first man in London to have it; Christopher Gibbs says that Robert had it before anybody else and then took more of it than anybody else, although the truth probably is that the source of the drug was Michael Hollingshead an extraordinary Englishman who had been experimenting with LSD for years in the USA and who wrote *The Man Who Turned on the World* about his mind frazzling experiences.

With the ever-present top quality stimulants and hallucinogens as a lure, Robert's glittering modern art exhibitions were becoming more star-studded than ever. At one, Jagger and Faithfull, the latest, hottest couple in town were giggling and having a mock fight that involved Mick pouring his champagne down her cleavage. Marlon Brando accompanied by a couple of young Thai girls was acting as doorman, standing by the gallery entrance and bowing to incredulous latecomers as they entered. Robert had Brando's belt in his hand, which seemed to hold an enormous sexual charge for him. When the VIP guests went back to the Mount Street apartment (known to all as 'the flat') for drinks, drugs and dalliances they saw Tony Curtis chatting with Tom Wolfe and Donald Cammell still going on and on about this film idea he had with his tame crazy criminal David Litvinoff, who was a friend of the Krays, in tow. It was the networking centre of the universe.

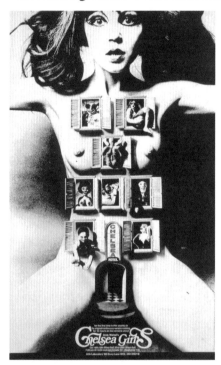

When the Warhol circus came to London with a print of Andy's film *Chelsea Girl*, it was of course to Robert's apartment that they headed. The address of the 'flat' was on the international grapevine. Fraser asked Keith Richards' sidekick Stash (Prince Stanislas Klossowski de Rola, son of the painter Balthus) to go and get hold of McCartney's film projectors so they could all view it. The Beatles all had projectors; it was their custom to hire in movies for private shows for themselves, friends and girlfriends; they thus avoided the hullabaloo that would have been caused by them turning up at cinemas. Ringo was a particular home movie fan with left field tastes; he liked Kenneth Anger, Bruce Conner and other stuff from the strange end of the American spectrum.

Semi-royals, of course, constantly dazzled Mick, and Fraser acted as his entrée into their world. He once took Jagger and Pallenberg to Wilton, the Palladian mansion outside Salisbury owned by the

Herbert family. Its occupant Henry Herbert, another member of the Chelsea set, directed *Emily* the soft porn film starring Koo Stark (who once had a relationship with Prince Andrew) and episodes of TV series *Bergerac* and *Shoestring* as well as performing his functions as the 17th Earl of Pembroke. The assembled guests stood slack-jawed as Henry showed off the family's Rembrandts, Reynolds and Reubens. Later, Cecil Beaton, the royal photographer who claimed to have had relationships with both Greta Garbo and Gary Cooper, took a picture of Jagger's posterior that now hangs in the Wilton guest room.

The Herbert family owned a villa in Tangier in Morocco. Robert frequently went to Morocco, as did many others in the clique; some went for the sun and others went for the sodomy; Noel Coward referred to Tangier as, "a sunny place for shady people". Paul Getty owned a palace in Marrakesh where Brian Jones was a houseguest as was the playboy drug dealer Comte Jean de Breteuil; one New Year's Eve, Lennon and McCartney just popped by to sing *Auld Langs Syne* in the desert. Availing themselves of the local dope, a writer who was also in attendance commented that the two Beatles were laid on the floor unable to stand or speak and that he had never seen so many out of control people in his life.

Talitha Getty and husband Paul had their photo taken on their roof with the Atlas Mountains and the massive mosque tower as a backdrop. He weas a djellaba and stands in the background; she sprawls against the wall in an embroidered caftan and white gaucho pants; it is likely they were both probably stoned out of their heads; they are young, beautiful and unbelievably wealthy, bohemian jet setters, the definitive rich hippies. The Patrick Litchfield photo is an icon of the period.

Anita Pallenberg says that once when she was in Tangier with Robert and Keith Richards, they spotted two perspiring men in dark suits wandering along the beach in the brilliant sunshine. Robert recognised them and chatted to them warmly, introducing Anita and Keith to his old mates Reggie and Ronnie Kray.

There was a long tradition of Tangier providing a bolthole for European and American bohemians. The writer and musician Paul Bowles had really blazed the trail when in 1947; he became one of the first of the city's international expatriates. He first visited in 1931 with his friend Aaron Copeland the composer, on the advice of another famous friend the writer Gertrude Stein. His presence (and the alleyway fleshpots in the northern Morocco port) was a magnet to numerous followers including Truman Capote, Tennessee Williams and Gore Vidal. The Beat writers Allen Ginsberg, William S. Burroughs and Gregory Corso followed in the next wave in the 50s; who with the exception of Corso, were homosexuals all. Burroughs was drifting after he had killed his girlfriend with a pistol in a drunken re enactment of William Tell's shooting of an apple from his son's head; to him, an accomplished junkie, the freely available drugs made Tangier impossibly attractive.

Brion Gysin, the originator of the cut up poetry technique and the *Dreamachine* (a device that utilised revolving lights to mess with the Alpha waves of the brain) was a resident too. Here he met and befriended Burroughs. In fact Tangier provides the backdrop for

Burrough's most famous book *Naked Lunch* when it is renamed the *Interzone*, a place where sex, drugs and murder can be found on every street corner, a place where the basest of desires could be indulged. In the years before World War II, Tangier was a free port administered by France, Spain, Italy and the UK and was designated an International Zone. Consequently, it became notorious for the activities of the numerous spies that were playing their own great game in the souks, massage parlours and coffee houses.

6

The Dreamachine

BRION GYSIN, was an artist and a mystic, the creator of the cut up technique, inventor of the *Dreamachine*, discovered the Master Musicians of Jajouka.

Burrough's friend Brion Gysin, born plain Brian, a British/Canadian who claimed he was a Swiss and who then became an American, was born in the grandiose Georgian Taplow House in Taplow, Buckinghamshire, which at the time, 1916, was serving as a military hospital and housed wounded Canadian soldiers (as well as soldiers' pregnant wives). He was brought up in the icy wastes of rural Canada and attended school in the UK where he was recognised as having a ferocious intelligence, but never knew his father who died in battle a few months after his birth; he was raised by an aunt and his mother. These factors, Gysin later blamed for the trajectory of his life: misogyny, homosexual promiscuity, enthusiastic drug consumption and precious little artistic fulfilment.

Perhaps influenced by the aristocratic chums he'd made at public school, he became ashamed of his lowly past and when a passport officer mistakenly spelled out his forename as 'Brion', he jumped at the opportunity to change his persona and kept the misspelled name (later, in Tangier when he was running the 1001 Nights restaurant,

Gysin affected the name Gysin von Liestal. William Burroughs, before they became friends, knew a fraud when he saw one and noted that Gysin, "doesn't have dime one", but ventured that he would probably get rich by acting rich). The school that inculcated in him snobbery also nurtured Gysin's budding homosexuality and a love (and talent) for art, the English language as well: he became editor of the school newspaper.

After school, Brion's travels began; he enrolled in the Sorbonne in Paris, hanging out in the Café Select in Montparnasse, which provided sanctuary to literary types during the day and 'Queers and mad queens from all over Europe", by night. In an interview conducted in 1982, Gysin described the café as a "sick Cage aux Folles". When he had once desired an expensive book by Henry Miller, lacking the cash, he simply sold himself.

A few years in Greece followed, where he contracted syphilis, read his Baudelaire and became a hashish devotee. In Athens, he encountered the supremely decadent Denham Fouts, an international male prostitute and opium addict, who provided sexual services to Europe's café society, amongst whom was Prince Paul, later King Paul of Greece. Fouts, who was also a large cocaine user lived in darkened rooms and would let white mice run all over him as he smoked opium in a jewelled pipe. Among his friends, were Truman Capote, Paul Bowles and Christopher Isherwood, who called him, "the most expensive male prostitute in the world" Fouts died on the toilet, aged thirty-five.

Learning from a master that he could live high on the hog if he played his cards right, Gysin toured the world on the 'princess circuit' as an international bum for hire and eventually washed up in Tangiers; he intended to visit just for the summer and eventually stayed twenty three years.

But it was while he was living at the Beat Hotel in Paris that he met William Burroughs again (Burroughs was working on *The Soft Machine* and *The Ticket That Exploded*) and Gysin told him that he considered the writing form was twenty years behind the art world in its use of random effects to create collages, and he taught Burroughs the cut up technique that later would chracterise his work.

'Cut ups' was originally invented by Tristan Tzara, a surrealist, who in the 1920's stood on a stage and announced to the assembly that he could compose a poem in five minutes made up of words drawn from a hat. The poetry purists in the theatre took this as a major affront to their art and Tzara found him self expelled from the surrealist movement as a consequence. Gysin took the technique and in 1959 wrote a poem called *Minutes to Go* comprised of (unedited) random cut up newspaper headlines that proved to be surprisingly coherent and meaningful. Numerous high-minded musicians including David Bowie, Patti Smith, Jagger, Laurie Anderson, Michael Stipe and even Iggy Pop have appropriated the style over the years and used it in the composition of their lyrics. The conceptual artist Genesis P-Orridge of Throbbing Gristle was a fan. Paul McCartney also experimented with the form and it was even, apparently, an influence on Keith Haring's paintings.

Minutes to Go was developed into a more focused and elegant word play technique, which he called 'the permutation'; a single phrase running through all existing possibilities of order, starting at the beginning, then the middle, then the end, then between all those places; words replaced with those phonetically similar but with different meanings that create a whole new set of completely strange and unplanned statements.

Below is an excerpt:

Rub out the write word

Rub out right word thee

Rub out word rite thee

Rub out the word right

Rub out right the word

Rub out word thee write

Rub the word right out

Rub the right out word

Rub the out word right

Word out right

Right word out

Out right word

Rub Out the Write Word by Brion Gysin. From Minutes to Go, by Sinclair Beiles, William Burroughs, Gregory Corso, and Brion Gysin (San Francisco: Beach Books, Texts & Documents, 1968), p. 62.

The polymath Gysin, considered to be one of the founders of the beatnik movement, a painter, an accomplished Japanese and Arabic calligraphist, a poet, a novelist, an historian, a radical filmmaker and an inventor, started messing about with sound cut-ups back in the 40s, whenever, basically, he could get his hands on a tape recorder. He worked with the Cambridge mathematician Ian Somerville, William Burroughs' constant companion and the man who would later run the recording studio in Ringo's flat making experimental music for Paul McCartney.

In 1960, Gysin showed off the techniques when he recorded some cut-up poetry for the BBC. The resultant work when broadcast, recorded the second lowest audience approval rating the corporation had ever experienced, an achievement in itself. Undeterred, he continued the experiments on paper, tape, film and canvas, accompanied by a heroin-charged Burroughs and fuelled himself by an abundance of local hashish. Paul Bowles wrote of Gysin and the other 'Beat Poets', "I can't understand their interest in drugs and madness".

Burroughs himself said of Gysin, "there was something dangerous about what he was doing". Burroughs would sit and watch Gysin furiously painting, filling his canvases with mystic symbols and calligraphy, literally trying to inject magic into his paintings and observed, "Bryon is risking his life and his sanity when he paints". He thought of Gysin as some sort of magician and insisted that he'd witnessed Gysin vanish on a couple of occasions. He told an interviewer "I can assure you it's one of the least astounding stories you'll ever hear about Brion Gysin". Other residents of the Beat Hotel bore witness to Brion's mysticism and also claimed to have seen him disappear.

The cut-up technique received acknowledgement elsewhere: Timothy Leary wrote, "The essence of anything is the cut up. Cut up words. Cut up pictures. Boil it down to the essence". In 1964, Marshall McLuhan wrote a piece called *Notes on Burroughs* in *Nation* magazine in which he mentioned, "Brion Gysin's cut-up method". J. G. Ballard became keen on the idea and Gore Vidal, who had met Gysin and referred to him as "a brilliant creature", thought that Gysin's influence had been key in making Burroughs and his work notable. The New York Times said that the cut-up method "actually knocks out logic and makes sudden room for images not seen in the vicinity of fiction before". However Jack Kerouac wasn't a fan, declaring that in his view the cut-up wasn't as interesting as the stream of consciousness passages that Burroughs employed elsewhere.

Gysin and Burroughs collaborated with Antony Balch on a film that utilised the cut-up technique. When *Cut-Ups* was shown at the Cinephone theatre in Oxford Street in 1966, the management complained about the huge number of personal items – handbags, gloves, briefcases, overcoats, hats – that the disorientated audience left behind in the cinema after the performances. Burroughs commented that the theatre "looked like a battlefield".

When Gysin developed the *Dreamachine* with the aid of Ian Somerville, any conservatives around him must have been driven to think that his sanity had finally deserted him. The machine consists of a cardboard roll the diameter of a vinyl album with geometric shapes cut from it and a light suspended in its centre. The tube is placed on an old-style record player and the deck turns at 45 or 78 rpm. This sets up a rhythmic flashing that the observer must look at through *closed* eyes.

The pulsating light stimulates the optical nerve and supposedly alters the brain's electrical oscillations. The patterns become shapes and symbols, flashing at between 8 and 13 pulses a second, which is the same speed as Alpha waves, the electrical oscillations that exist in the brain when the brain is in a state of relaxation. The colours swirl around and the viewer starts to feel that they are being surrounded by them. It was claimed that viewing a *Dreamachine* allows one to enter a hypnagogic state inducing drowsiness. It broke the sight barrier.

Viewers exposed to the machine quickly became terribly enthusiastic about its potential for creating altered states. The narrator on one of the Gysin, Burroughs short films comments, "Anything that can be done chemically can be done in other ways". Gysin himself imagined that one day, there would be a *Dreamachine* in every suburban house; families would gather around it in the evenings and watch it with their eyes closed. It would replace the TV altogether, and its viewers would instead watch internal programming. Allen Ginsberg was thrilled by the machine and enthused to Timothy Leary about it.

When it was exhibited at the Louvre's Musee des Arts Decoratifs, the Herald Tribune said that the "big hit of the show is certainly the *Dreamachine*. Like moths, the visitors are drawn to the whirling, flashing black cylinder on a turntable. A few minutes later some of them move back giddily. Others just wander away in a smiling trance".

Gysin made several attempts to get his machine put into production. Helena Rubenstein, the cosmetics manufacturer (and one of the richest women in the world) considered manufacturing it it as did the electronics company Philips ultimately to no avail; then Gysin found the money to take his idea to New York. Columbia Records looked at it and concluded there was potential but then seemed to be alienated by the futurist Gysin who told the board that records would one day be played without needles; that an electronic eye would scan a disc instead. John Geiger in his book *Nothing is True: Everything is Permitted: The Life of Brion Gysin* remarks, "Gysin was so far out front that there was always a real danger of people losing sight of him altogether".

In his time in NYC, Gysin stayed at the Chelsea Hotel, the bohemian redoubt, at that time, of the English pop artist Allen Jones, Arthur Miller and the ubiquitous William Burroughs who was in town to conduct some poetry readings. Other luminaries of the great red-brick building have included Dylan Thomas, Brendan Behan, Leonard Cohen, Tennessee Williams, Quentin Crisp, Arthur C. Clarke, who wrote *2001: A Space Odyssey* there, Allen Ginsberg, Gregory Corso, Sid Vicious and Nancy Spungen.

Ultimately unsuccessful with the *Dreamachine*, Burroughs and Gysin returned to London in 1965, where their reputations preceded them; they were granted only a one-month visa and were thoroughly shaken down by customs officers. They spent some time working together in Ringo Starr's flat where Ian Sommerville was doing cut-up recordings and Paul McCartney experimented with the *Dreamachine* and the cut-up lyrical technique. McCartney's biographer Barry Miles asserts that the sound recordings they did there were an influence on *Sgt. Pepper's Lonely Hearts Club Band*, which utilises half heard radio broadcasts and animal noises.

Another devotee of the *Dreamachine* was Kurt Cobain, a long term William Burroughs fan. In fact, a mysterious group calling itself the *Friends Understanding Kurt* (FUK) contacted *High Times* magazine after Kurt's death alleging that his protracted use of a *Dreamachine* had been responsible for his mental instability and by extension his suicide. Calling the machine "a dangerous trance-inducing contraption," and alleging that there had been a "string of suicides associated with the machine since the 60s". They went on to say that

Courtney Love had her suspicions that the *Dreamachine* may have been a factor in Cobain's deteriorated mental state and that Cobain may have been staring (with his eyes shut) at the machine for up to 72 hours at a stretch. This is all of course a hoax… or is it?

High Times was able to locate the San Francisco businessman who had sold the *Dreamachine* to Cobain. He stated that Kurt had spoken to him around twenty times in the six months before his death but then went on to scoff at the notion that he might have been using it for up to 72 hours at a time. However the supplier agreed that the machine could well have been a factor in unhinging Cobain.

Later, Gysin approached Jeremy Fry, the enigmatic son of the last chairman of the Fry's chocolate company and the owner of the hugely successful Rotork Engineering, a company that supplies equipment to the oil and gas industries. Fry promised to take the project on and give Gysin a royalty. But again Gysin was thwarted when, for some reason Fry lost interest and moved on.

Jeremy Fry: the grandson of the last Chairman of Fry's Chocolate, inventor, philanthropist, seducer, gave James Dyson his first break

Handsome, charismatic, with piercing green eyes, Fry swung both ways, as apparently did one of his close friends, the equally charismatic, handsome and bisexual Lord Snowdon. Fry led an extraordinary exotic life liberally sprinkled with lovers. He was at school at Gordonstoun, then flew with the RAF but couldn't go into the family chocolate business because his father Cecil Fry had, much to the chagrin of Jeremy's many aunts and cousins, sold the company to their arch rivals Cadbury. So, Fry Jr. part qualified as an architect before joining his brother in an engineering company that built components for the aviation industry, and developed, and built racing cars. However his fortune wasn't assured until he developed a valve actuator which, when housed in an explosion-proof housing, was snapped up by the oil and gas industries.

The company he started, Rotork Engineering, grew at a spectacular rate through the 60s and had manufacturing plants all over the world including a huge factory in the USA, which Fry built on swamp land and where he spent his spare time trawling for soft shell crabs. The money poured in and Fry was able to buy the vast, opulent Widcombe Manor, situated outside Bath where he and his wife Camilla held court. Cecil Beaton and Yehui Menuhin would pop in for tea, and Lord Snowdon, then Antony Armstrong-Jones, courted Princess Margaret there; the couple canoodled in a specially built suite that had its own jukebox (designed by Fry of course). With their other friends, they defined the 'fast set', and were regularly featured in the gossip columns and snapped at the airport coming back from skiing trips or safaris.

The kind of relentless energy that drove him to develop a new type of powered wheel chair, a flat-bottomed, high-speed boat, to invest in John Dunbar's Indica Gallery, to acquire and restore the Theatre Royal in Bath, to buy and restore an entire village in France, to found the company and finance the research that led to James Dyson's vacuum cleaner empire, also saw him motorbike racing, sailing, going on expeditions into the desert and chasing women, and occasionally men. In the early 50s Fry had been arrested and fined £2 for 'beguiling' a guards officer in Hyde Park. It was this indiscretion that led to an insistence by Buckingham Palace that he would be an inappropriate best man for the wedding of the princess and her dashing photographer beau. The papers reported that Fry was unable to exercise the role because of illness.

For his part, Lord Snowdon has repeatedly denied he was bisexual; however one tale is that Princess Margaret, whilst attending a function, was asked by one of the guests how was the queen. She is said to have replied, "Which one, my mother, my sister, or my husband?"

There is no doubt though that with his dark glasses and a Gauloises dangling from his lip, Snowdon presented a dashing image and was a sexually charged, serial seducer who probably never got round to telling Margaret that three weeks into their relationship he'd spent an evening boozing and sniffing amyl nitrate (poppers) down at Widcombe Manor, which had climaxed in a three-in-a-bed session with Jeremy and Camilla. Shortly afterwards, Camilla became pregnant and had a baby only three months before the royal wedding took place. The resultant child, Polly, is now in her late 40s and lives in a village in Somerset. DNA tests recently confirmed that her natural father was Tony not Jeremy despite her having been raised as a Fry.

Later in life, the indefatigable Fry moved into a rajah's palace in India where he planned to build a huge garden. When corrupt local politicians obstructed his plans, he simply knocked the whole thing down and shipped it hundreds of miles across the continent to a more conducive location. He lived out his last strange days as a virtual hermit in the vast palace.

Another one of Brion Gysin's contributions to the culture may also have unhinged a few. As a joke, he contributed a recipe for marijuana fudge to the *Alice B. Toklas Recipe Book* (Toklas, another resident of Tangier and the live-in lover of Gertrude Stein was a friend). Somehow or other the illegal ingredient got past the publisher's censors and the recipe was included in the cookbook. The publishers, at first enraged and then embarrassed had the last laugh; the book with the recipe for what has become known as Alice B. Toklas Brownies has never been out of print since. The recipe was immortalised in the film *I Love You Alice B. Toklas* starring Peter Sellers where hash cakes play a prominent role. Gysin was, needless to say, piqued that his unintentional contribution to the movie was unacknowledged and unrewarded.

In the early 50s, Gysin had became obsessed with a wandering band of musicians called the *Master Musicians of Jajouka* whose long drum and wailing pipe-based music is allied to a strand of Moroccan music where the players and their audiences experience ecstatic trance-like states. He travelled up and down the country watching them perform and in 1953 opened the 1001 Nights Restaurant in Tangier, which regularly served as a venue for them to play.

Gysin met Robert Fraser in 1966 and the exotic couple went on a Morocco road trip. When Fraser returned to London, he wrote to a client about his "extraordinary voyage to the Sahara with Brion Gysin". He also told Brian Jones about the mountain men and their trance inducing music; Jones was enthralled. The following year, Gysin and Jones met in Marrakesh and set off to hear the music of Jajouka. Jones was fired with enthusiasm for the music with its wild unconfined energy, unconventional musical structure and its potential to induce an altered state. Ever the experimentalist and always a sensualist, he soon discovered that taking on the assault of that music in the exotic location of a Moroccan mountain village while high on local hashish was about as far out as it could possibly get and resolved to come back and record the tribesmen as soon as the Stones' schedule permitted.

Unfortunately this was the good trip that turned bad for Brian when Keith Richard seduced Anita Pallenberg away from him. All the cast were present as the Shakesperean tragedy unfolded: Robert Fraser, Michael Cooper, Christopher Gibbs, Cecil Beaton, Jagger and Marianne. When Jones returned from the mountain, all his friends had deserterted him. It seems that Brian had assaulted Pallenberg the night before and that while he had been away exploring with Gysin, she had decided to start making eyes at Richards as they sat by the hotel swimming pool. Keith and Anita made plans and split together; the others discreetly retreated leaving Jones alone, distraught, betrayed and with a large hotel bill. He'd just experienced a very high high and now his bird had flown, an extremely low low.

Brian immediately called his new and only remaining friend Brion Gysin threatening to commit suicide; Gysin put him to bed and called a doctor to him concerned apparently (possibly presciently, possibly apocryphally) that Jones might end up drowning himself in the pool below his window. This event is often referred to as the moment when the dye was cast for Jones. He would never recover.

Brian nevertheless resolved to return to Morocco and in June 1968

again met up with Gysin. The femme fatale this time was Suki Poitier (who had been the girlfriend of Tara Browne until his death), but was now Brian's new girlfriend. Once more the journey was a drama; Poitier had overdosed on the way down and had had to be treated in a hospital for several days. Eventually, Jones, Poitier, Gysin and Gysin's long-term partner Hamri (who had been only 15 when he was introduced to and started living with Gysin who was in his thirties) again went to see the Master Musicians. Gysin was concerned about having a woman at the mountain village and persuaded Poitier to cut her hair short so that she might pass for a boy. As they reclined on cushions watching the musicians, a white goat was led past whereupon; Jones leapt to his feet and shouted, "That's me!" Later he realised that the food in front of them was goat; they were eating the very same goat they'd seen earlier and Jones commented, "It's like Communion".

Two months later he was back yet again, only this time he had bought with him a recording engineer from Olympic Studios and a lorry-full of recording equipment. Numerous tapes were made and finally the Master Musicians of Jajouka, sometimes accompanied by Brian Jones were recorded for posterity.

Unfortunately the Stones manager Allen Klein was less enthusiastic than Jones about the mountain music of the Sahara and left the tapes on a shelf. Jones would die before they were eventually released under the title *Brian Jones Presents the Pipes of Pan at Jajouka* in 1971. The cover is a painting done by Hamri; the sleeve notes by Gysin. For years afterwards there was a poster for the album pinned up on the wall in the Jajouka village and the local men would chant, "Ah Brahim Jones/Jajouka Rolling Stone/Ah Brahim Jones/Jajouka really stoned".

Suki Poitier was yet another of the golden ones that didn't make old bones; having endured the demise of Tara Browne, she was shattered by Jones's death, she stayed close to the Stones camp for a while but she and her new husband were killed in a hit and run car crash in Portugal in 1981. Another version of this story has it that she was driving the car along a coast road when her husband announced he wanted a divorce and she just drove over a cliff.

In 1972, Gysin was in London working on a screenplay for William Burroughs' book *The Naked Lunch*. Mick Jagger wanted to play the lead role but didn't like the choice of director. Brion approached Dennis Hopper for the job but history repeated itself, it was never made with Gysin's treatment and another potential moment of greatness eluded him. Then the shadows started to draw; Gysin was diagnosed as having colon cancer. He had to have his colon and anus removed and the massive irony that he, a homosexual 'receiver' should lose his undercarriage in such an unpleasant way didn't escape him; in fact it is said he found it almost funny. Then his friend William Burroughs' ex-boyfriend Ian Sommerville was killed in a car crash and Gysin was dragged to a low ebb, spiritually depressed and experiencing awful, constant pain despite ingesting considerable quantities of marijuana and bourbon, and having to learn to live with the ever present indignity of a colostomy bag.

Darkly moody and in pain, a brief high point came when, at David Bowie's suggestion, Iggy Pop sought Gysin out, sending him a letter carried by a liveried footman, with a backstage pass, and a limousine to take him to Iggy's gig in Paris. He took Gysin on stage in front of the 5,000 strong-audience and at the subsequent press conference placed Gysin at his side. Brion later wrote to William Burroughs alleging that Iggy, feigning a leg injury, had encouraged Gysin to massage his leg during the conference and then placed Gysin's hand on his erection, although this version of the event was more than likely built of fevered desire rather than actuality.

Bowie had used the cut up technique on his *Diamond Dogs* and *Low* albums. He told Rolling Stone in 1975, "I've had to do cut-ups on my writing for some time so that I might be able to put it back into some coherent form again. My actual writing doesn't make an awful lot of sense". He went on to acknowledge his debt in 1984, when he told *Musician* magazine: "Both Brian (Eno) and myself had always been interested in the Burroughsian concept - I should really include Brion Gysin here – of another world created from accident and severe logic adjustment".

Now a sick man: Gysin had developed emphysema, a souvenir from years of joint smoking and resolved to settle in Paris to die. He knew time was tight and like all old men, became constantly, bitterly aware that his friends were departing before his very eyes. William Burroughs' son, a drunk who had received a liver transplant and who had continued drinking was found virtually dead in a ditch; he later died in hospital at the age of 33. Gysin observed, "Not many of us get the chance to ruin two livers in a lifetime".

But there was to be a couple more hurrahs before his curtain came down. Keith Haring, the artist, made the pilgrimage to see Gysin, describing him as, "an incredible genius". He told *Flash Art* magazine that: "The work of William Burroughs and Brion Gysin came the closest in literature to what I saw as the artistic vision in painting". He borrowed a *Dreamachine* to show off in nightclubs.

Then Andy Warhol bought a couple of Gysin's pictures, which he had seen at Burroughs' New York rooms when having dinner there with Mick Jagger. This was the kind of recognition that Gysin had longed for all his life but by the time it arrived he was almost too ill to care.

There followed a strange incident when a mysterious benefactor called James Kennedy gave Gysin $4,000 a month as an advance on a commissioned picture – money that envigorated the dying man and enabled him to set up a Paris studio. Kennedy's real name turned out to be Jim McCann, the mythic, reputed IRA arms dealer who has a starring role in the story of Howard Marks's dope smuggling career and in the development of London's underground press. McCann, the self-styled 'Emerald Pimpernel' is wanted all over the world for drug smuggling and bombing activities. He'd learned that if you can successfully smuggle arms then it's not that difficult to smuggle dope. In the 80s, it is said he used to hang out with the IRA one day and the next he might be drinking with the film star James Coburn or John Lennon, which is conceivable if you go along with the FBI and MI5 who have both long thought that Lennon was making donations to the IRA. When the Gardai apprehended McCann on one occasion, he would only say, "My name is Mr. Nobody, my address is The World". Eventually most of the world got a bit hot for McCann and he fled Europe and was last seen in Argentina.

But in Paris McCann took up residence near the studio and when Gysin's health took a turn for the worse, rumours circulated that somehow Kennedy/McCann had made himself the sole beneficiary of all of Brion's writings and paintings.

Maybe because of this the painter, in 1986, the poet and piper Gysin died broke in Paris. Someone somewhere owns those amazing pictures and texts. By all accounts, especially his own, Gysin's career had been a disappointment, a failure. He had, he said, led "a life of adventure leading nowhere," and remains little known, apart from to a certain cognoscenti who still regard him as a powerful influence on their work and to pop culture.

7

Robert Fraser II

LIKE GYSIN, Robert Fraser's hopelessness with money meant that despite, or perhaps because of the opulence of his lifestyle, he was always broke. He had plenty of super-rich pop star friends and the temptation to hit on them for loans or to persuade them to buy a picture from him proved irresistible, and he often used or attempted to use them as a way out of his troubles. Christopher Gibbs used to buy things from him and then Robert would buy something from him in return but invariably Fraser's cheques bounced and Gibbs would sue his friend and not talk to him for months. Then, Gibbs says, he would forget that he wasn't supposed to be talking to Robert and they would resume relations, such was his character.

Mick Jagger says that although he knew that Robert was a hustler, he didn't really steal or perpetuate frauds but that Fraser's pictures always seemed a little too expensive. But, Jagger says, Fraser used to hit on the Beatles more than the Stones anyway, mainly because the Beatles had more money and possibly because McCartney in particular had more taste and was in the market. But Jagger lived to rue the fact he hadn't bought some of Fraser's 'expensive' pictures as he watched the price of them soar in the years to come. Robert did, after all, have immaculate taste.

Keith Richards didn't buy much in the way of art from him either but he was close enough to Robert to ask him to be his son Marlon's godfather. Robert accepted and organised a tantric baptism that involved a lot of Indians in turbans, chanting, herbs and rice. Marlon was given the baptismal name Marlon Leon Sundeep.

Fraser's connections would always prove invaluable. Another member of the Guinness clan regularly provided the Stones and their posh but broke friend with a stopover was Desmond, who ruled over the estate in Leixlep in Ireland. Desmond's mother Diana Mitford, regarded as the most beautiful of the Mitford sisters, divorced his father in the 30's and married the fascist leader Oswald Moseley father of Formula One's Max Mosely. She had carried messages from Moseley to Adolf Hitler before the war and a young Desmond had been taught how to do the Nazi salute and say Heil Hitler! in preparation for the day when he would meet with the Fuhrer, an event pre-empted by the outbreak of the war. Robert Fraser, Jagger, Christopher Gibbs and Paul Getty with his wife Talitha had also been regular visitors and savoured the opulence of the great house.

Fraser's relationship with his 'manservant' Mohammed kept the tongues wagging. The handsome young man would act the role of driver, gallery helper and butler but a visitor to 'the flat' talks of the time when they had once walked past the toilet door in the apartment and seen Mohammed sitting ostentatiously on the pan with his trousers round his ankles reading the paper; and how Mohammed would frequently go off on clothes shopping expeditions with Fraser's credit cards.

8

Paul McCartney is dead

ANOTHER STORY accounts for the rumour that emerged in the late 60's that Paul McCartney was dead.

Mohammed Chtaibi, a student had been the ward of Mark Gilbey, the multimillionaire heir to the Gilbey drinks company fortune. He had struck up a friendship with Robert and went to work at the gallery, covering for his new boss when Robert was off playing with his jet set pals and then went to live in the 'flat'. He also doubled as Robert's driver and drug bagman.

On this occasion in early 1967, Fraser and Chtaibi went by cab to Paul McCartney's St. John's Wood house for a party. When the Apple Scruffs – about twenty girls hanging around outside the house of their favourite Beatle - spotted the dark haired Mohammed, they briefly thought it was Paul and before realising their mistake became terribly excited. Once inside the gates and made comfortable, McCartney showed Robert a hollowed out book, which contained the stash, a whole range of chemicals including a bag of marijuana. Mohammed was deputised to start rolling a number of, what McCartney called 'Benson and Hashish B52 Bombers'. Then Mick

Jagger, Keith Richards, Brian Jones and Fraser's friend Christopher Gibbs arrived. The merry band got smashed and then decided to go off to Keith's mansion Redlands in Sussex and make a weekend of it (this is only weeks before the infamous Redlands bust starring Marianne Faithfull and the legendary imaginary Mars bar). Despite the fact that McCartney's Aston Martin and black Mini Cooper were available, for some reason they all tried to get into Mick Jagger's

Mini, which proved impossible so Mohammed was deputised to drive down in McCartney's Mini. This was a specially made Mini Cooper that had been fitted out with luxurious seating, a bar, smoked windows and wide wheels and was the only one of its kind in the country. Using two cars was useful, they reasoned since the Moroccan could transport the book with the stash inside it. Great idea. That would ensure that none of the pop star over lords would be nabbed in possession.

The two cars set off at high speed and were soon barelling out of town onto the motorway. Mohammed, who was very stoned, had a slight lapse of concentration while he was looking down and lighting a cigarette. What he didn't know was that in his hurry to get out of the gate at Cavendish Avenue, he had left the seat belt hanging out of the door and while he was looking down at the cigarette lighter had begun drifting across his traffic lane and into the path of a car in the next lane. The car to his side ran over the seatbelt and Paul's Mini was violently dragged further over towards the other vehicle. Mohammed instinctively hauled at the wheel to compensate but in that second, the other car came off the seatbelt and Paul's Mini was catapulted off the road where it smashed head on into a metal lamp that virtually cut the little car in two. Mohammed was left unconscious and bleeding.

When he awoke, he knew the police must be on their way and that if he wanted to avoid a spell in Wormwood Scrubs prison, his priority was to get rid of the book of drugs. He staggered from the wreckage and hurled the book down into a deep ditch. When the police got there, there were already many spectators and the word spread fast, first to London and then the rest of the world that Paul McCartney's Mini had been involved in a heavy accident and that a blood-covered guy who might well have been McCartney had been taken to hospital. Mohammed had to suffer having a lot of glass removed from his face and was then allowed to go home.

The following day, if he was expecting sympathy and praise for having quick-wittedly got rid rid of the stash, he was very much mistaken. Firstly Fraser gave him a tongue lashing for not arriving with the drugs and ruining the vibe of the party, then McCartney gave him a hard time because his beloved Mini Special was destroyed and worse it hadn't been insured.

As far as the rumour mill was concerned Paul was dead. Further speculation on his passing plagued him for years as fans played records backwards to hear 'Paul is dead' messages and spotted 'clues' on album sleeves. In 1993, McCartney was interviewed on Saturday Night Live and was asked if all those rumours about his death had been a hoax. McCartney replied, "Yeah… I wasn't really dead".

9

Robert Fraser III

JUST AS soon as he possibly could, the experimenter Fraser, hungry for yet another untried high got a heroin addiction and very quickly went from chasing the dragon to the needle. It was like he couldn't wait to get a habit, at the same time telling McCartney, "There's no such thing as heroin addiction, you've just got to have a lot of money". It was a time when there were very few registered addicts. Those that were only had to visit the doctor and ask nicely and they would be given grade 'A' heroin or cocaine on prescription, as a way of getting off the street heroin. The smart junkies, more than adequately supplied, were using some of their prescription personally and then selling the rest on. It was from these enterprising unfortunates that Robert, by way of Spanish Tony, was able to procure high quality drugs and the way that the National Health Service sewed the seeds of heroin addiction in the country.

The place to be was outside Boots the chemist 24-hour shop at Piccadilly Circus at the stroke of midnight when the junkies would rush the counter like shoppers in a sale to pick up their next day's prescription of cocaine or heroin. The area outside the shop (known for a hundred years as 'the meat rack') became a marketplace for drugs and rent boys and the whole area was littered with desperate

junkies, needles, young runaways and those preying upon them. Every night nefarious deals took place on the steps of the inaccurately named Eros (the statue is actually of Anteros) beneath the blaze of the famous Piccadilly Circus neon billboards that once promoted the health-giving properties of Bovril and then later, without a trace of irony, advertised Coke in flashing red and white neon - right above the chemist's door. Dope dealers made off with their stash; young lads wandered away with their new masters. The word spread; for a time London was attracting junkies from all over the world, pin cushions who wanted access to cheap high-grade drugs courtesy of her Britannic Majesty. The flotsam and jetsam washed up against Britain's shores.

Then came the well-chronicled Redlands bust. It was all the usual suspects, Jagger, Richards, Marianne Faithfull, a phantom Mars bar, Christopher Gibbs, Fraser plus an unwitting hippie from the Kings Road and a mysterious figure known as the Acid King or David

Schneiderman (aka Dave Britton) who split the scene of the crime at almost the same moment as the police and who mysteriously hadn't been searched, never to be seen again. This led to endless speculation that the band had been set up by the *News of the World* who had been working hand in glove with a jittery establishment's police force keen on taking a big pop star's scalp as a warning to us all.

Mick and Keith took the rap for some pills and some hash and were given prison sentences, reduced on appeal to conditional discharges. Unfortunately for Robert, he was caught with a bottle of pharmaceutical heroin that the others present couldn't believe he had with him; they hadn't suspected a thing. Heroin was so far still off the menu for the Stones.

Spanish Tony had boasted to Fraser and the Stones that for £6,000 popped in the right pocket, it might be possible for the charges to be made to go away. In the event the charges stayed right where they were, just the money went away. Fraser got six months in Wormwood Scrubs where he joined the LSD baron Michael Hollingshead and where they were both joined shortly after by the UFO Club's promotor John 'Hoppy' Hopkins, himself cruelly given a nine month

sentence for possession of a small quantity of marijuana.

Richard Hamilton, the artist who would later teach Bryan Ferry at art school, made the famous *Swingeing London* picture of Jagger and Fraser handcuffed together in the back of a police car. The *International Times* splashed a FREE HOPPY headline across its front page and beneath it stated that he was "in the hands of the enemy. Realise that they drink and get high and feel great, and you do other things and get high and feel great and they shit on you".

Later Oz carried a piece saying: "No matter how many arrests the police make, there can be no final bust, because the revolution has taken place in the minds of the young". It seems that the police were fighting an un-winnable war; they just didn't know it yet.

Prison was for Robert, having already endured the travails of Eton and the army, a breeze. Some reports have it that he actually enjoyed himself in the Scrubs, no doubt by availing himself of some of the man-on-man action that was inevitably occurring. The pain came with his eventual freedom for when he was released, his gallery was bust. But he rallied round; he still had the building; he could still depend on his highly influential friends and he knew how to sensationally tweak the tails of the art establishment and the press.

One of those friends was John Lennon who had left his wife and moved with Yoko into 34 Montagu Square, Ringo's flat, which was thus assured eternal status as London's premier rock pad (Chas Chandler and Hendrix had been asked to leave by the landlords, dismayed by the black walls). The couple made plans for an exhibition by John at the reincarnated Fraser gallery. The exhibition would be a collection of charity collection boxes, disabled mannequins wearing polio callipers and models of dogs with bandaged legs. There were a few drawings by Lennon and some of Yoko's; there were also 365 white helium filled balloons that were released, each with a tag asking the finder to get in touch with the couple at the Savile Row Apple HQ. It was a proper hippie 'Happening' and prompted Yoko to comment that, "The Robert Fraser Gallery was the driving force of the European avant-garde scene in the art world".

The next outrage featured the then little known Gilbert and George whose work was, at the time, universally regarded as beyond the pale, and who had become accustomed to rejection by London's galleries; however when they approached Robert begging him to show a couple of their pictures, which were brazenly named 'Shit' and 'C***', Fraser unflinchingly said 'yes'.

The resulting press furore, needless to say left him chuckling and extremely satisfied but his exhibitions, headline makers though some of them were, were losing their allure. At the end of the 60's, a decade that, in London at least, had Robert Fraser as one of its prime movers, he simply closed the gallery and went off to India, years after his favourite clients the Beatles had returned disillusioned by its offerings. Why? He'd had a spiritual awakening through studying Tantra and dance, he said, with the unspoken twin bonus that he would be able to lay his hands on lots of young Indian boys of course. Robert lived in a cave for a while; a cave in India being just about as far as you could possibly get from his exquisite apartments in Mount

Street, but he, in turn eventually experienced disillusionment of his own.

Fraser returned to London and took up residency in Coventry House on Leicester Square conveniently just across the road from the *Playland* amusement arcade which was, perhaps not coincidentally, a well known hang out for rent boys and runaways. Robert the roué, who ever liked to keep himself near potential prey, had a telescope fitted in his living room through which he would spot likely 'chickens'. Across the road, an employee of the arcade was on his payroll; Robert would telephone him, point a boy out and the employee would march the targeted lad across to the flat and wait for Robert to throw the door keys out of the window so the boy could be bundled in the door.

These were Fraser's binging, drinking years and his weight ballooned as did his dissolute desires. New York was a frequent destination for him and on his sex tours to Manhattan; he would dive straight into leather clubs like the Anvil or the choicely named Toilet where boys were buggered at the bar, where one night someone was crucified and muscle-bound men stubbed cigarettes out on his torso. Here Fraser could use and be abused 24 hours a day, a hell of his own imagining, but despite all the degradation he harboured a desire to once again have a cutting edge gallery full of glittering stars and media who would treat him with due deference and restore his rightful position as the modern art king of London; the toast of the town.

He'd have one more go he thought and took a lease in Cork Street, W1, opened a gallery and for a couple of years it looked like he had recaptured the old magic. One show, featuring Keith Haring, had break-dancers and pumping music; Haring painted the window shutters and gave away little signed sketches; it was a complete contrast to the other stuffy galleries to the left and right of him. Yet Robert was beginning to feel ill and so too was Keith Haring; the art lover and the artist were united in common predilections and now by a rather uncommon virus, paying the price for their hedonistic years of indiscriminate unprotected sex. There was something infinitely sad about the doomed gallery owner selling work by the doomed artist; a fin-de-siècle pall fell over the times.

Nobody knew what AIDS was then. There were murmurings from California of a sort of gay cancer that was baffling the medical profession but Fraser insisted he was OK despite all the obvious signs of his deterioration, making the excuse that he was suffering from recurrent malaria. Then he started going downhill fast but nevertheless stayed working. Toward the end he was, as usual, short of money and in danger of losing the gallery. Paul Getty 'loaned' him £100,000 money which Getty must have realised he had as much chance of recovering as Robert did his health. Fraser spent his final days being nursed by his mother in her house in Cadogan Gardens. One of the first in London to die of AIDS, even in death he was ahead of the pack.

Malcolm McClaren reckons that because Robert was so groovy, he made others groovy too; just by his association; he adds mischieviously that it is a "rare talent that only certain entrepreneurs have; stardust falls from them onto others, it makes ordinary people feel like stars and as a consequence they become stars; that some English artists were made groovier than they really were", while not of course specifically mentioning the extent of his own "grooviness".

10

Cars

JAGGER SAT outside the Scotch of St. James in his Mini looking at the front door of the club, waiting for his moment with the windscreen wipers flopping backwards and forwards. Shit, is that Keith Moon staggering around? Oh God he's wearing a Nazi uniform. Nice. And that's Keith's chauffeur, the one who wears a different wig every time you see him, arguing with him. Keith looks really out of it. He's getting worse man. I'm not getting involved in this, not when he's in that state. He'll push me into a puddle or something. I can't go in there with a wet arse. What's he doing? The chauffeur's trying to grab the car keys off him; he's trying to stop Keith taking that Bentley of his out for a drunken spin at one o'clock in the morning.

Christ, there's Paul. I can't get caught in a scene with Keith Moon when Paul's standing there. Thank God he hasn't seen me here. He's talking to Keith as well – trying to stop him driving. Moon's not listening, not even to Paul; he's a bloody lunatic; he'll kill someone one day.

Oh no, he's got it started. There he goes. Whoops-a-daisy, he's winged that Aston, oh and a Porsche. And here comes a Jag! No! He's hit that as well and sideswiped that Bentley. Bang, crash, wallop. Ricochet! There goes five year's royalties down the drain. He didn't miss one of them. Good work Keith. Oh, yes he did miss one; that blue one down there on the corner. What is that? Oh, it's a Bristol. I'd like one of those. George Martin's got one just like that. Perhaps it's his. I wonder if he's here tonight; a royal visit.

And Moon hasn't passed his driving test. No driver's licence; no insurance; just like Keith Richards, the other Keith... and Brian. Driving Bentleys around London drunk on brandy or bourbon with no driver's licences and full of pills. Those two and Moon have something in common, no respect for property; no respect for money... or for girls come to that. They should form a band together; the One Way Trip, that's a good name, or maybe we should get Moon the Loon to join the Stones...

Charlie wouldn't like that.

Moon will probably make that Wiggy chauffeur of his clear up his mess after him while he scarpers in a cab before the police get here and find all those pills in his pockets. He's done that before hasn't he? Smashed up all the cars outside the club. Just like Keith did when he ran into that bloke under the Westway in his German staff car then got Spanish Tony to sit there and take the rap while he ran off; the two Keiths, nutters the pair of them and what's the Nazi obsession all about?

Then Mick heard the megaphone barking from round the corner in Piccadilly. "This is the police. Get out of the road!" Then there was a screech of brakes and another crash. Mick chuckled; he knew that voice. It was the speakers. Moon has installed speakers and a microphone in the car so he could yell at people. It wasn't the police; it was Moon the Loon. Pete Townshend had told him that story; funny: Keith belting through a little village, somewhere in the shires in his Bentley shouting through the speakers that he was their new Conservative party MP and that they should know that hundreds of immigrants were moving into the village tomorrow. It scared the life out of them. Terrifying… terror… disruption, pandemonium; he thrived on it. Drugs, women, hotels, boozing, spending… a few drinks, a few more drugs… smash up your kit, smash up some cars!

Didn't he have a hovercraft that he used to drive to the pub?

Who killed the driver?

Moon's dangerous driving became a less funny affair when his car ran over his own driver and killed him. In 1969, he acquired an S1 Bentley and appointed an affable Irishman, Cornelius 'Neil' Boland to be its driver; of course being Keith Moon's driver also entailed other exhausting duties, keeping the bar stocked, occasionally being his bodyguard and more frequently his joker's assistant. As a bodyguard, Neil prevented Moon being battered by his father-in-law after Moon had broken his wife Kim's nose. As a chauffeur he often drove Moon on jaunts with 'Legs' Larry Smith the drummer with the Bonzo Dog Doo Dah band; as a joker's aide, he would be deployed to hide in department stores watching whie Moon and Larry, in front of a terrified shop assistant, tested the strength of a pair of trousers by ripping them apart; then when things started to turn ugly, Neil would arrive and say, "Are they one-legged trousers? They're just what I've been looking for," then ask the bemused assistant if the two legs could be wrapped up separately.

As stocker-up of the bar, he had every morning to fill the car with champagne, scrumpy cider, wine and tins of lager as fuel for the day's outrages. Larry Smith recalls touring around the west country, announcing to the public of Plymouth through the car's PA system that a lorry-load of snakes had just turned over around the corner and then they watched, pissing themselves laughing as the public scattered: or driving down the promenade bawling at the holidaymakers that there was a tidal wave coming but that they must stay in their shoes!

What does that mean?

Then when it was time for the pub, it would be Neil who would have to light the smoke capsule attached to Moon's shoe before he went in and gassed the customers and then it would be Neil who would have to bundle the drunken jokers into the car and speed away when the gags turned sour or the flashing blue lights arrived. Eventually all the shenanigans proved too much for Boland and he gave Keith three weeks notice. He'd had enough; he had a girlfriend and a new baby at home both of whom he never got to see; Boland usually had to sleep all day to try and keep up with a manic boss who usually wanted to play all night.

Keith agreed to perform the opening ceremony for a third rate disco in Hatfield as a favour to a friend. He would regret that decision for the rest of his life. As he, Larry Smith, Larry's girlfriend Jean Battye and Moon's wife Kim pulled up in the car park in the Bentley, Boland at the wheel, they couldn't have an inkling of the hell that was to follow.

The story goes that the disco crowd were predominantly skinheads (later denied) and that when they spotted the long hairs in the limo, there had been a few catcalls. Oblivious, Keith made a short speech, then tossed back some free drinks and danced to the music. Sensing that the mood was turning ugly, Larry and his girlfriend went to wait at the car; Keith emerged with Kim; he was trading insults with some of the skinheads and it seemd that a fight was inevitable. Boland had the car started and ready to go but the rowdy youths pelted the car with coins and gravel and arrayed themselves in front of the Bentley preventing it leaving. It's here that accounts of events get murky; it seems Neil got out of the car to try and calm the crowd down and that Keith, who had no driving licence, no insurance and was plastered drunk, slipped across into the driving seat, hit the accelerator and drove the Bentley through the crowd for some yards down the road, then opened the driver's door and waited for Boland to get back in the car. The fight moved round to the front of the car and then the Bentley suddenly lurched forward into the crowd. It was then that Keith was informed that somehow Neil had fallen under the car and his head had been crushed under its wheels. The body couldn't be extracted until the fire brigade arrived and jacked the car up. A devastated Moon was taken to the police station and kept over night. He was released when the lawyers arrived and smoothed the ruffled feathers of the police department.

Pending the inquest, Moon went off on a European tour with the Who; he attended the inquest on his return and was partially exonerated when the jury returned a verdict of accidental death. The police charged a number of the youths with causing an affray and when Moon appeared at the ensuing court case, he pleaded guilty to the charges of driving while drunk with no licence or insurance but offered in mitigation that his party had been threatened with violence and that he had only driven under duress. "I just do not know what would have happened had I stayed in the car park", he stated. "The mood was getting worse all the time". Unbelievably, the magistrates gave Moon an absolute discharge; he even escaped paying costs and having his licence endorsed. Those accused of causing an affray however, were not so fortunate; the magistrate threatened them with Borstal training but in the end handed down a range of fines.

It's true to say that the sad event haunted Moon for the rest of his days and it has been said that it contributed in a considerable way to the increase in his manic behaviour, heavy drinking, drug use and eventual destruction. He always blamed himself for Boland's death and would often burst into tears at the mention of Neil or that fateful evening, however there is one who doesn't blame Keith Moon at all and that's Boland's daughter Michelle who was three when her father was killed. Michelle has set up a web site dedicated to the events of that night under the heading 'Keith Moon was not driving'. She says that she tracked down one of the youths convicted of affray, Peter Thorpe. On the site, she prints a copy of the email that Thorpe apparently sent her in which Thorpe alleges that one of the youths leaving the disco had, as a joke, asked Kim Moon for a lift home, and that Kim had told the person to 'fuck off'. Thorpe agrees that he and his mates threw coins at the car as it was leaving and that the driver had jumped out to confront them; he also agrees that there was a fight, which moved around to the front of the car. He then says that it was Kim who took the wheel and drove the car at the crowd; Thorpe was 'thrown' over the car's wing. They shouted for the car to stop but by then the damage was done and Neil was dead.

Michelle Boland then claims that she went to Hatfield to interview Thorpe, a "nice, respectable family man', and that Thorpe had stuck by his allegations; he had a very clear view of who was driving the Bentley at the moment of the accident and that "it was definitely not Keith".

Later, Kim Moon exited the abusive relationship she had with Keith and married the ex Small Faces keyboard player Ian McLagan; she then exited life when she was killed in a car crash in 2006. It seems she had run a stop sign and her car had been hit by a truck. So it seems, the truth has gone to the grave with her and her ex husband Moon the Loon, that is unless any of the other occupants of the car ever change their stories. However Moon persistently claimed that it was he who had been driving, even in intimate moments when it might be expected that he would confess all, if the truth were different to his account. Pamela Miller (later to be known as Pamela Des Barres), the infamous Los Angeles groupie who alleges relationships with Mick Jagger, Jimmy Page, Jim Morrison and Keith Moon wrote in her book *I'm With The Band*, that she had been in bed with Keith indulging in a long night of passion and role playing when Keith took on the persona of a priest; a priest that suddenly started confessing his own sins, one of which was killing Neil Boland. "He broke down and started to cry," she states, "calling him self a murderous fuck". She adds that over the next few years of her relationship with Moon that he confirmed the story several times and that he would burn for eternity for killing his driver.

But that sad and sobering story hadn't happened yet and Keith Moon was still behaving like kid in a toyshop, albeit a drunken kid with some very expensive toys and some very exotic adult friends.

One time Mick recalled, he had been sitting with Lennon and Paul when Keith had come over and told them all that he'd been drinking with Bruce Johnson from the Beach Boys, at the Waldorf earlier that evening and, that they should all go with him and meet him.

A real live Beach Boy! In London!

Despite the illustrious prospect, Jagger, too scared of Chrissie's reaction, couldn't go because he was meeting her later on, but Lennon and McCartney jumped at it. Apparently Johnston freaked out when he saw the two Fabs strolling into the lobby but by then they'd become a bit awe stuck too. It was funny seeing Lennon impressed by meeting somebody else since he was king-of-the-fucking-world. He was the same when he met Dylan. Neither of them had known how to talk to the other so Dylan just played it ice cool and Lennon reverted to fast talking, cartoon Liverpool yobbo "Y'know like wack?" and was stand out rude which he always was when he was nervous.

Then Johnston played them the *Pet Sounds* album and they were swept away. What did McCartney say? That *God Only Knows* was the best song ever written? Praise indeed.

But he thrives on a bit of peer pressure does McCartney; give him his due. Didn't he go home that night and write *Here There and Everywhere*? Britain's premier songwriting answer to the talented Beach Boys went home inspired and knocked out a worthy adversary to the 'best song ever written' in 24 hours of nervous competitive energy. What would the Beatles greatest fan Brian Wilson say was the better of the two tracks? It's a tough call. God only knows those bloody Beatles make it seem so easy.

As an aside, one of the backing singers on the *Pet Sounds* album was Johnston's old band mate Terry Melcher, with whom he'd played when they'd gone out as double act called Bruce and Terry, just before the Beach Boys days. Melcher, who was Doris Day's son and who had produced her hit song *Move Over Darling* as well as the first two albums for the Byrds, was to become enmeshed in the Charles Manson murders. Manson aspired to be a singer, always had, and Melcher had rejected him at an audition. Bad move. Manson had harboured a grudge ever since and he was definitely the wrong guy to upset.

Because Melcher, with his wife Candice Bergen had once stayed in the house where the murders took place and had known Manson, it was alleged that he had been the original target for the Manson gang who had only murdered Sharon Tate, her unborn baby and the others merely because they happened to be there – poor blameless victims in the wrong place at the wrong time.

Paul never seems particularly bothered by bloody Keith Moon, nor does John. What have the two Fabs got in common with Moon - apart from sharing the services of Dr. Robert the vitamin B12 injecting rock rat pack medic? "Oh and did I put some amphetamines in that?" Moon makes them laugh; he especially tickles Ringo… Ringo loves Keith Moon. Him and the Loon get on like a drumkit on fire.

Drummers…

Funny isn't it, driving; Brian Jones could never drive either; always slamming that Bentley into other cars, or the wall, off the wall, and then getting Spanish to take the blame… and Lennon… he can't drive either; terrible driver, blind as a bat (Lennon had once insisted on driving a Mini to Scotland with Yoko, Julian and her daughter Kyoko against all advice; three days later he asked the Apple office to deliver something bigger – an Austin Maxi. Shortly after, Lennon drove off the road into a ditch; all of the car's occupants were injured; Kyoko required four stitches, Yoko fourteen and Lennon seventeen. The car, complete with its bloodstains was crushed into a cube and shipped down to the house in Surry where it was put on a platform as a garden sculpture).

You can tell a lot about a man by the way he drives. Mick's little crash in the midnight blue Aston seemed slight by comparison. Clapton couldn't drive either; no licence, never passed a test; turned his Ferrari over in his own driveway. Jeff Beck could drive; he used to build hot rods. Him and Keith Moon once raced through the underpass at Knightsbridge in that lipstick coloured Rolls, doing a hundred miles an hour with Keith playing the Beach Boys flat out. Moon slowed down next to a cyclist and yelled through the speakers at him: 'Dismount immediately!' The shocked guy nearly went over the handlebars.

Hendrix! God knows what he's like behind a wheel, driving in London on the left side of the road. Still he can play a guitar upside down so…

McCartney can drive though. Baby you can drive my car.

Someone else who was handy behind a wheel was June Bolan, who before she married Marc used to run Blackhill Enterprises, managers of Pink Floyd, office in Alexander Street, W2. Five years Marc's superior, the beautiful June Childs was just what he craved, a mother, lover, manager and driver. Their eyes met; sparks flew and they fairly immediately set up a love nest in the back of June's van which was parked outside Marc's parent's Wimbledon prefab. The smitten pair didn't emerge from the steamy van for four days. It's said that they were so in tune with each other that they would sometimes just sit cross-legged opposite one another and stare into each other's eyes, in silence, for twenty minutes at a time.

But they couldn't live in a van forever, so June found them a flat at 57 Blenheim Crescent, Ladbroke Grove for £2 8s 6d a week and put the name 'Bolanchild' on the doorbell. They were married in 1970 (after Marc had had a brief liaison with Marsha Hunt) and the guests were Mickey Finn, the percussionist, and his girlfriend, Jeff Dexter the DJ, another old Mod and an old friend of Marc's, and Alice Ormsby-Gore, later to be Eric Clapton's girlfriend; a passer by was co-opted to take the wedding photograph.

When Marc made a bit of money (at one point T. Rex record sales accounted for about six percent of the total British domestic record market), June accrued a 4.2 Jaguar, a Daytona Ferrari, a white Rolls Royce with blacked out windows, a Radford Mini, and an AC Cobra. June knew her wheels.

It's a shame she wasn't driving on that night in September 1977 when Marc's Mini driven by his second wife Gloria Jones, took off and hit a tree. He'd never learned to drive because he'd always feared he would die in a car crash. The night that the news of Boland's death was announced, his house was looted; the looters had known Marc wouldn't be coming home.

11

Macca and the men (and women) with holes in their heads

"WHO TOLD Lennon about the trepanning?"

"Well I didn't. What's he said?"

"He came bounding in the other day with a big smile on his face and said, 'Are we all gonna get out heads drilled then Paul?' Then he fell around laughing. And now he won't stop going on about it. You know what he's like… a dog with a bone. Keeps on and on, taking the mickey non-stop".

"Perhaps he secretly thinks it's not such a daft idea. Perhaps him and Yoko have been talking about it and secretly he wants to get it done. They're into anything at the moment those two. You can see it can't you, 'John and Yoko say, drill your head for world peace'".

"No, he's just taking the mick. I know he is".

"Well, I didn't tell him anything about it because I don't know anything about it, which means you must have told him yourself".

"I did say something the other night when I met that bloke. I wish I'd kept my mouth shut now".

"What bloke?"

"That bloke Joey Mellen. I met him at Michael Hollingshead's house in Pont Street, you know the World Psychedelic Centre as they call it. I'm gonna have to stop going round there; it's gonna get busted soon. I just know it is. Anyway Mellen's got this theory that if you take LSD then you must eat a boiled sweet every half an hour. In that way, you keep your sugar levels up and you never get a bad trip. He says bad trips come from low sugar levels in the brain, which is why you get horrible hallucinations and the fear, but if you do the sugar thing then you just get the high; the nice bit".

"But then all your teeth fall out".

"He even had an answer for that; something about calcium levels dropping, so you have to drink a glass of milk".

"Who is this Mellen chap?"

"He's one of that lot, you know, Michael Rainey, the Ormsby-Gores. He met them all in Torremolinos where Rainey's sister has got a nightclub. I think they had a kid together. He's one of those Eton/Oxford types who smoke their first joint and then flush their expensive educations down the toilet and go off on a personal enlightenment trip that they never come back from".

"Well you did the enlightenment trip thing, didn't you?"

"Alright wise guy, but at least I came back".

"You came back; Lennon came back but I'm not sure about George…"

"Anyway, this Mellen bloke ended up in Ibiza hanging out with a strange Dutch hippie who had trained as a doctor – another one who threw his education away – and had all these sugar and LSD theories.

He'd been taking acid in the 50s and later on he was something to do with the white bicycle thing in Amsterdam. He also reckoned that we'd all be a lot happier if we'd stayed on all fours".

"What do you mean?"

"He reckoned – the Dutch bloke; Huges I think his name is – that the day we stood up on our back legs, is the day when we became anxious and unhappy and started worrying about God. When we stood up, some of our brain blood sort of sunk downwards. Apparently we haven't quite got enough blood in our brains".

"So monkeys are happier than we are".

"Have you ever seen an unhappy monkey".

"Not on the Typhoo TV advert".

"It was PG Tips".

"Aah, the power of advertising".

"Anyway, then he goes on to say that the way to achieve a permanent state of happiness and some sort of long term youthfulness is to get a third eye".

"What, like a spiritual third eye?"

"No, I mean drill a hole in your head".

"Christ, I thought you were joking".

"No I'm not. That's what trepanning means. The bloke Mellen's had it done. He reckons the Dutch bloke Huges has had it done and has found happiness – given up smoking, drinking, acid, marijuana, the lot. Mellen says he keeps talking about lifting ourselves above gravity's drag.

"Here, guess what he's called his daughter".

"Who?"

"The Dutch bloke".

"Hole in the Head".

"No… this is before he had that done".

"What?"

"Maria".

"What's funny about that?"

"Her second name".

"What Huges?"

"NO, her middle name".

"I dunno. What is it?"

"Juana. Maria Juana".

"Shit man".

"No shit".

"How do they do it then".

"Do what?"

"Drill holes in their heads".

"Electric drills but Joey Mellen said the first time he tried it, he used a hand drill and fainted before he'd finished. He says there's no pain at all, just a schlurping noise when you break through and a sort of gurgling. There's a spurt of blood, then it stops. But get this; you have to chisel a little dent first, so that the drill can start off, like a little hole, otherwise the drill just wanders around all over your head".

"What happened then?"

"He said he felt brilliant".

"I expect he did. It's the same as beating your head against a brick wall – nice when you stop".

"No, I mean he feels good all the time, never gets depressed; feels like he's fourteen".

"You sound pretty keen on all this; like you're planning on getting it done. No wonder Lennon's taking the mick".

"Ha ha. Of course I'm not getting it done. It might mess up me hair. And who would I get to chisel the dent in my head? Lennon? Linda? But you have to admit, it's quite interesting isn't it?"

"It doesn't bloody interest me".

"Here, you'll never guess who else is into it?"

"What, apart from you?"

"No. You know what I mean. Anyway… Julie Felix".

"Julie Felix? The folk singer? Didn't you go out with her?"

"No… well, not exactly".

"What? She's had it done"?

"Well that's the sixty four thousand dollar question. I don't think so but no-one knows, but get this; she used to share a place with that poet chap Lawrence Ferlinghetti who came over for the Albert Hall poetry thing, and they knew the Dutch weirdo and Mellen and they all used to sit round and discuss it. She's even written some songs with Mellen; three tracks I think; one called Brainblood-something or other".

"Christ. No wonder she's not in the charts these days".

"It gets weirder. Then this guy Mellen's girlfriend, Amanda goes and gets it done. And, she does it to herself; she drilled her own head and they filmed it – it's called *Heartbeat in the Brain*. Someone told me that when you show the film to an audience, half of them fall off their seats and faint. It's one of Bernardo Bertolucci's favourites apparently. And here's the really weird bit: apparently, all through the operation, all the way through the drilling, she has this strange, sort of beautiful smile on her face – completely tranquil – drilling away, and smiling".

"Crazy. You say Mellen is a friend of the Ormsby-Gores and Rainey?"

"And Sir Mark Palmer and Lord Timothy Willoughby whatever his name is, you know, the one who fell off his boat in the Mediterranean; and Joshua Macmillan, the old Prime Minister's grandson. He died of drink and speed".

"What the Prime Minister?"

"Yeah, probably?"

"Well that's obviously another reason why Lennon is taking the mick; he thinks all those hippies are fairies and pixies doesn't he?"

"He should talk. He was on the David Frost show the other night and him and her got into a bag. He's obviously trying to make a point about something or other, but I'm fucked if I know what it is".

"Maybe he should get his head drilled".

"Maybe we all should".

Joey Mellen is now running a gallery. He and Amanda Fielding (who performed her own trepanation) are separated. Mellen met and married Jenny Gathorne-Hardy, who also has had the operation done. It was performed by Joey and a friend; she is happy that she had it done, telling the *Independent* newspaper in 1995: "It was as though for years I'd been a puppet with my head hung down, and now the puppeteer had taken hold of my head string and was gently pulling it up again."

Amanda Fielding met and married Lord Neidpath who was once an Oxford Professor and who during his time had occasion to teach Bill Clinton. The good Lord has also undergone a trepanation operation (for which they had to fly to Cairo and part with £2,000). There have, he says, been ongoing beneficial effects. Amanda now heads the Beckley Foundation, dedicated to the understanding of consciousness and altered states. She has run for Parliament on two occasions, with the manifesto 'Trepanation for the National Health' which espouses that the potential benefits of trepananing should be scientifically investigated. Currently, this research is taking place at the Sechenov Institute for Evolutionary Physiology and Biochemistry in St. Petersburg.

Joey Mellen and Bart Huges talk about bad reactions to LSD

Mellen: What's the worst flip-out you've ever seen?

Huges: That was one who after taking LSD for six successive days ended up totally incapable of surviving, incontinent and unable to chew or swallow the food I put in his mouth.

Mellen: What happened to him?

Huges: He went via a hospital to a mental hospital and was there for a year. When he came out his wife couldn't stand him and left him. Before his state deteriorated he begged me to trepan him, but I said that I couldn't consider such a thing. What was the worst you have seen?

Mellen: I remember one in Ibiza who flipped gradually over a period of some weeks. He began by taking acid every day and in the course of that he learned how to maintain the state without acid by doing deep breathing exercises. He started giving away all his possessions, including his passport, paid for his coffee with lumps of hash and gave his watch to someone who asked him the time. He thought he controlled the tides, the temperature and the "rhythms". Next, while continuing to behave politely, with a lot of smiles, he stopped talking altogether. In the end he just stood on a balcony for days staring out over the sea, not eating, drinking or sleeping, until he suddenly left his post and walked off at a brisk pace. He was picked up by the police throwing stones at a building and sent to a mental hospital, where he was given electric shock treatment. He was released after a few weeks, reconditioned but not his old self.

12

The men who turned on the world:
Acid, Hollingshead and Esam

IN THOSE days there were only two main sources of LSD in London. The first was Michael Hollingshead, famed as *The Man Who Turned on the World*, the Executive Secretary for the Institute of British-American Cultural Exchange in New York who, in 1960 acquired one gram of d-Lysergic Acid Diethylamide Tartrate-25, simply by writing to the Sandoz Pharmaceutical Laboratories in Basel, Switzerland and ordering it. When it arrived (with a bill for $285), Hollingshead processed it and laboriously amassed in a 16oz mayonnaise jar enough LSD to unhinge 5,000 of those unwary enough to try it.

The mayonnaise jar full of trips has now entered hippie mythology like 'Owsley's acid'.

When manufacturing the first batch, Hollingshead, inevitably now and then, dipped his finger into the mixture and took a lick, then at some point in the evening things began to unravel and he went off on a fifteen-hour trip. For most, that might have been just the salutory slap in the face they'd needed to resolve to never go anywhere near the mayo jar again, but Hollingshead was made of sterner stuff and had become curious about what had just happened to him. To this extent, merely in the interests of research of course, he undertook "many, many acid sessions" and recorded his experiences.

Astonished by the profundity of the trips, he now badly needed to discuss the disturbing and extraordinary things he had seen with somebody else, but who? Nobody he'd ever heard of had been where he'd just been. No one... Well perhaps one, Aldous Huxley. Huxley, father of the hippie movement, the British author of *Brave New World*; Huxley had reputedly taken peyote at a dinner with Aleister Crowley back in 1930. This experience had awakened in him a desire to research the effects of hallucinogenics, which he considered had broad implications for society and mankind in general. After Huxley was given mescaline in the early 50s he increased his efforts to experiment with drugs, and probably self-administered LSD in about 1955. He regarded his experiments as a 'search for enlightment' and was a pioneering explorer of 'inner space'.

After his death on the 22nd November 1963 (he died on the same day that Kennedy was assassinated), Huxley's books could be found beside hippie beds all over the world; his essay *The Doors of Perception* inspired the name of the band The Doors and his face appears among the illustrious throng on the cover of the *Sergeant Pepper* sleeve. His experiments with hallucinogenics continued to the very end; Huxley famously begged his wife (by way of a note, he could no longer speak) to inject him with LSD as he lay on his deathbed. She had dutifully administered 100 micrograms of the drug and then repeated the dose a couple of hours later as he undertook his last great trip.

However, in Huxley, Hollingshead had obviously discovered the right man to discuss his own recently discovered brave new world. Huxley listened, fascinated by stories of Hollingshead's production methods and mental experiences and then suggested that perhaps he should speak with an acquaintance of his, Dr. Timothy Leary. Leary, he explained, had written papers on the induced visionary experiences associated with psilocybin, the synthetic of the sacred mushroom of Mexico.

By now Hollingshead was either stoned on grass or out of his head on LSD nearly all the time, including during his working day; this was way beyond mere research; he'd allowed his work to suffer and when he met visitors he was often incoherent, babbling about the rottenness of British culture, insulting the Queen and talking of 'Kingdoms yet to come' and a 'Golden Dawning'. It became clear to him and others that he had to resign from his job as soon as possible.

Hollingshead rented some rooms in Cambridge, Massachusetts near where Timothy Leary worked, and arranged to meet Leary to discuss the effects of LSD and what he thought he might do with the remaining 4,975 trips he still had in the mayonnaise jar. Leary suggested that Hollingshead should move into his attic room and conduct some experiments there. The first of them included the jazz trumpet player Maynard Ferguson and his wife Flo; Hollingshead took spoons-full of the brew, Leary hung back warily observing the effects. Half an hour later, Flo, who had been laying on a sofa, sat up, with a huge smile on her face, and started waving her arms at Tim. "You gotta try this, Tim, baby. It's f-a-n-t-a-s-t-i-c!"

"Yeah, really, Tim", added Maynard, his face all lit up. "It really gets you there —wow—it's really happening, man.... "

Leary took the first step on a life-altering course that would eventually lead him to a thirty-year jail sentence. When he recovered from the trip, he wrote of the experience in his book *High Priest*, "'It has been five years since that first LSD trip with Michael Hollingshead. I have never forgotten it. Nor has it been possible for me to return to the life I had been leading before the session. I have never recovered from the shattering ontological confrontation. I have never been able to take myself, my mind and the social world around me seriously. Since that time five years ago I have been acutely aware of the fact that I perceive everything around me as a creation of my own consciousness".

These first experiences grew into the Harvard Psychedelic Project where Hollingshead, Leary, various doctors and a number of students researched hallucinogens. Part of their work involved dosing hardcore criminal recidivists at the Massachusetts Department of Correction. They established that, "very few of the inmates who underwent the intensive LSD or psilocybin sessions ever came back". By that, we must assume they meant 'came back' to prison, rather than 'came back' from the trips.

There followed years of sessions in various institutions set up by curious philanthropists, including a spell at Millbrook, a 64-room mansion on a 2,000-acre estate, donated by a drug enthusiast benefactor. On any evening many of the rooms were occupied by people experimenting with their own minds, often with profound and sometimes with hilarious results; on one occasion, another jazz musician, Charlie Mingus spent several hours jamming to a sink tap, as Hollingshead explains," Charlie Mingus and I were in the kitchen one evening, high on LSD, and unaccountably the tap started making yowling sounds followed by bangs. Charlie got out his bass and played *arco* in counter-point to the sound coming from the water tap. He seemed to know exactly the pattern of the sound. 'I am conducting the sound,' Charlie told me. 'I've taken it over. I've tuned into the vibrations and resonate to them".

And they weren't just using psiloscybin and LSD. A contact with NASA "resulted in us obtaining some JB118, the space drug officially on the secrets list." In one evening's experimentation with this designer hallucinogenic, Hollingshead perceived that he had turned into a crow.

The widely held belief that American institutions were experimenting with acid has become part of folklore. There were even stories that the CIA were planning to put LSD in Russian or Chinese reservoirs in the event of war, and surely it would be a fool who thought that it hadn't crossed their minds. However one allegation seems to have some currency - that the CIA encouraged the hippies to use LSD because it took the steam out of the anti-war demonstrations. It's hard to concentrate on peace marching and civil rights issues when you are staring at patterns in the carpet.

The various institutions that they had been involved with eventually became wary of Leary and Hollingshead dosing criminals and students with extremely strong hallucinogens, and sources of funding began to dry up. It was, for Hollingshead, time to return to London, and in 1965 he set up the World Psychedelic Centre in a large, high ceiling-ed flat in Pont Street, Belgravia.

He was, however, still determined to continue his 'research' and had brought with him boxes of psychedelic literature including the *Tibetan Book of the Dead* and, the legendary magic mayonnaise jar that incredibly still contained a thousand or so trips; LSD wouldn't be made illegal in Britain until the middle of 1966 and it is possible that it was down to Hollingshead alone that the legislation was pushed through when it was.

The centre was attended by a Who's Who of 60's notables starting with Hollingshead's partners Desmond O'Brien, already getting a reputation as one of the most far-out LSD exponents in London and who had been described in the Sunday People newspaper as 'Mr. LSD'; and Joey Mellen, one of the first people to trepan (drill a hole) in his own skull.

Associates of the World Psychedelic Centre included Victor Lownes, who co-founded the Playboy empire with Hugh Heffner and who once boasted of having five women a day, sometimes two at the same time, Julian Ormsby-Gore, the film maker, Alex Trocchi, the philosopher-writer junkie who once shot up in the Indica bookshop in plain view of the customers but yet had moralistically been responsible for getting Marianne Faithful into rehab; Julie Felix, the folk singer who had a big hit with *If I Could (El Condor Pasa)* as popularised originally by Simon and Garfunkel, Jo Berke who worked with R.D. Laing the radical psychiatrist, Feliks Topolski, the painter, John 'Hoppy' Hopkins, the writer and photographer, Ian Somerville, the multi-media expert who worked in McCartney's studio, Roman Polanski, the film maker, Bart Hughes, the eminence grise of the trepanation movement, Sir Roland Penrose, a director of the Tate Gallery and a friend of Picasso, William Burroughs, Donovan, Paul McCartney, Christopher Gibbs and Victoria Ormsby-Gore. One visitor talks of watching Mick Jagger trying to roll a joint on his knee in the Pont Street living room while battling with Michael's cat which was jumping all over him.

By then Michael had discovered yet another drug, DMT (dimethyltriptamine) - a violent hallucinogen that worked in a short sharp burst and wore off after a few seconds instead of the six to eight hours a strong acid trip usually takes. DMT was the drug of choice on the set of Donald Cammel's film *Performance* and, it is said, it was the DMT that made the making of the film such a wild, verging on impossible experience.

Hollingshead's pioneering 'experiments' were making his character and his behaviour increasingly frayed around the edges. There was the added problem that he had developed a heavy Methedrine (amphetamine) addiction. Although Methedrine wasn't at the time illegal, the doses he was taking were enormous – up to seven-syringes-full in one day (on the days when he was awake) then he would stay up and work frenetically for days on end finally collapsing into a virtual coma. Consequently he was suffering violent mood swings. He was also chain smoking grass and marijuana and taking large (500 micrograms) doses of acid three times a week.

Yet again his drug use had clearly gone far, far beyond mere academic research. Hollingshead had once commented, "There is some possibility that my friends and I have illuminated more people than anyone else in history." However, it seems every time he illuminated someone else, he was lighting himself up as well, over and over again. He had become possibly the most drugged man in history (who wasn't in some sort of hospital). Hollingshead had rewired his mind.

"In vain I tried to kick the habit, but it was impossible", he said. "The monkey was on my back and I could not remove it. I began to believe that it was all somehow a cosmic plot in which I was the victim. I had nightmares which nearly scared me to death. I reached a point where communication with other people was impossible. I saw the whole world conspiring against me. I was literally out of my mind and living in some kind of hell of my own making. And, worst of all, there was no one I could turn to for help, for there was no one I trusted; such were the effects of this poison I injected into myself".

His friends could see he was coming unglued; he'd become an embarrassment, babbling and incoherent. They started avoiding him and his house in Pont Street where the noisy parties ran non stop, with the windows wide open and the lights full on, comings and goings at all times of day or night, with strung out hippies screaming in the street, chauffeurs in Rolls Royces arriving to pick up packages for rock star clients who were either too lazy or too incapacitated to do their dirty dealings for themselves.

The crash was a long time coming but when it came it was devastating; the *Sunday People* ran the headline, 'THE MEN BEHIND LSD—THE DRUG THAT IS MENACING YOUNG LIVES" and beneath it was a lurid tale about the comings and goings at the World Psychedelic Centre. A highly paranoid Hollingshead was tipped over the edge and went on the run... but not without first forcing down his throat enough drugs to kill a pink elephant. He drove across the country out of his mind with fear and ultra strong hallucinogens, sometimes having to stop because he couldn't focus his eyes on the road. At some point he went on a five-mile high-speed dash across fields and railway lines and almost ran over a cliff in an effort to escape the lights from the police car that he was convinced was chasing him, only to find that he had been running from the reflection of the full moon in the car's rear window.

On his return to London a limp Hollingshead suffered another blow when he found out that Timothy Leary had been busted trying to get marijuana into the US from Mexico and the lawyers were talking about a 30-year jail sentence; then the Pont Street flat was busted and he and those that were present were arrested for marijuana possession.

Foolishly, Hollingshead decided to defend himself in court and naturally opted to be on LSD when he did it. While other users of the drug usually suffered visions and unrealities, Michael only seemed to be suffering from the giggles; his unrespectful wisecracks in court didn't impress the judge and helped garner him a stiff sentence of 21 months; he was rapidly despatched to Wormwood Scrubs whereupon he was interviewed by the governor who wanted to know why such an intelligent and literate man like himself had resorted to drugs. He replied, "Just lucky I guess".

Later, other casualties of the police war against drugs were to join him. 'Hoppy' Hopkins, Robert Fraser and other friends of the Centre were all imprisoned on drugs offences. The cells were being packed with intelligent young men who had made the mistake of getting caught in possession of drugs, often referred to as the 'victimless crime'; the Establishment fight back against the perceived hippie menace was in full swing.

If dangerous drugs were on the streets they were also in the prisons; well they certainly were after Michael received a visit from Stanley Owsley the infamous American LSD chemist and creator of 'Owsley's acid'. After the visit, Michael suddenly had a stash of LSD, which he shared around the jail. One of his keenest customers was George Blake the double agent who was five years into a massive sentence of forty-four years for spying for the enemy (Russia). Maybe the LSD inspired him because Blake never finished his draconian sentence; he escaped from the Scrubs with the aid of a motley bunch of CND supporters and quasi anarchists who had been inside with George and had taken pity on him. Blake is still alive and lives in Moscow.

Once out of prison, Hollingshead hit the hippie rail, travelling in the US, Norway, Tonga and spending a bit of time on a spiritual sojourn in Nepal, where having rebuilt his psyche he resolved to return to the UK and join a monastery. The suggestions that he was a British Intelligence agent are a bit fanciful; after writing his book *The Man Who Turned on the World* and other LSD related articles he went quiet. Considering the rigours of his life, it is perhaps unsurprising that Hollingshead is no longer with us. One theory is that he died in South America in the late 70s.

Hollingshead left behind a daughter Vanessa, a comedian who lives in the USA where she has built a successful career for herself despite at the age of five having stayed with her dad at Millbrook the New York mansion where he was conducting drug experiments and picked up a dosed sugar cube that she found lying around, ate it and took a trip herself. Her mother, aghast that such a thing had happened took her away from dad and fled to Manhattan but she couldn't claim the moral high ground for long because she then she became a speed dealer. Vanessa now includes in her repertoire wry jokes about her drug-addled parents, including one about how they all used to take family trips together without ever leaving their home and another a true story that on one occasion, mum persuaded little Vanessa to take some speed so she could tidy the apartment faster.

Another early source of LSD in London at that time was a New Zealander blow-in to town, John Esam, who may well have been getting it from Hollingshead. But wherever he had found it, Esam had a lot of it and he was opening doors of perception of his own in the flat within the 101 Cromwell Road house, a windowless, cardboard shack that he'd knocked up in one of the upstairs corridors; 'box' was a more apt description of his accommodation.

The Cromwell Road house, close to the West London Air Terminal was London hippie central for many years. Nigel and Jenny Lesmoir-Gordon, friends of Syd Barrett and Roger Waters from Cambridge, seem to have been the original 'alternative' residents and they had sublet rooms and parts of rooms (or even part of a corridor in Esam's case) to a whole range of peculiar tenants – exotic vagrants who blew into town from all over the world with little but '101 Cromwell Road' written on a scrap of paper.

At the top of the now demolished house were Syd Barrett and any other members of Pink Floyd who had nowhere to stay that night. George Andrews, an American poet who co-wrote *The Book of Grass: An Anthology of Indian Hemp* was over in the corner. Duggie Fields, the artist was with Syd in both Cromwell Road and in Earls Court (the flat with the striped floorboards which is pictured on the sleeve of Syd's album *The Madcap Laughs*).

Duggie had been friends of Simon Posthuma and Marijke Koger, a.k.a. *The Fool* who had regularly visited Cromwell Road. It was they who did the original (rejected) sleeve for the *Sergeant Pepper* album and who had painted the fabulous pavement-to-chimney-pot-tall mural on the Paddington Street side of the Apple shop on the corner of Baker Street. When the mean-minded neighbouring shops, perhaps apprehensive about the tribes of Beatle fans that swarmed over the area, complained about the lavish mural, they were forced to paint it over.

Amsterdam-ers Simon and Marijke were truly beautiful people who'd come to London wearing equally beautiful clothes that were just so right for the times; sequins, battered lace and rich velvets in abundance. Originally they'd planned to be stage designers having gone broke running a boutique in Holland, and by good fortune they went cap-in-hand to just the right people, two theatre publicists who had among their clients the Savile Theatre, then owned by Brian Epstein.

Bingo, they were instantaneously thrust into the inner circle of the Beatles, who, becoming as they were, increasingly tired of the procession of young hopefuls that came to them asking for a little bit of money for this project, or a great deal of money for that, were, like all young men, always in the market for some new clothes, The Beatles were all soon draped in Fool-designed costumes.

The *All You Need is Love* TV broadcast is made all the more lovely because of the Fool's designs. The exquisitely decorated long coats, scarves and foppish cuffs the Beatles modelled sum up the period. The Beatles had always looked good but on that film, they reached a rich-hippie apotheosis that even extravagantly dressed audience members like Mick Jagger, and a prancing Donovan couldn't emulate.

The Hollies, The Move, Procol Harum and Cream rushed to get dandified by the costumiers to their royal highnesses the Beatles. Cream had the Fool decorate Eric Clapton's famous Gibson SG as well as Jack Bruce's six-string Fender bass and Ginger Baker's drum kit. The cute Amsterdamers also did the sleeve for *The 5000 Spirits or The Layers of The Onion* album for the Incredible String Band, an intrticate vibrant monument to psychedelia.

The Beatles, ever self aware, recognised that they looked particularly spectacular on their worldwide broadcast of the *All You Need is Love* film; shortly after it's broadcast, The Fool were designing a piano and a gypsy caravan for Lennon (the caravan, originally intended as a gift for Julian which ended up on Lennon's own island Dorinish), painting murals for Paul, on George Harrison's Mini and also all over the walls of his Esher home. The Fool were everywhere man, designers by appointment to the hippest band in the land.

However, contrary to popular belief, they didn't paint the psychedelic designs on John Lennon's Rolls Royce. One source suggests that a friend of Lennon's, Donovan's mate Gypsy Dave did the work. Certainly the designs look unlike the Fool's other work and are more reminiscent of gypsy or bargee design. In any event, the sight of the psychedelic Roller so enraged a passer-by that the lady attacked Lennon in the street with an umbrella because she thought the paint job was a sacrilege.

When the Beatles originally decided to open the Baker Street boutique, The Fool were given £100,000 to transform the shell into a place where beautiful people just like them could buy beautiful clothes that they had designed. Despite its rich, glamorous proprietors and the creative breath of life the project received, sadly the shop only lasted eight months and when it was closed in a storm of finger wagging told-you-sos directed at the Beatles, the design team, the Fool, unwittingly associated with disaster and ridicule seemed like they were very inappropriately named indeed, and their star went into a rapid decline

They fell from the Beatles' firmament but both Simon and Marijke are still in business, he in the Netherlands and Marijke on the west coast of America. Marijke's art is still stimulating; Simon is publishing a book about his life entitled *A Fool Such As I*, which inevitably includes stories of their circus days at Apple.

As an adjunct to the Apple Shop, the Beatles founded the short-lived Apple Tailoring (Civil and Theatrical) in a shop at 161 Kings Road. One of its co-directors was John Crittle, an Australian who came over in the vanguard of Aussies (Germaine Greer, Martin Sharp, Richard Neville, Bruce Beresford, Barry Humphries) all of whom had been attracted to the bright lights of 60s London and who had later become known as the 'Larrikins of London'. Originally, the handsome Crittle had been involved in the *Hung On You* boutique and then partnered Tara Browne in *Dandy Fashions*, but his maverick ways often alienated his partners.

John's friends were many though; Crittle was at hand when Peki D'Oslo, the one time muse of Salvador Dali - Amanada Lear in an earlier carnation - was summonsed to appear before Marlborough

Street Magistrates Court on a cannabis possession charge (she had been arrested by police during a raid on the *Dandy Fashions* shop. Brian Jones sent his chauffeur Brian Palastanga with a limousine to get them safely to and from the court, ostentatiously showing his solidarity with all his famous victimised friends who were also being swept up in the 1967 push to nail some pop stars and rid the streets of the demon drugs). John Lennon must also have liked Crittle because he once drew a pen and ink picture of him that was subsequently sold by Bonhams auctioneers in Tokyo and did well enough at the sale to provide Crittle with a Bentley.

And the beautiful people liked Crittle's clothes as well as Crittle; under his stewardship, Dandy Fashions sold a red rose covered silk jacket to Hendrix, and to David Bowie the silver lame suit he wore when singing *Space Oddity* in the short film *Love You Till Tuesday*. But like the retailer, the bespoke shop didn't last; the Beatles pulled the plug on Crittle's tailoring company when the accountants took control at Apple; John went back to Australia.

When John, a chain smoker, died of emphysema in 2000, it was revealed that he was the Prima Ballerina Darcey Bussell's natural father. Darcey admitted that she had vague memories of Crittle once driving her up the Kings Road in a Rolls Royce but had no relationship with him as a teenager or adult. Crittle apparently made several attempts to contact her later in years but despite having one telephone conversation together, the two never met again.

The landlord of 101 Cromwell Road, Nigel Lesmoir-Gordon hadn't wanted to be running a hippie haven; he'd only originally moved to London to become a filmmaker. One of the very first films he made was of Syd having an acid trip. Christopher Case, Robert Fraser's gallery assistant was also resident in the weird house - another psychedelic voyager. It was a house that Floyd's manager Peter Jenner says, 'was run by heavy, loony messianic acid freaks. Syd got acided out. Acid in the coffee every morning, that's what we were told. He had one of our cats and they gave the cat acid.' One of the leaders of those 'heavy, loony messianic acid freaks,' which Jenner refers to, was John Esam.

Esam had made his way to London in the early 60's by way of the Greek islands and coincidentally the acid arrived at pretty much the same time as he did. And also in from Athens came Dan Richter, a mime teacher and the editor of an avant-garde poetry review who, for some years moved around the John and Yoko axis and who starred as the bone-bashing ape with ideas above his space station in Stanley Kubrick's sci-fi epic *2001*, in the *Dawn of Man* opening sequence. Lennon would later comment: "2001 should be played in a temple 25 hours a day".

Known as 'the Spider', Esam was a poet who had performed at the ICA with William Burroughs, Brion Gysin (originator of the cut-up word writing technique and inventor of the *Dreamachine*, a stroboscopic light machine that it was said could encourage alternative mental states), and Daevid Allen (who later performed with Soft Machine and Gong).

Esam and Richter with Barabara Rubin had been largely responsible for setting up the Albert hall poetry readings with Allen Ginsberg et al. "We had been used to going to poetry readings in small places like the Better Books shop ran by (Barry) Miles or Ronnie Scott's", said Richter. Then one day we were sitting opposite the Albert Hall; we smoked a joint and this crazy idea came to us, 'let's put on a reading there… in the Albert Hall. Let's rent the Albert Hall'. It was crazy. So we walked across the road and asked if we could hire the place and amazingly they said yes. We found the money, a few thousand dollars… I think my wife's father had cashed in a pension or something like that and we put the reading on".

The tall, thin, intelligent, drug cool Esam with black hair smoothed down flat on his head and intense, piercing eyes was a striking figure and people attest to how he had an aura about him. Although that expression is over-used by many people about many people in those days, in this case it seems there was a certain amount of truth in it. One friend Virginia Clive-Smith (Virginia, who among other things designed covers for one of the Firesign Theatre comedy team's books) said, "John was like a spaceman…

this incredible character who laid everything that moved and had the most extraordinary magic about him. He would take people over totally. He would create such energy around him that he was fascinating, almost the way a cobra fascinates a bird".

Perhaps the aura in the eyes of those beholding him had something to do with the 'several thousand' acid tabs that a friend of his (Hollingshead?) had brought in from the USA.

Suddenly there was a lot of activity at the house. Lots of junior hippies were gathering to listen to weird music and sit at the feet of these senior freaks who in turn sat beneath Tibetan tapestries and dispensed tales of the east, consciousness expansion and spiritual enlightenment, while the kids smoked joints that knocked them to the floor and occasionally downed brain shuddering glass phials of LSD. Eventually even the police twigged that something strange was going on at 101 Cromwell Road and one night they walked straight through its wide-open door into a smoky room filled with gaily dressed people in various stages of mental derangement. Esam, despite his astral gliding mustered a grasp of reality from somewhere and quick as a flash, swept up a bag full of acid-soaked sugar cubes and flung them out of the window into the garden. A policeman with quicker reactions than even Esam caught the bag as it flew towards the blackness and the game was up.

The cops knew they'd got hold of something, after all Esam had tried to ditch it so it must be important, but they weren't quite sure what it was. When tests confirmed that the sugar lumps contained LSD they became excited, then they were much disappointed because at the time, the substance was still legal. But talks with their scientists threw up a fiendish angle. LSD, the boffins reasoned, was a semi-synthetic derivative of a substance called ergot, a parasitic (and in certain circumstances poisonous) fungus. Eureka! They deduced that Esam was not a mere drug dealer; he was in fact a poisoner!

He was charged under the Poisons Act with conspiring to produce a toxic substance which people were ingesting, the penalty for which would be far worse than that for a mere drugs offence. Whatever the sentence for hashish possession or dealing might have been in those paranoid times, the penalty for the production of poison might, only just, fall short of hanging.

The case went to the Old Bailey and for the hippies, it all started to become very unfunny. Things started unravelling, in fact, it all became exceedingly heavy, not least because there were a further 4,000 trips hidden in a door handle in another flat and the police were making dawn raids. Everybody freaked out. There was a flurry of activity and a number of the scene's protagonists fled the UK for Ibiza and other destinations unknown and waited for the heat to die down.

The case against Esam turned into a dispute between each side's scientific experts - about the nature of ergot, what type could be considered a poison and whether you could extract Lysergic acid from it. The white coats put their heads together. One observer said that the government's argument could be characterised as, "if you boiled instant orange juice, you'd wind up with an orange" which was a clearly unlikely result. Eventually the police scientists had to give way; in fact complete harmony broke out among the experts and they informed the judge that they were unanimous that there was no real justification for calling LSD a poison at all.

A few freaks un-freaked. The case against him dismissed, Esam had escaped the prospect of a cell of Wormwood Scrubs but unfortunately his free spirit seemed to have escaped as well. Chastened and battered by his experiences, Esam returned to New Zealand, and lay low avoiding all things narcotic for many years, last heard of living in a retreat, Oregon House in California where he is a student of the works of the spiritual teacher Gurdjieff - best known for his theory of 'the Fourth way', philosophies concerned with attaining higher levels of consciousness. Daevid Allen, who saw him in recent years, noted that Esam didn't look in the best of health. Dan Richter confirmed early in 2008 that Esam had had health issues but was on the mend.

Asked to recall those times and his friend Johnny Esam, Dan agreed that Esam was a charismatic man but added: "there were a lot like him around at that time though. Although there were relatively few people involved in that pre-1965 scene, nearly all of them were busy creating: poets, writers and artists. It was primarily a literary scene; the rock 'n' rollers came later. The music was jazz. I never thought Johnny was a drug dealer; he was just involved, like the rest of us, in trying to expand our minds, expand our consciousness, getting turned on and getting excited about the future. There would be poetry readings and then someone would stand up and announce a manifesto. It's hard to look back at that period with a pair of eyes from today.

None of us thought of ourselves as dope dealers or criminals. It was a free time and London was absolutely a good place to be. There were a lot of places like the Cromwell Road house that were kind of notorious. The time was charged with electricity. There was a new world, a new reality, a new truth and the pace of change; the world took a leap forward. We all thought we were changing the world. We wanted to live high; you know, we thought we were like Zen monks or something. After the poetry reading the hip/beat scene exploded. We had to turn away thousands of people. It was a big thing that had happened. This was no longer a small movement among the literati, just among the intellectuals and this was happening in London. It was like somebody had dropped some magic dust on the world".

Richter's view is that the world was changed. "You have to remember how it was", he says. "Women were second class citizens, blacks were second class citizens. There was an insane arms race; it was basically sexist white men with money and power and nobody else mattered. At the start of the 60s, half of Africa was colonised by European countries. We were the ones that brought things like this to people's attentions. We were the ones who went out on the streets and got our heads cracked fighting for civil rights. The world we live in today is very different; a black man and a woman running for president of the United States and that is a direct result of what was happening in the 60s".

13

'Magic' Alex, the Maharishi and the Nothing Box

"HAVE YOU met the Greek bloke; Lennon's new guru?"

"What's his name?"

"He's got three names; he's sometimes called Yannis, then he's Alexis and then sometimes just Alex".

"That's handy if you're being chased by the tax man; you can run in three different directions".

"I want three different names".

"You've already got two: Paul and Macca".

"Yes, but they're not grand enough. They call Elvis 'the King' don't they? I think they should call me 'Prince Paul'".

"What about 'Pope Paul'".

"You're jokin' aren't you?"

"So are you".

"That's true".

"What does he do?"

"What does who do?"

"What does the guru do?"

"Guru do? He does electronics. He's one of John Dunbar's oddities, did a kinetic light show at the gallery".

"What's the hell is a kinetic light show?"

"I didn't go so I don't know; it's lights moving about I think. Brian Jones saw it and was very impressed apparently".

"Was he tripping?"

"He would have been at some point that day knowing Brian. You want to know what else the guru reckons he could build?"

"A robot Ringo?"

"No, we replaced Ringo with a robot years ago. No, he says he can build a house that can float".

"That's a houseboat".

"No, I mean one that can float through the sky".

"You've been reading too many Dan Dare comics".

"Or he has; a lot of it sounds like science fiction. He can talk up a storm can Alex, Yannis or whatever he's called. He reckons he's going to build us a new recording studio... at Apple, here, in the basement, and get this; he reckons it will be a 72 track".

"Seventy-two track? There's no such thing".

"Well, there is in his head. All we have to do is pay him forty quid a week and he'll build us a studio and loads of other stuff".

"Sounds like he'll be building himself a bank balance along the way".

"Yeah, but what if he pulls it off? Seventy-two track. Then it'll be 'bye bye Abbey Road'".

"You won't be able to walk to work anymore. How many tracks is Abbey Road?"

"We recorded Sergeant Pepper on an eight-track".

"So 72-tracks would be really something".

"Really, really something".

"What does George think?"

"Which George? Harrison or Martin?"

"Martin".

"George Martin is doing his nut. He refuses to believe anyone knows more about recording equipment than all those white coat blokes with biros up at Abbey Road but they've got 16-track studios in the States now so…"

"That's still not 72".

"True".

"And that would be a helluva wide piece of tape presumably".

"Also true".

"As wide as a bog roll".

"More like two bog rolls… and that's not a very nice thought: our music being associated with toilet paper… Anyway, while he's working on the plans for the super studio, Alex – or should I say 'Magic' Alex as Lennon has started calling him – has been knocking out these little boxes with weird flashing lights on them".

"And what do they do?"

"That's it. That's all they do; they flash. Lennon loves his; he just sits there tripping watching these randomly flashing lights all night".

"But what's the point?"

"That's it; there is no point, just entertainment for tripping millionaires. That's why he's calling it the 'Nothing Box'".

"So you're paying him to produce Nothings, but how much does each Nothing cost?"

"Well certainly not nothing because nothing's for nothing but I think I deserve a free one as we've given him a job and a workshop... or the 'laboratory' as it is to be known".

"What goes on in there?"

"I haven't been in but apparently there is all sorts of weird shit".

"How weird is the shit?"

"Erm, he's gonna make a 'phone that will tell you who's calling you before you pick it up".

"Now that would also come in handy if the tax man was after you".

"Or Yoko..."

"Indeed".

"...And stereo speakers that are kind of wallpaper... oh, and a huge sun that he wants to hang outside the boutique in Baker Street. Trouble is, he says, it needs us to put in a load of cash".

"Goes without saying; what did you say to that?"

"Lennon is all in favour. You know what he's like: 'Give him anything he want; he's my guru'".

"Predictable, but what did you say?"

"I said, 'if you can do it then we want one'".

George Harrison partnered advertising copywriter Terry Howard in Sybilla's nightclub, conveniently situated (for the Beatles and their popstar mates) in Swallow Street, through an arch just off the bottom of Regents Street W1. Howard could only afford the costly venture, even with a Beatle as a partner because he had a profitable sideline as a society photographer, scamming debutantes and the like by snapping them at their coming out balls, selling a set of shots to them and their mothers, then selling another set to the newspaper gossip columns.

A character who was often seen out and about with The Fool – in George Harrison's nightclub and many others was John Alexis Mardas (Yannis Alexis Mardas), who Lennon dubbed 'Magic' Alex.

Mardas was a blonde-haired Greek whose father held a cabinet post in Greece's dictatorship government, yet another waif washed up against the banks of the Thames drawn by the Beatles and London's Xanadu, but unfortunately he'd omitted to obtain a working visa and was soon in trouble wth the Greek embassy. Despite the bother, Alex quickly ran into the walking-talking hippie conduit John Dunbar; he installed a kinetic light show at the Indica Gallery where he met Brian Jones. The Stones used some of his lights on a tour they were doing, and Jones introduced him to Lennon who was so enamoured of Alex's schemes and wheezes that he told the other Beatles that Mardas was his new 'guru'. An Apple attorney was rapidly deployed to sort out Mardas's visa and work-permit problems and suddenly Yannis was at the living-breathing heart of hip London.

Boasting skills in the embryonic world of electronics, Alex was poo-pooed by George Martin when he announced that if he only had the money he could build a 72-track studio (at a time when the best that London had to offer was Abbey Road's eight-track). Mardas was given to wandering around the Abbey Road console room inspecting the gear and tutting. However, despite George's scepticism, such was the band's faith in Alexis that he was given the time and money to try and pull off some of his incredible claims.

Mardas was put in charge of Apple Electronics on a wage of £40 a week and a share of the profits and during the time he, in theory, was supposedly building the biggest, most technologically advanced studio in the world. Meantime, he kept the Beatles in his thrall (particularly a wide-eyed Lennon) with an array of gee-gaws including the 'Nothing box' – a small plastic box with randomly blinking lights - plastic apples with radios inside and luminous paint. Other visionary products would be a telephone you could tell who to call and wallpaper loudspeakers. Also the Apple shop would, if only they'd give him the money, benefit from a huge artificial sun hanging out above Baker Street. Paul McCartney's response to such claims was typically dry: "Well, if you could do that, we'd like one," he said.

The Beatles installed Alex in a 'laboratory' in Boston Place the road alongside Marylebone Station, which coincidentally is the road that the Beatles run down in *Hard Day's Night* (Alex himself appears for a moment or two in another Beatles film *Magical Mystery Tour*).

When the Beatles and their partners went off to India to the Maharishi's ashram, they took along a tribe of similarly questing devotees including Mike Love of the Beach Boys, Donovan, Patti Harrison's sister Jenny Boyd (who was Alex's flatmate), Mia Farrow and her sister Prudence (who inspired the Beatles song *Dear Prudence*) and Alex. After a few days, Alex suggested to the others that there was a 'rat' in the ashram. He began murmuring that the Yogi was taking more than a spiritual interest in Ms. Farrow and other attractive members of the group. Cynthia Lennon alleges that this was because Mardas thought that the band was falling under the Maharishi's spell and he felt that this was some kind of threat to his own influence as the band's 'guru'. Though the accusations have never been confirmed by Farrow and have been completely denied by George Harrison, Lennon believed his friend's story and was instrumental in calling the whole thing off, prompting the remaining Beatles to flee back to London (Paul had already left).

Later Lennon stated in interview that the Beatles track *Sexy Sadie* with its line 'You made a fool of everyone' was originally called *Maharishi*.

Another version of this story is that the Maharishi had wanted Magic Alex to build him a radio station so that he could spread the transcendental word over the airwaves. Unfortunately for Alex, the Maharishi had, before becoming a swami, received a physics degree from Allahabad University and was therefore fairly familiar with all the gadgets Alex had in his 'magic' box and was unimpressed by the ensuant lack of progress in the radio station project.

Subsequently, Alex went off to Greece with Cynthia Lennon, Donovan and Jenny Boyd. Lennon didn't go, making the excuse that he was busy recording. When the party got back to Kenwood, Lennon was sitting cross-legged on the floor with a strange-looking Japanese woman called Yoko and her slippers were sitting outside their bedroom door. Cynthia fled to the flat that Mardas and Boyd shared, her marriage over.

Back at Apple HQ, Magic's studio was considered unusable by the band; furthermore the Patents Office rejected many of the patents Alex had applied for on behalf of Apple Electronics on the grounds that all he'd done was adapt pre-existing devices. A doubting George Harrison said, "Alex just read the latest version of *Science Weekly*, and used its ideas." Incoming Apple boss Allen Klein quickly closed Apple Electronics; then it was revealed that back in Athens Alex had been a mere TV repairman. It was estimated that Apple Electronics went down £300,000 out of pocket.

George Martin was so annoyed at the Beatles for being, as he saw it, duped by the charismatic Greek that he thenceforth distanced himself from the production of their next album, then called *Get*

Back, and to a large extent left the mixing to Glyn Johns; eventually the tapes were passed, against McCartney's wishes, to Phil Spector.

Alex moved on; his previous clients had been only rock's aristocracy; what about the real thing? His next venture included the Shah of Iran among other royals; Alex became connected with ex-King Constantine of Greece who had met him through Alex's new Greek wife (John Lennon had been joint best man with Donovan at the wedding). Together, they set up a company that built and sold bulletproof cars to VIPs and royalty, utilising the King's friends and relations as customers or agents. Among the illustrious crew was the Sultan of Oman and Constantine's cousin Prince Philip, who took delivery of Mercedes limousines armoured by the company.

Duncan Campbell, the investigative journalist writing in the New Statesman in 1979 said that the Sultan's ex-SAS protectors wanted evidence that the limousines were as bullet proof as they were claimed to be and took one of the Mercedes 450 saloons out into the desert for a shoot up. One bullet, it's said, punctured an air cylinder, which set the petrol tank ablaze; then it exploded leaving the car a burnt out wreck. King Hussein of Jordan conducted similar tests and was told that the bulletproof metal just wasn't, and that the armoured glass when hit with a bullet, showered the interior of the car with shards of glass.

Despite the set-back Alex's royal connections held him in good stead; when Prince Juan Carlos of Spain, another of Constantine's cousins wanted a secure communications system set up to enable him to be in contact with his palaces from wherever he was, be it in his helicopter, his car or his yacht, it was Alex, the ex-TV repairman who got the contract. Campbell doesn't say how successful the system was but hopefully more so than the 22 limousines that went to Oman, Jordan, Spain and Iran.

According to Campbell, Mercedes Benz, realising that the vehicles were inadequate, denied approval of the conversions and in turn the West German government refused to grant them roadworthiness certificates.

Another bizarre tale connects Mardas to one Panos Koupparis who, amongst other things is a researcher into paranormal activities and claims to have seen the death of Princess Diana before the event, in the bottom of a coffee cup in a kebab restaurant in East Dulwich. In 1989 he was imprisoned for allegedly attempting to blackmail the Greek Cypriot government. In what became known as the 'Nemo' case, a letter conspicuously dated April 1st and signed Commander Nemo had been delivered to the Cyprus High Commission in Mayfair stating that there were deposits of the highly toxic dioxin hidden in specific sites all over the island and that they would be electronically dispersed unless the Cyprus government paid over $15 million. A short while later, Koupparis went to the High Commission in Mayfair claiming he knew how to detect these sites and render the weapons harmless. All he needed was a fee of about £25,000. He was unsurprisingly arrested.

It then transpired, that an employee of Mardas's company chauffeured the car Koupparis had been driven in that day, and it was later revealed that Mardas had employed Koupparis at some point;

Mardas was called as a witness for the prosecution at the trial. Koupparis served time but was released after it was determined he had been temporarily insane at the time of the event, the result of the mis-prescribing of anti-depressants and other medications.

In 2004, Christie's sold a number of Alex Mardas Beatles souvenirs under the title, 'The most significant collection of Beatles' memorabilia to come on the market in over 10 years'. Star lots include a coloured felt pen drawing by John Lennon, a letter, signed, from John Lennon to Alexis Mardas, *Happy Fish* a wash, pen and ink drawing by John Lennon, a leather collar worn by John Lennon throughout 1967 and 1968 and a custom-made Vox Kensington guitar, used by John Lennon and George Harrison in 1967 and given to Magic Alex by John Lennon as a birthday present.

Mardas stated that the sale proceeds would go to a charity in Greece.

On 21 August 2006, the Independent newspaper made this statement:

"On 14 June we inaccurately referred to Mr Mardas's involvement with the Beatles' company, Apple Electronics Limited.

Mr. Mardas was not an employee of this company but a director and shareholder. He was not sacked by Apple Electronics but resigned his directorship in May 1971, retaining the shareholding until he gave it to Apple Corps some years later.

We accept that he did not claim to have invented electric paint, a flying saucer or a recording studio with a "sonic force field" or cause his employers to waste money on such ideas.

We apologise to Mr Mardas for these errors."

14

The Chelsea set and Kings Road in the 60s – the trendiest boulevard in the world

THE tribes of 1st century Chelsea weren't going to just lie down and let the Romans walk into their manor and start charging them taxes. Perhaps they were anarchic ancestors of the hardy pre-Abramovich Chelsea supporters that still to this day inhabit the area, for it seems the Ancient Brits of SW3 put up something of a scrap in their attempts to prevent the legions wading across the wide shallows of the Thames from Battersea. The skulls, bones and Celtic weapons found when the foundations of Battersea Bridge were being dug out attest to a ferocious mid-stream battle. In the face of such stiff resistance, the Romans were forced to bring up to the front line their secret weapon.

The plucky Chelsea defenders, perhaps painted in blue woad, squinted and stared in disbelief through the river mists as a huge and terrifying monster lumbered towards them through the reeds, whereupon it hauled itself up the mud and gravel bank. It was an armoured elephant, which had come half way round the world; from sub-Saharan Africa by ship to England, it had walked up through the

Elephant and Castle to the Thames and the pachyderm was now heading in the general direction of Fulham. The colour drained from the defenders' blue-painted faces; they had never before seen a beast, especially one coated in armour before, so they fled.

The victorious invaders gazed around at the green and pleasant land they had just captured, saw that it was good and planted some vegetables in it. Thereafter, for hundreds of years, the fields of Chelsea were London's western larder.

So abundant were the salmon in the clear waters of the Thames so the legend goes, that Henry VIII had a pet Polar bear on a long leash that he would allow to go on a daily fishing expedition into its shallows. Through the nursery gardens and fields of sheep ran a rough track that meandered for several miles parallel with the river from St. James down to Putney Bridge, but when Charles II needed to go to his palace at Hampton Court, he usually opted for the royal barge. It was a lot quicker than travelling by the track, the earth surface of which was either dry and rutted, making his coach lurch around and causing the horses to trap their hooves; or when it was wet, turned to a quagmire that sucked against the carriage's wheels which often required all within to alight and put a shoulder against the machine to make it move at all.

It was when Charles commenced his relationship with the young Nell Gwynne that he started paying particular interest to the track that ran along the Thames in the area known as Chelsey, for halfway along it was a house named Sandford Manor which made the perfect hideaway for his ex-fruit-selling mistress far from the prying eyes of the royal court. The site of the manor is reckoned to be in modern day Waterford Road SW6, near to the recently closed Gasworks restaurant, the erotica-filled rendezvous used by the gangster John Bindon and Princess Margaret and where April Ashley used to wait on table.

Whenever Charles had business in Hampton Court (which seemed to be more and more frequently as his passion for Nell increased), he could reach the top end of the river path easily from his palace at Whitehall. The trouble was that it sometimes took hours to reach Sandford House (it was said that an overheated Charles once frenziedly rode his horse right up the main stairs of the manor, straight to m' lady's bed chamber, such was his pent up ardour). After one of these lengthy stops to water the horses, invariably his party wouldn't reach the great gates of his palace in Hampton before nightfall.

The answer, he reasoned, was to turn the sheep path into a track that his coach could negotiate with ease. This would require considerable expenditure and lots of gravel so he raised the taxes and dug for his gravel beneath Chelsey itself, which rests on a bar of the stuff (the word Chelsea might even mean gravel; it could be a corruption of 'chesil' as in Chesil Beach - an old Anglo Saxon word for gravel). From these pits the stones were hauled up to the site of the proposed road where teams of day labourers tamped them down.

After its completion, Charles reasoned that the ordinary public should be prevented from using his expensive road because they would only only drive their goats and ox carts along it and spoil its surface. So, from then, right up until 1830, only those who had a special copper token with the monarch's head on it were allowed to use what was originally a private trysting trail.

From such base motives the Kings Road was built and it has kept its air of the raffish and the royal ever since: highly fashionable at the eastern end and for much of its length but at about the World's End kink, traditionally becoming a place of lowlifes, thieves and whores. Once described as "a village of palaces", the most famous boulevard in the country has long been a place where bohemians, drunks, aristocrats, artists, avant-gardists, criminals and superior tarts indulged in drinking and chicanery.

Save for boat building there was little industry in the area. A notable exception was to come much later when a sanitary engineer set up a business that came to be three shops, a yard and a brass foundry based in Marlborough Road. It was here that Thomas Crapper, plumber by appointment to Queen Victoria, Edward VII and George V, built his celebrated flush toilets. The company moved to 120 Kings Road where it remained until 1966.

The city was dark, with its closed in alleyways, inadequate street lighting, wartime blackouts, and pea soup fogs (which all gave cover for party time for the capital's homosexuals); and in the early to mid 1960s, any splashes of colour were few indeed. The early sixties were really black and white: many of the films were – *Hard Day's Night* for one; many of the photographs were – look at David Bailey's *Box of Pin-Ups*, iconic shots of the faces of the time. Terence Stamp, the Beatles and the Kray twins stare out in glorious monochrome. Think of the Who in their earliest incarnations; the band may have been wearing bright pop art clothes, but they looked black and white to us. There was no colour in the newspapers and little in the magazines; colour TV didn't arrive until 1967.

If you'd looked down a darkened King's Road late one night in 1964 and seen a badly parked car of vivid revellers, laughing and squeaking, echoing in the distance, perhaps pointing at the swanky modes in *Bazaar*, Mary Quant's first shop (where Andrew Oldham had once talked himself into a job); they would have stuck out like birds of paradise in the swirling river mist-covered, sleeping street. Entranced, you may have rushed towards the attractive dazzling figures, only to see them jump into their Mini Moke and dash giggling away like will o' the wisps as you faltered and slowed to a disappointed halt, raised your collar to the wind and trudged slowly on into the funereal gloom of Fulham.

Was that Cathy McGowan, the Queen of the Mods, you'd seen swinging her legs into the rear seats? Could that have been Eric Burdon beside her? When McGowan had applied for her job at *Ready Steady Go* and been asked by her interviewers what was more important to teenagers, sex music or fashion, she had responded, "fashion". It was the right answer. When Burdon met her, he thought she was, "the girl of the day".

Another glamorous Kings Road bird of paradise was the occasionally glimpsed actress Diana Dors sweeping past in her powder blue open-top Cadillac convertible, her peroxide hair so stiff with lacquer it was like a conning tower in the breeze. The legend was that wild parties regularly happened at her town flat just above unglamorous Safeways supermarket, where two-way mirrors on the bedroom ceiling allowed guests to watch other unsuspecting guests having sex.

The imported Cadillac was as exotic as it got at that time; all else was muted Morris Minors, Standard 10s and Ford Prefects in Henry's obligatory black. Even Chelsea's purring Rolls Royces were as black as the tarmac.

The shops were still a throwback to the days of Chelsea being a village outside London. There were butchers and ironmongers, Jones the grocer, with its glass-topped biscuit tins; Sidney Smith's the drapers and a Woolworths with sweets spilling over its counters. There was an art shop that still thrives, Green and Stone at number 295 whose directors had once been Bernard Shaw and Augustus John; however, even then the main emphasis of the business was picture framing and not the selling of oil paints and palettes to romantically starving artists. Nonetheless, the road built for a King had had always boasted lightning flashes of great glamour, even occasionally of the Hollywood variety.

The Pheasantry is now a PizzaExpress but even the modern-day excess of signage can't hide the incongruous French style façade of 152 Kings Road, SW3. Originally Georgian, in 1881 it was taken by the Joubert family who owned a company of cabinet-makers keen to cash in on the home building aspirations of the wealthy families moving to the area then known as 'The Cadogans'. They turned the façade of the building into a billboard for their extravagant French a la mode designs and nowadays the front wall remains a plaster patisserie in amongst the Georgian brick geometry. The talented Felix Joubert made superb furniture and his skills were noted by Sir Edward Lutyens who commissioned him to make miniature furniture; picture frames and even suits of armour for the famous Queen Mary's Dolls' House, which is on permanent display at Windsor Castle.

The land on which the Pheasantry stands was originally Box Farm where pheasants were bred for the monarch's pot. The birds were sold from the house. Later it was a fashionable restaurant with apartments above and workshops below. In the early 1900s, the *Spirit of Ecstasy* lived there; that is to say Eleanor Thornton, the favourite model of the sculptor Charles Sykes who achieved an exquisite immortality when she posed with her knees bent and her arms stretched back in an ecstatic impression of a winged angel so that Sykes who from her ideal figure, could sculpt a mascot to go on the prow of the Rolls Royce motor car where she would for ever vanguard the wealthy in six coats of chrome.

In the 20s and 30s, the building housed a ballet studio where Alicia Markova and Margot Fonteyn took the lessons; the mirrors and the practice barre have been preserved and are on the first floor in the restaurant. Augustus John, Chelsea's eternally pre-eminent artist, the post-impressionist, art shop owning, philanderer and eternally thirsty epicurean, dominated the restaurant and drinking club that the premises housed from 1932 onwards, under the stewardship of Rene de Meo. Among the revellers were the queen's portraitist Annigoni, the poet Dylan Thomas, his wife Caitlin, the singer Gigli and the polymath Peter Ustinov. The atmosphere must have been thick; Caitlin Thomas always insisted that Augustus John had raped her and that she only married Thomas to escape John; she asserted that she felt no attraction to Dylan especially after the drink had bloated him beyond recognition.

Conveniently situated a stone's throw from Peter Jones, the posh person's department store in Sloane Square, Humphrey Bogart and Lauren Bacall sprinkled some stardust over the Pheasantry when they had a romantic dinner a deux there after a shopping spree. The house speciality was shish kebab cooked on hot coals and skewered on a sword.

In the early 60s the Pheasantry club dining room membership fee was 10s 6d for artists, fifteen shillings for ladies and a guinea for gentlemen.

Later in the 60s, the Pheasantry became an artists' colony with a club in the basement and the inhabitants were a Who's Who of the period. The mysterious David Litvinoff who counted among his friends Francis Bacon, Lucien Freud, John Bindon, George Melly and Reggie and Ronnie Kray had been instrumental in recruiting some of the building's exotic residents and lived in one of the flats himself. He was a very well connected, colourful gangster of whom Melly said, "he understood entirely the excitement of violence", and was employed as a script consultant by Donald Cammell who was locked away in 23 Lowndes Square, Knightsbridge with Jagger, Pallenberg and James Fox taking powerful hallucinogens and making *Performance*.

One of the apartments in the Pheasantry is used in the film *Blow Up* in the scene where David Hemmings looks through a window and watches a couple having it off.

David Litvinoff, the pop stars' pet villain

Described by Christopher Gibbs as "a mercurial, wandering Jew - intelligent, under educated and terribly funny", David Litvinoff moved effortlessly through the demi-monde where criminal met artist. He could talk up a storm and his colourful conversations would veer wildly from this to that; he was a natural to act as the advisor on the Mick Jagger film *Performance* with his intimate knowledge of the London underworld, its spielers, brothels, dodgy pubs and drug dens; its hard men, psychos and whores. In fact, some attribute the style of the movie, its leaping editorial style and stream of consciousness, entirely to Litvinoff who's given on-screen credits as both dialogue coach and technical advisor.

When the well-spoken, well-bred actor James Fox, a strange choice for the role of Chas - a gangland enforcer with a broad sadistic streak - had been recruited, the film's director Donald Cammell determined that his star needed to be shown the sights of the east end and the Old Kent Road and its inhabitants, and to be generally 'toughened-up'. Litvinoff and John Bindon delighted in taking him on a tour of the haunts of the undesirables including the Thomas A Beckett boozer and boxers' pubs where 'the chaps' were in abundance. There is even an allegation in Tony Sanchez's book *Up an Down with The Rolling Stones* that Fox was taken at the dead of night to see a couple of burglars demonstrate how they might, theoretically, carry out a job.

Another 'advisor' worked on Fox's physical fitness – skipping, sparring and working out – and, by all accounts, Fox developed a decent left hook, once leaving a sparring partner covered in blood. Before the toughening process had commenced however Fox was given to arriving on set in floppy hats, long hair and scarves; it was quickly explained to him that 'the chaps' would never be seen dressed like that, so Fox had a haircut, started wearing snappy suits at all times and more and more became Chas.

When the Redlands bust occurred, Litvinoff took it upon himself to find out who had squealed to the police about the antics of his new friends the Stones and their entourage to whom he now felt a sense of loyalty. He sniffed around, asked questions and noted that the same name kept coming up, a casual acquaintance of the band who had, perhaps, seen an opportunity to make some money from a national newspaper. Litvinoff, fresh from working with John Bindon on *Performance* and knowing Bindon's propensity for explosive violence took him along on a raid to check the unnamed man's alibi. The story goes that they beat a confession out of the suspect and then reported back to an unsuspecting Jagger, who had no knowledge that there had been retribution meted on his behalf. Jagger was, of course horrified by the situation, immersed as he was in a court case that might have seen him imprisoned.

Litvinoff crops up again in the Stones story when Brian Jones died and the Stones had to turn their imminent Hyde Park gig into a requiem. He knew the pefect poem for the occasion, Shelley's *Adonais* about the death of Shelley's friend Keats; Jagger it read on stage at the Hyde Park gig while a host of sweltering butterflies were released from a box and flopped around him.

One of the Krays inner circle, Litvinoff used to go pulling boys with Ronnie Kray and may even have had an affair with Ron, but it seems their relationship soured, if not for the absence of love then probably because of the gambling debts Litvinoff ran up with Ron's firm. Apparently a long outstanding £1,000 was the last straw as far as the twins were concerned and David found himself suspended upside down in and alleyway behind their club near the Derry and Toms building in Kensington High Street (later Biba) while Ronnie ran a sword (a long-favoured weapon) through Litvinoff's teeth causing a grinning gash either side of his mouth and virtually splitting his's face from ear to ear. This scene was depicted in the film *The Krays*, that starred the Kemp brothers Gary and Martin, and the way Christopher Gibbs relates the story, while Litvinoff was being mutilated he could hear the CND marchers coming up the road singing *Corinna Corinna*. Such was the code of the fraternity of 'chaps', that the assault was never reported to the police.

Litvinoff disappeared at some point, on the run from his murky past. He first went to Wales and then to Australia, eventually returning to London. Depressed by the idea of becoming middle aged, one report has it that he killed himself with sleeping pills in Christopher Gibbs' Cheyne Walk mansion. Another suggests that David had been writing a book about the Krays and their accomplices and that when the twins got wind of it, they had him got rid of; his body dumped in the Rainham marshes; Litvinoff would probably have preferred it that way. Live by the sword, die by the sword.

Germaine Greer lived downstairs in the Pheasantry, writing *The Female Eunuch*, while a fellow Australian, the pop artist Martin Sharp was above painting the cover for Cream's *Disraeli Gears* album. A friend and neighbour, another Australian Robert Whitaker was arranging photoshoots with the Beatles. Whittaker had travelled with the Beatles for two years and taken many of pictures of them some of which became the basis of the *Revolver* album sleeve. It was really Whittaker that opened Swinging London's door for Sharp and Oz editor Richard Neville. When Oz started, Whittaker was at hand; one of the most famous pictures he produced for the magazine depicts a female sitting on a flying toilet, as she relieves herself over the Houses of Parliament.

There were other artists and 'interesting' characters around the house; Philipe Mora the film director and the writer Anthony Haden-Guest to name but two but the Pheasantry only entered into mythology when a room became vacant and Eric Clapton moved in.

Martin Sharp

Sharp had worked on the original Australian version of *Oz* magazine with Richard Neville in the early 60s. When the two of them were busted for obscenity (Sharp had printed a near-the-knuckle poem he'd written about party gatecrashers and he and Neville had been photographed peeing into a sculptural wall fountain), incredibly they were given prison sentences. They appealed and got off but chastened they decided that claustrophobic early-60s Australia was too conventional for two free spirited youths who wanted to publish a "magazine of dissent" so together they went off on the hippie trail to Nepal, and thence on to London where the biggest buzz was.

Esconsed in the Kings Road, Sharp soon found the Speakeasy club where one night, he came across a musician who needed some lyrics. As luck would have it, Sharp happened to have some lyrics lieing around. Fortuitously he had just happened upon Eric Clapton who had just started Cream with Jack Bruce and Ginger Baker, and Sharp's lyric, *The Tale of Brave Ulysses* made it on to the B-side of their single *Strange Brew*. Sharp and Clapton became friends and when a room in the Pheasantry became available Clapton moved in. Soon Martin was designing the psychedelic sleeves for Cream's *Disraeli Gears* and *Wheels on Fire* albums. Robert

Whittaker did the photo shoots. Clapton's girlfriend, French model Charlotte Martin moved in with him (and when she moved out, it was to have a relationship and a child with another guitar legend Jimmy Page).

As well as designing record sleeves, Sharp was art director and chief cartoonist for the British *Oz* magazine, painting illustrations and covers including the famous Bob Dylan cover which has iconic status as one of the definitive pictures from the psychedelic era alongside another Sharp painting, that of an 'exploding' Jimi Hendrix based on a Linda McCartney photograph. An *Oz* spread entitled *Plant a Flower Child* and the *Blowing in the Mind* Bob Dylan cover when turned into posters, made Sharp and Neville a healthy pile of money and now originals of Sharp's 60s work are highly prized among collectors of ephemera from the period and are widely bootlegged.

Most importantly, Sharp's savage pictures were making powerful statements about what he considered was really obscene in western society. There weren't many magazines that would take the notorious photo of the Vietcong suspect being shot through the head and put it on its cover. Oz did, but not before Sharp had splashed it in blood red ink and inscribed on it THE GREAT SOCIETY BLOWS ANOTHER MIND.

Enraged, the establishment, in the shape of Detective Sergeant Pilcher (who figures elsewhere in this book), took one of his small revenges on behalf of the nation's morals; he thundered up the Pheasantry staircase, searched Sharp's flat, found a lump of hashish and dragged him off to prison for possession. The fact that the original intention had been to nail Eric Clapton offered little solace to Martin who, after his sojourn in the cells, was fined the maximum amount.

When Clapton told Sharp he should go to see Tiny Tim, who was that night playing alongside Peter Sarstedt, The Bonzo Dog Doo Dah Band and Joe Cocker in a London concert, Sharp was bewitched by the highly eccentric six-foot-one, falsetto-singing ukelele player. He took it upon himself to get involved with this unique character and became Tim's music producer, friend and patron, and over a 12-year period recorded hundreds of tapes of Tiny Tim singing and playing, as well as designing sleeves for his records and his costumes (Tiny Tim died in 1996 suffering a heart attack while singing his biggest hit *Tiptoe Through the Tulips* on stage).

With the Oz magazine closed down and its management doing time for corrupting the nation's morals, Sharp, who had crossed half the world to come to what he'd regarded as a wonderful place, decided that London's swinging was all but over; he returned to Australia to paint and exhibit his work as well as starting a campaign for the restoration of a local recreational area, Luna Park under Sydney Harbour Bridge.

Germaine Greeer

One of the more striking figures of the scene, Germaine Greer lived in the Pheasantry in Chelsea only a couple of days a week. The rest of the time she lived in Leamington Spa working at the University of Warwick where she was Doctor of English. Described by the New York Times as 'six feet tall, restlessly attractive, with blue-gray eyes and a profile reminiscent of Garbo', she wrote for Oz magazine under the name Dr. G. At the same time, such was the cross fertility of the times; she wrote a gardening column for *Private Eye* under the name Rose Blight. Not your normal gardening writer, she was as happy writing about growing daffs as she was a feature for Oz about an obviously indispensable item, the hand-knitted Cock Sock, "a snug corner for a chilly prick", as she dubbed it. Richard Neville, ever keen to get his kit off, modelled the woollen tube.

Greer saw her job at Warwick as part of a planned subversion as she told *Rolling Stone* magazine in 1971. "I'm still into converting the straights. That's why I teach. I guess the university doesn't really know about all the things I'm involved in. I don't push it down there. I only make occasional references when a line in a poem is like smoking or taking mescaline".

In 1969, she and two expatriate Americans Jim Haynes and Bill Levy, together with the editor Heathcote Williams founded *Suck* magazine, which probably needs no detailed analysis of its content especially when you know that it needed to be based in Amsterdam to avoid prosecution under the British censorship laws (a prudence that *Oz* should perhaps have considered).

It was for *Suck* that Germaine asked Keith Morris, who did photo shoots for *Oz* to take some explicit pictures of her. The late Morris, who had trained with David Bailey was, like many, intimidated by this lanky overwhelming presence, so he did as he was told and took the pictures despite his lack of relish for the close up nature of the work. When the magazine published the shots of her nether regions in all their glory, Greer, realising that she had perhaps 'over exposed' herself was furious, but of course the genie was out of the bottle. She left the magazine in protest.

Morris's career prospered despite this set back. Nick Drake, then unknown asked him to take a few dozen shots of him for promo reasons and Morris was, from then on, the only photographer allowed near the enigmatic, shy Drake. He also photographed Fairport Convention, Richard Thompson, Jimi Hendrix, Janis Joplin, BB King and Marc Bolan.

The two Americans from *Suck*, Levy and Haynes, were really quite early pioneers of, and had the effect of galvanising the 'scene'. Haynes had set up the Drury Lane Arts Lab, an experimental theatre group, knowledge of which once spread abroad then became a pilgramage and was mimicked by David Bowie in Beckenham. Levy, who had sailed over in on the Queen Mary in 1966, was and still is a resolute gentleman of the underground press who describes himself as a "point man for the zeitgeist". Over the years he has served for: The Insect Trust Gazette, International Times, Suck, The Fanatic, High Times and Penthouse Magazine. In Holland where he lives, he is known as the Talmudic Wizard of Amsterdam. On his Amsterdam radio programme he is known as Dr. Doo Wop; he remains an old school hippie.

Effortlessly passing from the establishment halls of academe to the anti-establishment pages of the underground press, Germaine Greer also found her way into the beds of some of the notable pop stars of the time and often referred to herself as a 'supergroupie'. Although physically and mentally intimidating, there's no doubt that some of the big boys in the pop profession, all ego pumped, regarded her as an irresistible challenge and felt compelled to have a crack at the statuesque Aussie, thus reinforcing, the old adage that there's nothing so sexy as brains... especially when there are a great pair of breasts beneath.

Under the title *The Universal Tonguebath: A Groupie's Vision* and under the byline Dr. G, for Oz, she conducted an interview with herself and explained how deathly a concept monogamy is, how she is determinedly promiscuous and how most of the pop stars she had had were at the top of their game. Naturally you can't really imagine Germaine settling for the roadies or the bass player from the support band, although there may have been occasions when she dallied with some stars-in-the-making. "I guess I'm a starfucker really", she wrote... because all the men who get inside me are stars. Even if they're plumbers, they're star plumbers. Another thing I dig is balling the greats before the rest of the world knows about them, before they get the big hype". She probably didn't mean plumbers.

On the cover of that issue of Oz, she is pictured undoing the flies of Vivian Stanshall, singer with the Bonzo Dog Doo Dah Band.

"Supergroupies don't have to hang around hotel corridors," she once said. "When you are one, as I have been, you get invited backstage. I think groupies are important because they demystify sex; they accept it as physical, and they aren't possessive about their conquests."

She once encountered Jimi Hendrix in the Speakeasy and challenged the long limbed guitarist to an arm wrestle. It must have been quite a sight as they went at it head to head - they were both bearing fulsome Afro hairstyles at the time – the fiery feminist and the dynamic new rock god. Maybe Hendrix was just doing the gentlemanly thing pretending he was losing or maybe he was making devious plans for Germaine for later in the evening because the strapping Ozzie beauty slammed his arm down on to the tabletop scattering the drinks and ashtrays. Of course Hendrix was left handed and we don't know which arms the combatants were using in the struggle, and there could have been a side bet and a wily Hendrix was just playing into her hands as it were…

Commenting on those pop stars that denigrated the groupies, Germaine said, "Most of the musicians who did this were small-time types; you never heard of Eric Clapton or Jimi Hendrix or Mick Jagger going on like that". Promoting herself as the plaything of rock stars is pretty hard to square with the fact that she had written the women's lib tract *The Female Eunuch* only two years earlier but it confirms her role as the "saucy feminist that even men like" - as *Life* magazine described her on their cover when it ran a feature on the professor.

It's alleged that Greer also went on a mission to seduce John Peel, and Mick Farren of the Social Deviants (another Afro wearer) admits that he was on her list of conquests although she contends that the chasing was all quite the other way round, saying, "They have to come to me. I make a point of not being part of the slag heap, or meeting them from the audience side of the footlights". Another famous affair was the Italian film director Frederico Fellini.

Germaine has nobly and notably never kissed and told about her interesting sex life and now that she has more come to resemble the respectable, bespectacled academic and commentator that the soubriquet Doctor Greer conjures up and has entered the ranks of Britain's national treasures, she might have mild concerns that some of her many conquests (those that are still living anyway) may, at some stage, kiss and tell about her.

Somewhere along the way, Greer got married, to Paul du Feu, a handsome muscled man whom she'd first seen in builder's overalls drinking Guinness outside a Portobello Road pub. Despite the attire, du Feu was in reality an occasional magazine columnist and cartoonist but Germaine saw only a rough-hewn builder and turned on the twin spotlights of her sex drive and intelligence. In a short while they were wed but stayed together for only three weeks during which time she cheerfully admits to having committed many adulteries. "In three weeks of marriage, it's true to say I was unfaithful seven times" she told ABC television.

However, the sheer presence of Germaine in du Feu's life projected him into the spotlight; he became the first male nude centrefold for *Cosmopolitan* magazine in the UK and had a book published entitled *Let's Hear it for the Long Legged Woman*. Somewhat surprisingly, after the three-week marriage, du Feu met and married another powerful, high profile woman, another six-footer, the civil rights activist, actor and writer Maya Angelou with whom he had a more successful relationship spanning eight years. Germaine, naturally, vocalised her opposition to the marriage.

By the early 70s Germaine Greer was rich, with property in the UK and Tuscany in Italy. Apart from Rupert Murdoch, Dame Edna Everage (and latterly the two *Crocodiles, Hunter* and *Dundee*), she was the only living Australian that the Americans could put a name to. Writing for many periodicals including *Esquire, Harper's* and *Playboy*, as well as the UK national press. Greer, giddied by her celebrity, said to the critic Kenneth Tynan, "If I peed on the paper, they'd print the stain".

Germaine was also a big hit on the American speaker's circuit. The measure of her financial success came when Richard Neville, the besieged proprietor of *Oz* magazine was facing a jail sentence on obscenity charges, Greer felt unable to give evidence on behalf of her old friend at the trial, he says because she was tax exiled in Italy and to return would leave her liable for an in iniquitous British tax and substantially financially the worse off.

Since then, her life has been lived out on our TV screens, in her books or in newspapers. She wrote one lament about the father she barely knew and another about the fact that having a child of her own has eluded her. In 1986, she cast a jaundiced eye over the 60s a period of social and sexual liberation when she was so active and noted that the participants were, "just rich kids playing... we were never really going to change anything".

Another Pheasantry occupant, the Anglo-American Anthony Haden Guest would have been a Baron if he hadn't been born out of wedlock. Instead, that honour fell to his half brother Christopher, the actor who played Nigel Tufnell in *Spinal Tap* ("but this goes up to 11") who is married to Jamie Lee Curtis. Anthony is a writer and cartoonist who in the mid 60s was drawing the *This Way Out* cartoon for the *Sunday Telegraph* and writing columns for the other Sunday broadsheets, although his main talent seemed to be an uncanny ability to be present at every significant social occasion on the calendar. This attracted nicknames like "Unwelcome-Guest", "Uninvited-Guest", and "The Beast." His friend Taki Theodoracopulos wrote in the *Spectator* magazine in 1997 that Haden Guest had attended some function or another every night for the last 35 years. He's still doing it so that's quite possibly 47 years by now.

One friend speaks of once seeing him sitting naked on the piano in the Chelsea Arts Club; who knows, a lot of exotic activity has happened within those walls, but the most energetic clubbing period for Guest was in the 70s when he was resident in New York writing for *Vanity Fair* and the *New Yorker* magazines (he'd moved to the USA when he lost his studio in the Pheasantry). He almost took up residency at Studio 54 during its most debauched period, utterly unhindered by the red velvet rope barrier, and could be seen night after night gossiping with Liza, Andy, Truman or Bianca. Unlike many attendees and despite his ferocious social life he seems to have been able to recall a lot of the goings-on and wrote the definitive book of NYC's decadent disco years, *The Last Party: Studio 54, Disco and the Culture of the Night.*

The famously bibulous Haden-Guest is widely believed to be the model for Peter Fallow, the drunken British journalist exiled in New York in Tom Wolfe's novel *Bonfire Of the Vanities.* Despite his love for New York, he maintains a wistful affection for London, saying recently to Jonathan Leaf of New Partisan "New York, yes, it has changed - and not for the better in the last ten years. It's come to have a deeply anti-bohemian culture. London has more tolerance for idiosyncratic behaviour – wearing pyjamas when you go to collect the newspapers, strange hobbies".

Hung on You on Chelsea Green was among the big four Chelsea boutiques. *Granny Takes a Trip,* Mary Quant's *Bazaar* and Vivienne Westwood's *430* are the others. Of them, only *430*, the old *SEX* shop Westwood ran with Malcolm McClaren survives today. Michael Rainey and Jane Ormsby-Gore ran *Hung on You* when they weren't gallivanting around the countryside in gipsy caravans looking for the Holy Grail. *HOY* was where young men gathered to buy white shoes, chiffon scarves, purple trousers and striped blazers. The proprietors were interested in Byron and Spencer's *Fairie Queen* so there were billowing shirts with frilly fronts and big sleeves and leather jerkins. The Beatles and the Stones were regulars, 'three of those and four of those please'.

Jane's father David Ormsby-Gore had been the British Ambassador to Washington in the Kennedy years (in fact Kennedy and he were distantly related) and it was under his stewardship that the UK and the USA had one of its closest relationships. In fact when Bobbie Kennedy was assassinated, Ormsby-Gore attended the funeral as one of the pallbearers. There was even talk of a romance between him and Jackie Kennedy after John Kennedy died. Referred to by the Kennedy clan as "our kind of Ambassador", one of his stunts was to smuggle fine Cuban cigars to the family via the diplomatic bag.

When he returned to live in London in 1965, it was said that the Ormsby-Gore family were themselves the British equivalent of the Kennedys and that with their re-appearance they had restored some of the glamour to Chelsea. The children, Jane, Alice, Victoria and Julian were at the heart of the new 'in crowd'. David, the father took a seat in the House of Lords as Lord Harlech and those of a certain age will be very familiar with his name having seen it many times as the signature on the British Board of Censors classification certificate at the start of any movie of the period.

Mick and to a lesser extent the other Stones first became close friends to the daughters and then the Lord and the Lady. The family house in Wales proved attractive to the social climbers in the band and both Jagger and Jones were visitors. David, as they knew the Lord, was close enough to the band to be present when the Stones launched their *Beggars Banquet* album with a lavish reception in the Elizabethan Room in the (appropriately named) Gore Hotel, Kensington. The band were dressed as beggars, while 120 journalists and other assorted media folk were served a seven-course banquet in candlelight by full breasted serving wenches. The tables groaned with boar's heads, cucumber and artichokes marinaded in Canary wine and flagons of claret and mead.

After the hearty repast, clay pipes and snuff were distributed and those assembled drank to the success of the album and the forthcoming publicity campaign. Mick, wearing a frock coat and top hat thanked the guests and then opened a gold confectionary box by his plate. Inside was a custard pie, which he flung into the face of Brian Jones who had been sitting next to him. At the same time, the guests were being given similar custard pies and an epic pie fight of *Tiswas* proportions ensued in the luxury surroundings. Lord Harlech was well and truly pied, an event that seemed to give him inestimable pleasure.

Granny Takes a Trip, Hapshash and the Coloured Coat

Ten years before the Sex Pistols started hanging out in Malcolm McLaren and Vivienne Westwood's shop *Sex*, *Granny Takes a Trip* at 488 Kings Road opposite the World's End pub was the regular haunt of all the significant figures of British rock and roll. Nigel Waymouth and Sheila Cohen were the original proprietors; Cohen had amassed a collection of antique clothes and bric-a-brac that formed the basis of the stock. Jonathan Aitken describes the contents of the shop in *The Young Meteors* and as usual didn't quite get it, "Charleston dresses of the 1920s, Victorian bustles from the 1880s, Boer war helmets, African fezes, Arab head-dresses, Chicago gangster suits from the Prohibition era, military uniforms... Victorian feather boas, an early gramophone, in short everything that would seem totally out-dated and absurd is found within the four tiny walls of *Granny takes a Trip*".

He also points out that the name of the shop is a drug reference, which might not have been that necessary to do in 1967.

It was when Cohen and Waymouth took on John Pearse, a Savile Row tailor as a partner that the range really developed and pretty soon *Granny* was clothing all the young dudes who flocked to the shop as much for the experience and the networking as to buy; Syd Barrett asking for more sequins to be sewn to a velvet jacket; Hendrix buying a powder-blue antique Hussar's jacket adorned with gold braid; Keith Richards putting a record on the old Wurlitzer juke box that stood in the corner belting out the latest tunes. There was a beaded glass curtain at the door; there were swirling marble patterns on the wall that provided a backdrop to the rails of highly coloured clothes, and a lace curtain at the entrance to the single changing room. Drug dealers threaded quietly through the racks doing some retailing of their own.

But it was the exterior of the shop that assured *GTAT* would enter modern history as the greatest of the London boutiques. One day the entire façade was painted with the face of Hollywood film actress Jean Harlow – the 'Platinum Blonde;' on another day a 1948 Dodge saloon car was bursting through the front window, half in and half out of the shop. Over night the shop would be transformed by a new façade; once it was covered in stars, strewn from the street up the concrete steps and all over the windows and walls; while on another occasion a huge Sitting Bull glowered from the frontage. The humble dry cleaning shop next door with its utilitarian aluminium windows looked impossibly drab by comparison but was grateful for the bonanza of extra business it garnered as the result of its location beside the grooviest clothes shop on the planet. It was an outrageous display of retailing creativity that nobody had seen before and the shop blazed a trail for other shopping 'experiences' like *Mr. Freedom, Sex* and *Paul Smith*, becoming a meeting place for the young and beautiful cognoscenti. Mary Quant had of course had her own exciting and surreal window displays at *Bazaar*, referred to by George Melly as "a banner, a battle cry, a symbol of the new sophistication". And aided by Andrew Loog Oldham, she had on one occasion dressed the bald-headed window mannequins in swimming suits and had them all playing white instruments wearing round goggle sunglasses. On another occasion they had a model dressed as a photographer suspended by its feet from the ceiling, taking pictures of a parrot also suspended at a crazy angle. They hired beautiful girls to carry sandwich boards up and down the Kings Road, which proved to be a sensation.

Although such stunts and displays might not cause much more than a ripple of excitement these days, back then they created a furore and shoppers travelled miles to go to *Bazaar* and *Granny Takes a Trip*.

The two pioneering stores' close proximity to *Hung on You*, which at some time was housed in the *430* shop, was part of their success; you could do them all in one afternoon.

Just up the road in Kensington and Knightsbridge, *Biba* appeared; it had the same shocking impact. Its creator Barbara Hulanicki recalled that every hour or so she'd have to go and wipe the nose marks from the front window.

Nigel Waymouth's talents as a designer bought him to the attention of Jo Boyd and John 'Hoppy' Hopkins who needed some posters made promoting their club the *UFO (Unlimited Freak Out)* that they were preparing to open below the Blarney pub at 31 Tottenham Court Road, W1. They introduced Waymouth to Michael English thus creating the partnership *Hapshash and the Coloured Coat* whose posters have legendary status in the world of psychedelia. Waymouth explains the chemistry and the techniques they employed, "Expensive gold and silver inks had not been used much on street posters before we made it a regular feature of our designs. We also pioneered the technique of gradating from one colour to another on a single separation. The effects were startling bringing an explosive vitality to the fly posters on the London streets. Nothing like it had been seen before or since. Looking at a whole block of some twenty or thirty of a single *Hapshash* poster was a powerful visual shock. It was not long before people started tearing some of them down to decorate their own walls. It was eye candy to match any psychedelic experience.

In October 2000 the Victoria and Albert Museum put on an exhibition of the *Hapshash* posters and designs, including many of the original artworks. These posters are now collector's items and fetch high prices at the auction houses. 'High Art' the definitive guide to psychedelic posters said, "They designed some of the most dazzling, beautiful and original psychedelic posters as good as anything produced in San Francisco and Detroit".

The ex-Ealing student English describes the work he did with Waymouth as "the bright, brilliant colours of pop flowing organically into the sexual shapes of art nouveau". They confessed to *Oz* magazine editor Richard Neville that all their inspiration came from taking acid trips.

The duo were particularly inspired by the art nouveau work of Aubrey Beardsley and had been to see a show of his work at the V&A Museum. The late George Melly had also been in attendance and commented that he was "surprised to find it packed with people" who he said were mostly "very young". He added, "I had stumbled for the first time into the presence of the emerging underground".

Everyone loved the UFO posters including The Who, Hendrix and Pink Floyd and they all wanted the duo that had so accurately encapsulated the times to make posters for them too.

So closely were the young artists associated with bands and the music scene that they decided to make some music of their own and enlisted the insane/genius producer Guy Stevens to help them produce an album, which was released under the name *Hapshash And The Coloured Coat - Featuring The Human Host And The Heavy Metal Kids.*

Stevens appears on the album as 'The Human Host". On it is a track called *H-O-P-P-Why?* a dedication to their patron John 'Hoppy' Hopkins of the UFO. The second and last album the duo made, *Western Flier*, featured Groundhogs' guitarist Tony McPhee and a pre-Womble Mike Batt. Highly experimental and demonstrative of the pent up madness of Stevens (who once told Charles Shaar Murray, "There are only two Phil Spectors in this world and I am one of them"), the records are regarded as cult classics of the genre and gave a taster of the Kraftwerk-style music that was to follow.

Granny Takes a Trip survived for a few more years after Waymouth left to concentrate on the poster and sleeve design business. John Pearse had departed for Rome to join the Living Theatre group. Sheila Cohen sold the business to an American partnership but it closed in the mid-70s at about the time that Malcolm McLaren was staking his claim to the lower reaches of the Kings Road.

Nigel Waymouth, living back in the UK after a long spell in San Francisco, continues with a career in painting. He is an accomplished portraitist and has done commissions for the royals, Diana Rigg, Tom Hanks, Rupert Murdoch's wedding and many more. Copies of some of the *Hapshash* posters are available from his web site.

15

The Alternative

WE START to see a pattern here. While the 'grey' people sat at home watching the *Black and White Minstrel Show* and *Dad's Army* on TV, their children were organising their own parties at *UFO, Middle Earth* and student bars right across the country. Instead of shopping at Burtons the Tailors and Hepworths, the children had started opening their own clothes shops. They were also opening bookshops full of books that only their contemporaries wanted to read, and galleries with exhibits only they wanted to walk around and wonder at. Instead of going abroad with Thompson's Holidays, they were taking the hippie trail; instead of propping up the bar at the Hare and Hounds they were popping pills in the Bag o' Nails (the club named after Ben Jonson's "The Bacchanals").

In a 1967 edition of The Observer, contemporary commentator Peter Fryer described the west London basement dwellers and their ilk as a "new society". He was one of the first to note a scene "of several thousand people, mostly under 30, who have their own vocabulary, dress, stimulants, entertainments, publishing houses, communications network, posters and shops - all as different as possible from those of the older generations".

Everything had to be part of the new vibe. It was around now you started seeing hairdressers at trendy parties. The posters on the walls advertised gigs that your parents wouldn't be able to find let alone be allowed into. Then came the Apple organisation, which was for its architects, the first toe in the water of a full-on attempt at recreating society. There would be clothes, electronic gadgets, music, books, poetry, films and TV, all with a youth orientation, all shot through with a revised set of ethics; an evolving liberalised morality.

McCartney had part-financed the Indica gallery, the Indica bookshop and the *International Times* newspaper, an effort which, when put alongside the Beatles' plans for Apple amounted to an impressive contribution to the culture, a system that existed entirely outside the old frameworks. It was a deliberate attempt to subvert conventional business practices. There were to be no men in suits, no adults at all basically, because with adults you just couldn't have fun. The kids had broken into the engine room and were pulling the levers of power. The way they saw it, the days of the old Tories running Britain and the Empire from the clubs of St. James and Pall Mall were numbered.

These were lofty ambitions. Apple took a full page ad in *Oz* magazine, written by Miles, to explain their credo: "Paul McCartney asked me to point out that Apple is not in competition with any of the underground organisations, rather it exists to help, collaborate with, and extend all existing organisations as well as start many new ones. The concept as outlined by Paul is to establish an 'underground' company above ground as big as Shell, BP, or ICI but there is no profit motive, as the Beatles' profits go first to the combined staff and then are given away to 'the needy'".

Wow man.

All before it became a time of mischief, pulling the lion's tail and fucking with the Establishment

The Entrepreneurs

Forget all the spiritualism and the navel gazing, who was making money in the 60s? Entrepreneurs. Everywhere new things were opening up; Island Records was one of the first independent record companies, dedicated to signing new young artists and able to survive without the patronage of huge electronics businesses (EMI and Decca), that seemed to be run by chartered accountants and industrialists. Its proprietor Chris Blackwell a youthful go getter, was the son of a Jamaican plantation owner who, while having a fine time as a water-ski instructor in Montego Bay, heard a cabaret band that he figured needed to make a record. Without hesitation, he put them in a studio in Kingston and pressed a record in New York, which he then hawked around shops from the back of his car. The trunk was soon emptied, and emboldened, he signed more local talent. It wasn't long before he noted that his records were selling better to the Jamaicans in London than the Jamaicans in Jamaica, so in 1962 he upped sticks and opened Island Records in London.

Two years later, *My Boy Lollipop* by 15 year-old Millie Small became a worldwide hit and Blackwell's label prospered. When touring with Millie, he came upon another 15 year-old, Stevie Winwood who was playing with a Birmingham band that eventually became the Spencer Davis Group. *Keep on Running* was followed by *Gimme Some Lovin'* and *I'm a Man*, and when the band split and Winwood formed Traffic, Blackwell had a label that was as happy releasing progressive rock, as it was rhythm and blues and reggae.

The Island artist roster was formidable and is a constant testament to the label owner's impeccable taste. His label remains the foremost independent label that the UK has ever produced: in the 60s/70s, the 'white' side of the label boasted Free, Cat Stevens, Spooky Tooth, Robert Palmer and Mott the Hoople. On the 'black' side were Bob Marley and the Wailers, Toots and the Maytals, Burning Spear, Third World and Black Uhuru. When Island licensed Chrysalis Records and EG, its eclecticism broadened with the addition of Jethro Tull, Procol Harum, King Crimson, Emerson, Lake & Palmer, Roxy Music, Bryan Ferry and Eno on board.

In the 80s and 90s, the good taste flowed like a river and Grace Jones, Ultravox, U2, Tom Waits, The Orb and Pulp all made significant releases on Island.

As well as acquiring one of the juciest artist rosters of any label ever, Blackwell built the British end of the *Manga* anime film business along the way, before selling up in recent years to concentrate on building high-end holiday resorts in Jamaica and the Bahamas. That portfolio includes *Goldeneye*, the property once owned by James Bond author Ian Fleming and from whence the film title is derived.

But back then Blackwell also created the import label Sue Records run by Guy Stevens, a pivotal figure in the 60s/70s - one third of the *Hapshash and the Coloured Coat* band, resident DJ at the Scene and later on the man who would produce the Clash album *London Calling*. Among Sue's releases was *Mockingbird* by Charlie & Inez Foxx, Bob & Earl's *Harlem Shuffle* and tracks by Elmore James, Ike and Tina Turner and Lee Dorsey. Stevens would play these tracks at his Monday hops at the Scene, which was the hang out of the stars and which by 1964 had become the centre of the mod world; they would do the pills and the jumping around as Stevens spun the imports and turned them on to this new thing called Motown.

It was Guy Stevens who brought Berry to the UK for his first tour; he was also president of the Chuck Berry Appreciation Society, and had a say in the UK releases that Pye International put out including those by Chuck as well as Bo Diddley and others on the Chess and Checker labels. Along the way, Stevens, who today remains a little-known figure, named and produced Mott the Hoople (he conducted one of their sessions wearing a Lone Ranger outfit); then he may have donated names to both Procol Harum and their biggest hit *Whiter Shade of Pale* (one version of the story suggests Stevens may have had a cat called Procol Harum; another version says that the cat was owned by a Welsh acid dealer called Ash). However naming things was clearly Guy's gift; when the Rolling Stones needed a name for their latest album release, Mick went to Guy who said, "What about *Sticky Fingers?*"

Unfortunately, a spell in prison for cannabis possession – another long-haired pop musician incurring disproportionate judicial wrath - seemed to send Stevens off the rails and during the long years before his career was given second wind when he produced *London Calling* for the Clash, he would be found propping up the bar in The Ship, the muso pub just up from the Marquee Club in Wardour Street, Soho, sustained by the £100 a week that Warner Brothers was paying him to stay away from their building.

One of the classics, *London Calling* restored Guy's status and kept him in clover for a short while but really, it had been a leap of faith on the part of Joe Strummer who had insisted to the band and their dubious manager that Stevens was up to the job despite all appearances. In fact Stevens was completely burned out when he'd made the record and it would prove to be his swansong. Parked back at the bar in the Ship, he spent endless nights reliving the moments, shifting the liquor, waving his arms about and falling off his stool; the booze was going to get him, especially in that unique pub where the staff always remained coolly aloof to the antics of the fairies, mods, beats, punks and the falling-down-desperate that alternated night on night. The customers looked like whichever band was going to grace the Marquee stage that night; in the daytime the Ship would be full of the local film studio staff, lost tourists and thirsty sex shop customers but during the evening it would pull on another mask. On any dark damp Monday night in the 60s, in the corner by the toilets you might possibly have seen Bowie blowing smoke in Hendrix's face as Rod Stewart bought the drinks, while ten years later – same pub, same corner, you may well have witnessed Lemmie helping Chrissie Hynde kick in the front of the jukebox.

Poor Guy needed prescription drugs; then he started treating them as fun too, washing them down with his whisky, and part of the same sad malaise. An overdose did for him, just like it had Keith Moon. He died unrecognised then, and remains largely unrecognised now. Considering the breadth of his achievements, incredibly Stevens was only 38 when his spirit rose through the roof of the Ship to settle on a stool in the VIP bar of rock and roll heaven.

Two more influential 'hippie' entrepreneurs of the time were Richard Branson, who had started a student newspaper and then a record retailing business that would grow into multi national companies which now has plans to put hotels in space, and Tony Elliot who started Time Out magazine, a hugely influential handbook for those seeking details of political trends and events as well as what was on at their local cinema. The guys behind Oz would go to prison before one of them, Felix Dennis, who was famously told by the judge during the sentencing in the Oz obscenity trial that he would be given a shorter sentence than the others because he was "very much less intelligent", started Dennis Publishing, so successful that it now sees him in the top 100 wealthiest people in the country (a large part of Dennis's estimated £750 million stems from his shareholding in the computer reseller Microwarehouse), where of course, he joins Elliott and Branson.

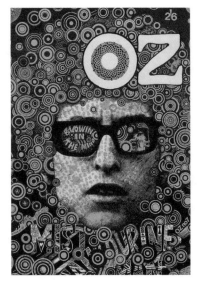

When the judge at the *Oz* trial made the foolish mistake of repeating his assessment of Felix's intelligence in the Spectator magazine in1995, he should perhaps before he opened his mouth, have taken into account the fact that he was outside court privilege; Felix sued the magazine and won.

Having abandoned the pleasures of crack cocaine, boozing and skirt chasing, he has transformed himself into a prolific and respected poet writing books and performing his material on stage; he has homes in Mustique, New York and London. Among his many accomplishments, including the planting of a forest named after himself in the Midlands, is that he was the first man to say the 'c***' word on British TV on the *Frost Show* in 1970 (the waspish theatre critic Kenneth Tynan had been the first to use the word 'fuck' on TV during a debate about censorship in 1965).

Another long hair who made it big in business was Peter Asher, who was so nearly Paul McCartney's brother-in-law and had been half of the singing duo Peter and Gordon before he put some money into the Indica gallery then went to work at Apple as A&R man. Asher signed and produced James Taylor whose first album wasn't a big seller, but convinced of Taylor's potential he resigned his job and went to work for Taylor as his manager. Asher found his big success producing a string of huge selling albums for Linda Ronstadt and a whole string of albums for other artists including Neil Diamond, Diana Ross and more recently even Morrissey, yet he remains an archetypal 60s figure, alleging that Mike Myers modelled Austin Powers on him.

Among others, Ossie Clark set up his design firm, Zandra Rhodes hers; John Stephen was the lord of Carnaby Street and everybody seemed to be in a band. The biggest of the band managers even started making money, lots of money. There were Floyd's managers Peter Jenner, and ex LSE lecturer Andrew King, The Who's Kit Lambert and Chris Stamp, and Brian Epstein of course. In 1967, Chris Wright and Terry Ellis started the Ellis Wright Agency, which managed Jethro Tull before it grew into Chrysalis Records. Harvey Goldsmith became the world's biggest gig promoter while another prominent member of the self-employed, Howard Marks, became the world's biggest dope smuggler. And all the big gigs everywhere were being promoted by Harvey Goldsmith.

This new spring had arrived with the Beatles and they continued to surge forward, pioneering musically, stylistically and now spiritually, leaving bands like the Beach Boys and the Stones desperately trying to hang on to their coat tails. The Stones in particular felt the pressure to come up with something that would at least let them draw level, if not pull ahead of their close friends and deadliest rivals. Although, perhaps they should have been content to remain in second place, because they undoubtedly benefited from their brutal competition with the greatest band in pop history; it made them try so much harder; it made them what they are. But they couldn't resist mimicry of the great ones; the Beatles' influence was pervasive. To many, *Satanic Majesties* was a pale *Pepper* imitation; the sleeve was a definite tribute/rip off. After the *White Album*, the Stones issued *Beggars Banquet*... in an (off) white sleeve. The Beatles did *Let it Be*; the Stones did *Let it Bleed*. They were either praising their heroes or taking the piss.

In 1970, John Lennon, perhaps jaundiced that his band had broken up, looked back at the rivalry and railed, "I would just like to list what we did and what the Stones did two months after, on every fucking album and every fucking thing we did". The Stones eventually took the lead in the race but only after their arch rivals had turned on each other and imploded in a welter of writs. But there wouldn't be much time to celebrate; now the Stones would be pitted against new rock titans: Pink Floyd, the Who and Led Zeppelin.

But three or four years earlier, back in the days of innocence, back in the days of the two-horse race, it had seemed that it was only the favourites the Beatles who had the vision, the drive, the potency and above all the cash to energise what was more and more being spoken of as a revolution. Coffee bars in London, Paris and San Francisco buzzed with dreams and plans. Everyone knew that something was happening, that something was coming; the air crackled with possibilities.

But in reality, while the red-led French students became radicalised and tore up the cobble stones of Paris to pelt the police (it's not really that surprising that the students got the hump. President de Gaulle had referred to the flower of French youth as "shit in the bed"), and although there were a couple of noisy demos in central London, the coffee bar habitués of Chelsea weren't really alive with talk of communism or Marxism: they weren't that political at all. The pretty things were talking individualism, free love and communal living. They weren't so much battling a tyranny as cocking a snook at their daddies.

Looking back at what is often regarded as a hippie-dippy dream: it's easy to sneer at the maidens-and-dragons graphics, the little bells, the dubious hair and the brocade waistcoats. The whole period is redolent with the potential for ridicule. No one really had a clear philosophy; no one could spell out exactly what all the children wanted. All they knew was what they didn't want. No old rule; no old God; no old school tie and no old clothes (unless they were old army tunics or Victorian lace).

And it wasn't just stoned ex-public school hippies loon dancing in a field and spouting about karma; don't forget that the dry, acerbic Lennon hadn't needed much encouragement to tag along with the Beatles to the Maharishi's ashram in search of spirituality. It was he who'd written *All You Need is Love* and talked of the potential for 'another way' even though he would eventually crop his hair short and reinvent himself as our denim clad working class hero.

A more political, radical 'Hoppy' Hopkins theorised that we could only have a new society if the record companies got together and set up their own bank - and this is 40 years before the creation of Virgin Money which, though an offshoot of a once hippie record label, is just another bank with no brief to attempt to change society for the better; just one to make more money for its owners.

Hang outs and heavy pets

The Casserole restaurant, opposite Paultons Square near World's End on the Kings Road, was an ordinary bistro until Rudolf Nuryev was seen in there. Then Nicki Haslam turned it into a Bedouin tent and the clientele started dressing up a bit. In his autobiography *Red Carpets and Other Banana Skins* Rupert Everett tells the story of popping in for a snack and a power nap and waking up to see Lady Diana Cooper, Bianca Jagger and Andy Warhol sitting opposite him. There was a gay club called The Gigolo downstairs. In his 1967 book *London Dossier*, Len Deighton warns his readers, "Don't go down there if you like women".

But if you did like women then the Kings Road was, back in 1964 as ever, the place to be as observed by John Crosby, a New York Herald Tribune columnist who wrote, "Take a look at these girls, striding along in their black leather boots, their capes, their fur hats, their black stockings with wild designs. They look like something out of Alexandre Dumas with that challenging walk and those challenging clothes. All they need is a sword, these girls. They look like they're looking for trouble with a look-at-me cockiness that is a thorough menace to male drivers".

The pursuit of individualism coupled with Chelsea's reputation as the refuge of the English eccentric is finely evidenced by the story of the Kings Road lion. There aren't many pet shops left in the UK now and even if you could find one it is unlikely that anything living and breathing bigger than a gerbil will be available to buy, but there was always a rumour that Harrods would you get you anything legal you desired, even an elephant if you could afford it.

John Rendall, a close friend of Princess Margaret's one-time lover Roddy Llewellyn, heard the story of the Harrods customer who, while mischievously testing the theory, asked the salesman if he could obtain for her a camel and the unflappable salesman had blithely replied, "One hump or two madam?" Determined to test the theory for himself, Rendall visited the top people's store's wildlife department. No camels were in evidence but he couldn't help but notice a male lion cub sitting there.

It had only taken 250 guineas to bag the beast, and for a year, Christian the lion cub (Christians and lions – ha ha), who went from 35 pounds to 185 pounds in the period and was probably no longer to be classified as a cub, lived with Rendall in his flat. He acted as a mascot for Rendall's *Sophisticat* furniture shop and either sat in the window scaring passers-by or wandered around the shop scaring the customers. "Christian often lunched at the Casserole opposite

Paultons Square, where he met Mick Jagger and the rest of the Stones, David Bailey and Marie Helvin, Amanda Lear, Justin de Villeneuve and Twiggy", Rendall told the Times in 2006. "He was

 exercised every day in the Moravian graveyard behind Lindsey House on Cheyne Walk".

Rendall used to drive around with Christian in the back of his Bentley and the lion would often demonstrate a remarkable sense of humour by obligingly terrifying the hippies as Rendall told the Daily Mail in 2007, "Sometimes, he'd see people staring at him through the back window of the car, keep very still on purpose - and then, just when they were convinced he was a stuffed toy, he would very slowly turn his head and freak them out".

Eventually Christian was considered too big for the Kings Road, especially after a couple of incidents, including one when he affectionately reared up putting his front paws on a lady guest's shoulders and inadvertently ripped the front off her dress leaving her clad only in bra and pants.

Realising the lion had to go, Rendall made contact with George Adamson, the lion expert who, with his wife Joy and Elsa the lion had been featured in the film *Born Free*. Together they flew Christian down to Kenya and released him into the wild where he prospered and had cubs of his own. There is on You Tube a film of a reunion between Rendall and the lion, a few years later when the huge beast, now father of a pride can be seen approaching the long-haired young man quite tentatively, before bounding forward, placing his huge paws on Rendall's shoulders and hugging him. The touching footage (complete with syrupy soundtrack) has been watched many millions of times.

And Christian wasn't the only big cat padding through the mansions of London. Soho club owner Paul Raymond kept a pet cheetah about the house, which at 6 o'clock every evening would be ushered into a van and taken over to the Raymond Revue Bar to appear in the shows, purring and slinking between the long legs of the dancers.

Up the road at the Clermont casino, Lord Lucan might be at the bar talking to Jemima Khan's father Sir James Goldsmith and racing driver Graham Hill, the club's owner John Aspinall strolling past both his distinguished and manifestly undistinguished members holding a snow leopard on a lead.

The Clermont club at 44 Berkeley Square used to be the London home of the Regency dandy Beau Brummell. When it opened its doors as a casino in 1962, in through them walked the ubiquitous Princess Margaret, followed by a pack that included Peter Sellers, Roger Moore, Tony Curtis and heavyweight boxing champ Joe Frazier. Its owner, John Aspinall, who later owned private zoos, had since the 50s been running illegal high roller gambling sessions in some of London's finest mansions, houses that he borrowed from his friends especially for the occasions.

When the gambling laws changed, Aspinall was able to take his activities above ground and, along with some willing partners, bought the Mayfair club. Soon the power elite of the time was elbow-to-elbow at the chemin de fer tables drinking free whisky and chatting to beautiful girls in the opulent Berkeley Square surroundings. Little did they know that while they were being entertained, they were also being fleeced, very efficiently, every evening, in a marked card scam that ran for years at the club and which was introduced to Aspinall by London crime boss Billy Hill, an associate and one-time mentor to the Krays. The scam was finessed by other sham gamblers planted by the management, including one, perhaps aptly called Louis the Rat, and the fiddled earnings were colossal; it's been suggested that the Earl of Derby lost £40,000 in an evening; at a time when you could buy a new Jaguar for £1,200.

Brian Epstein was a regular at the club, handing over the keys of his silver Bentley convertible to the doorman on entry, who would leave the car parked just where it was, right outside the club front door, a magnet to every well heeled passer by who would know from the car's livery that the Beatles manager was in that night.

On occasions Brian would lose £10,000 - £15,000 in a night, hurling good money after bad while knocking back balloon glassesfull of vintage brandy, puffing on a cigar and crunching up amphetamines as his losses increased. Then, embrassed, he would swear who ever accompanied him into silence; he didn't want the Beatles to know that on average he was losing £5,000 a week.

Mark Birley who ran the legendary society club Annabels in the basement of the Berkeley Square building and who had been a friend of Aspinall became disgusted by the extent of the scam. There had for some time been a staircase that led directly from the casino to his club beneath so that the delicate club members didn't even have to set a well-heeled foot in the street. In anger, Birley had the backstairs sealed off.

Aspinall's zoos became notorious; over a twenty-year period the press reported that five keepers had been killed by some of his more ferocious animals; indeed Mark Birley's son Robin was severely disfigured, when he was mauled by one of the zoo's tigers.

The full story of the con at the Clermont club can be read in *The Hustlers: Gambling, Greed and the Perfect Con* by Douglas Thompson. The film rights of the outrageous tale have been optioned by Martha Fiennes, sister of Ralph and Joseph Fiennes, who suggests that her brothers may play cameos in any eventual film.

Rock 'n' roll, dazzling fashion, drink, drugs, crooked gambling dens, fast cars, sex and wild cats; 60s London had it all.

Having freed Christian the lion, Rendall himself fled into the wild with his girlfriend Lady Sarah Ponsonby, niece of the Earl of Bessborough. Together with her brother Prince George Galitzine, they set up a commune for fellow aristos, musicians and artists in a rambling country house at Surrendell Farm near Malmesbury in Wiltshire. Another resident was Roddy Llewellyn, who had been hounded out of London by the press because of his association with the (as yet un-divorced) Princess Margaret; he had a nervous breakdown as a result (it seems Margaret had a nervous breakdown too and may even have attempted to commit suicide although this has been denied by Buckingham Palace). Forced to flee the camera's gaze, Llewellyn sought refuge on the farm where he found peace and set to tending to its gardens. The Princess used to visit him there. "I was a very bad hippie", he told the *Daily Telegraph* in 1977. "My job seemed to be to clear up everyone's mess. They'd be in bed till midday, and I'd be up at the crack of dawn trying to cook breakfast and wash up. I chose to get the garden into shape. I cleared it by throwing nuts into the brambles for the pigs to rootle. Then we ploughed, rotovated and started to cultivate". Another notable who used the commune as a retreat was Dame Helen Mirren who apparently lived at Surrendell Farm for years when she was working at the Royal Shakespeare Company in Stratford.

16

The Princess, Black Power and the Bank Job

ANOTHER retreat for the London jet set was the Princess's Les Jolies Eaux on the island of Mustique, a ten-acre plot given to her by Colin Tennent, the island's then owner; it played host to many London luminaries. The Mustique beach house was to some extent Swinging London-on-sea as the likes of Lionel Bart, Peter Sellers, Martin Amis, Mick Jagger and the gangster John Bindon shared drinks, beach towels and even the (sun)bed of HRH. It was even suggested that Dusty Springfield had once visited and had a dalliance with the Queen's sister.

Bindon was famously photographed sitting next to Margaret wearing an 'Enjoy Cocaine' emblazoned T-shirt and later boasted to his girlfriend ex-model Vicki Hodge, the daughter of Sir John and Lady Hodge, that he had bedded the princess (Hodge might have been seeking revenge when she too bedded a royal when she had a tryst with Margaret's nephew Prince Andrew in the early 80s).

PM, as Margaret was known, was apparently fascinated by Bindon's working class accent peppered as it was with rhyming slang and outrageous stories of the underworld, but above all, she was amazed by his party trick. Bindon would persuade a willing female to get him aroused and then hang five pint-pots from his foot-long manhood. The laughing psychopath became her favourite champagne pouring 'bit of rough'.

Back in London, Bindon refused to comment on the rumours of a relationship, real or imagined, with the Princess but hinted that from time-to-time he would get a call from Kensington Palace requesting his presence. He said he would dress smartly for these occasions and

a car would pick him up, take him off to the palace and then deliver him back home later in the evening. What took place thereé can only be speculated about except that Wensley Clarkson in his biography entitled *Bindon* alleges that a source close to Kensington Palace staff told him that there was frequently a smell of marijuana in the corridors whenever Bindon was in attendance.

On another occasion, he had been picked up by a car in less convivial circumstances; Bindon claimed that he had been leaving his mews flat one day when four burly men in a Rover Coupé asked him to accompany them for a chat. They weren't the usual underworld figures he'd reasoned; they were lean, hard and intelligent and, he said, they gave him a message in no uncertain terms: keep quiet or suffer the consequences. Convinced that he'd just had a talking to by MI5 or some equivalent 'heavy mob', the hard man Bindon was sufficiently intimidated to keep his trap shut about any royal liaisons and took his secrets to the grave.

Interestingly, a recent film called *The Bank Job*, written by Dick Clement and Ian Le Frenais, starring Jason Statham alleges that a raid on Lloyds Bank in Baker Street, London in 1971 when £500,000 was stolen, was actually a front for the security services to gain possession of some compromising photographs of the Princess in Mustique. Known as the 'walkie-talkie bank job' because the participants were seen using walkie–talkies to communicate with each other, it states that black activist and murderer Michael X, a Trinidadian gangster who had sidelines as an enforcer for Peter Rachman the slum landlord, running prostitutes and drug dealing, somehow came across the steamy photos, deposited them in the bank and tried to blackmail the British establishment with them. According to the film, the raid made the headlines in the national press for three days before the government issued a 'D' notice, effectively a gagging order preventing the press from making any further speculation about the case. Issuing 'D' notices happened extremely rarely and only in circulstances when it was considered that state security was under threat.

However, other sources say that four men were imprisoned for the crime but no-one is quite sure who they were and where they did their time, the inference being that the security services themselves did the raid, that the money taken was a device to cover the real reasons for the raid, that the robbers that were imprisoned never existed and that quite possibly the pictures were of Princess Margaret and John Bindon.

One of the real-life (actually real-dead) characters in the film is Gale Ann Benson, the daughter of the broadcasting magnate and Conservative MP Captain Lenny Plugge. Gail had been the girlfriend of an American Black Power leader Hakim Jamal (a magnetic character who often told people that he was God) whom she had met at a dinner party hosted by Vanessa Redgrave. Hakim had led her first to his bed and then into the world of the London Black Power movement led by Michael X aka Michael de Freitas who fashioned himself on the American human rights activist Malcolm X. But had the real seducer been Gale; was she really a British spy?

While visiting the commune run by Michael X in Trinidad, Gale had been set upon by a number of men, One of whom was de Freitas; they hacked her with machetes and buried her alive in a hole on the beach. The fim suggests that Benson had been murdered because the Black Power group thought that she was an MI6 agent who was spying on the Black Power movement and specifically on Michael X to make sure that he wasn't concealing any further photographs of Bindon and Princess Margaret.

Of the gang that murdered Benson, nearly all were quickly dead themselves: one turned witness for the prosecution; another drowned mysteriously at sea and a third, Joseph Skerritt was murdered by Michael X. Two more were given death sentences; one was hanged, and the other escaped the rope by the skin of his teeth when he had his sentence reduced to life imprisonment.

Hakim was later shot to death in Boston. Michael X escaped prosecution over the crime although everyone concerned knew that he had done it. Ironically, he was eventually hanged for another murder, that of his former accomplice Joseph Skerritt. Mysteriously, government information about this case and Michael X remains embargoed from public view until 2054.

The story of Bindon, the princess and the bank raid becomes a web that takes in the black power movement, John Lennon, the originator of pirate radio, the security services, slum landlords, the Profumo Affair, the underground press and murder in the Kings Road.

Michael X aka Michael de Freitas aka Abdul Malik

When John Lennon moved on from pleading for universal love to extreme thoughts of violent revolution, he came across Michael X who preached black power politics from his base in Notting Hill. Skilfully, Michael balanced his high-minded activism with a parallel and more lowbrow career collecting rent and conducting evictions for the notorious slum landlord Peter Rachman (paradoxically many of those he evicted were black). He was also pimping, pushing and running gambling houses. Despite his ill concealed criminal activities (he had once served 18 months for urging his supporters to shoot any black woman they saw with a white man), he seemed to hold certain wealthy white men under some kind of spell. This was the time of 'radical chic'; the stars were sucking up to the various groups that professed to represent the opressed; over in America, the composer Leonard Bernstein was entertaining the Black Panthers at his opulent Manhattan mansion; a short while later Marlon Brando would reject his Oscar out of sympathy with native Americans. Jane Fonda had meetings with the North Vietnamese government and became 'Hanoi Jane'.

When Michael X had needed money to open a Black Power commune on the Holloway Road, known as the Black House, he tapped up a young millionaire dropout called Nigel Samuel. Everyone liked Nigel but agreed that Nigel was nuts; usually stoned out of his head, he'd once sat and watched four floors of his Eaton Square offices burn and collapse after setting the room alight with a joint. The dope and the drink, especially in combination turned him into a cheerful mess, a soft touch for the constantly cap-in-hand underground and he was frequently hit upon to bail out Oz magazine, to pay the wages at IT magazine, to start a record company so that Mick Farren's band the Deviants could get a record out, or to pay the rent at the Drury Lane Arts Lab.

Samuel's surfeit of cash came from his family who owned the Portman Estate, 110 acres of posh London real estate north of the Marble Arch end of Oxford Street. His father had commited suicide so Nigel was being watched over by the family solicitor, chairman of the Arts Council, director of the Royal Opera House and general bastion of the British establishment, Lord Goodman who was often depicted by Private Eye as a sinister 'power behind the throne' in 60s/70s Britain. The lawyer and his charge were chalk and cheese and

Goodman provided minders to the young hippie millionaire ostensibly to drive him around town in his Lotus or his Ferrari but with tacit instructions to the minders to imprison Samuel in hotel rooms at any time when his spending or his erratic behaviour started to cause concern. Goodman would sometimes stop Samuel's allowance as a punishment for some incursion or another, an act that would so infuriate the young man that he would fly into a giving frenzy; throwing thousands into crazy, doomed projects while conversely becoming enraged if he thought a restaurant had overcharged him by a pound.

When Michael X came across this nice, white, impressionable and awfully rich young man, his eyes lit up; he began making plans for Nigel and once he'd sunk his hooks into the young man, they stayed in; Samuel became the paymaster to the Black House and much else besides, writing cheques for just about anything that Michael instructed him to, including trips to Trinidad or Timbuctoo in private planes. It's hard to imagine how Lord Goodman, the appointed guardian of the Portman millions felt about this, he the protector of all things British unable to prevent Portman money aiding the rabid Michael X, a declared enemy of the state. Another irony was that Samuel was giving money to Oz and IT magazines, both of which had been accused by Goodman of being obscene publications with recommendations that the police close them down.

However, Goodman the white knight of the establishment, the protector of British morals, may not have been all he seemed; it's an interesting footnote that when the good Lord died, the then Lord

Portman made an allegation that Goodman had stolen £10 million from the family estate, although ultimately the matter was never pursued, the full story remains untold; there were too many skeletons in that particular wardrobe.

Samuel may have been fleeced by the so called black activist but he fared better than another associate of the Black House, Marvin Brown, a businessman who upset Michael and was beaten up and ordered to wear a spiked collar, then led around the house for days while its occupants threatened him and extorted money from him.

Another white, rich and perhaps naïve financier was John Lennon; it was the time that Lennon and wife went from bed ins to sit ins, from long haired peaceniks to street fighters. Their new stance required a new image and haircuts were the starting point. He and Yoko were shorn and donated yards of their hair to the Black House, which was to be auctioned off for the cause. One wonders where the tangled mat of Mr. and Mrs. Ono Lennon's barnet is now, since in 2007, an anonymous bidder paid $48,000 for just one lock of Lennon's hair, which had been kept as a souvenir by Lennon's hairdresser in the mid 60s.

When the Holloway Road house mysteriously burned down, Michael X and four colleagues were arrested for extortion; Lennon paid their bail. It's further alleged that when Michael was up on the later murder rap, Lennon sold his famous white piano, the one on which he'd written *Imagine,* to help finance his defence. It didn't help and Michael X felt the hangman's noose in 1975.

Captain Lenny Plugge, pioneer of commercial radio, artist, sculptor, inventor of the Stereoscopic Cinematograph and owner of the Lowndes Square house where *Performance* was filmed

In 1925, Captain L.F. Plugge (which he pronounced as 'Plooj') rode the lift to the top of the Eiffel Tower with a radio transmitter, pointed it at England and started broadcasting music. It was because of early infractions into the British airwaves like this that the following year, the government sat down in Geneva with representatives of the sixteen participating nations, and carved up Europe's airwaves between them. An enraged Lenny Plugge wasn't having any of that and, some eight years before Radio Luxembourg started broadcasting he was in Normandy, with his transmitter, playing music to the south of England and, in 1930, he set up the International Broadcasting Company as a direct competitor to the BBC. It supplied airtime on stations in France and Spain to advertisers in the UK, the first ever radio station to broadcast advertising to the British audience in English. It was very profitable.

Lenny became extremely rich. His flagship station was Radio Normandy, which had among its staff Roy Plomley, the creator of Desert Island Discs and other pioneers of radio. In the years before the second war, Captain Plugge was selling British advertising on radio stations right across Europe. Such was Plugge's enthusism for commercials that it's often said that the expression to'plug' a record or product originates from Lenny's surname, although that claim is dubious. Unfortunately, the war closed most of his broadcasting capability down; by the time the war was over, many restrictions had

been put on the industry and he was unable to recommence his massively profitable activities.

The celebrated model April Ashley, born George Jamieson and one of the first Brits to undertake a sex reassignment in Casablanca in 1960, met Lenny at a party in the latter part of the 60s. She spoke of a "short and tubby" man "wearing thick round spectacles through which he peered at you as if trying to descry a mountain top a great way off. Though in his mid-seventies he was bursting with eagerness so that this, along with his attempts to catch sight of the top of one's head, conspired every few moments to lift him off the ground in little hops".

Plugge, she says, claimed to have invented early electronic curios Television Glasses and the Stereoscopic Cinematograph. He told her that he was going to buy a tower in Rome because he had decided to become a sculptor and then went on to detail some of his extraordinary and profligate lifestyle. He'd once lived at the club Les Ambassadeurs just off Park Lane, which he regarded as his town house and which was run by a staff of thirty footmen in powdered wigs. He had a house in the country, somewhere near Chatham where he had been the MP between 1935 and 1945. He also had a flat in

New York, moored a yacht in Cannes harbour and owned the *Performance* house at 23 Lowndes Square; oh, and two flats in Dolphin Square… and his tower in Rome.

Lowndes Square is one of London's smartest streets, home to the super-rich; currently a three-bedroom apartment there will currently cost you around £4 million to buy or perhaps £10,000 a week to rent. The road runs south from Knightsbridge parallel to Sloane Street. Roman Ambramovitch owns some houses and a couple of flats there, a few doors down from the location of the film *Performance*, residences that he paid many millions for and from which he has plans to carve out one massive residence. It is estimated that the eventual property will eventually cover eight stories, three of them underground. There will be a cinema, an indoor pool and obviously a gymnasium, and it may, when completed be worth £150 million. Oh, and it's handy for the Chelsea ground at Stamford Bridge just down the road.

The *Performance* house no longer stands but, as is evident from the film, it was once a huge, rambling, run down mansion with access to a massive private garden. It was, in fact, only used for the interior shots for the movie; the exteriors were shot at 25 Powis Square, Notting Hill which in the late 60s was itself a run down area, now populated by London's smartest media folk and surviving city boys with the ubiquitous 'interesting' Russian on every corner.

In his post-radio days, opera was Lenny's abiding passion, (as well as women, including Princess Margaret who he counted among his friends, and April Ashley, who at that time was gender unspecific).

With him, April attended a performance of *Carmen* with the Bolshoi Ballet at Covent Garden; she noted that when the curtain calls came, Lenny hurled bundles of flowers at the stage scattering mud all over the set. It seems he had ripped up the flowers from Lowndes Square on the way to the show and had deliberately left clods of earth on them to assist with their propulsion and the direction. "I find a little weight helps them to travel," he told her.

Plugge's company IBC is significant in the musical history of London. He moved its headquarters from its original Hallam Street address to 35/36 Portland Place, W1 and those offices would later house BBC Radio 1, a channel that had directly benefited from the Captain's pioneering work. Beneath was the famous IBC recording studio, where The Who, The Kinks, The Rolling Stones and Jimi Hendrix all made some of their best recordings.

Sadly Plugge would outlive both his daughter Gale who was murdered and her twin Greville who was killed in a car crash in Morocco. Lenny eventually died in Los Angeles on the 19th February 1981 at the age of 91; his life spanned from cavalry charges to Concord, from the birth of radio to the birth of U2.

17

John Bindon

A NASTY piece of work, John Bindon would drink heavily in any number of establishments up and down the King's Road and was prone to picking on unsuspecting pub customers and beating them to a pulp just to amuse his mates, on one occasion cutting off a man's arm with a machete. However, this propensity for unpredictable explosive violence, rather than repelling the Chelsea pop stars and bar fly actors, only seemcd to attract them. One night, film director Ken Loach, scouting for a psychopath to play the abusing husband in his film 1967 *Poor Cow,* observed Bindon mouthing off in a Fulham pub and recognised instantly that he'd found his man.

The brutality Bindon brought to the role impressed friend of the Rolling Stones film director Donald Cammell who, the following year, employed him to play a gangster in *Performance*. Bindon, happy to be typecast as the thug he was, appeared in two more iconic British movies *Get Carter* in 1971 and *Quadrophenia* in 1973 as well as making regular TV appearances in *The Sweeny, Softly Softly* and other cop shows.

During the filming of *Performance*, Bindon and his mate the other real-thing gangster on the team, David Litvinoff maintained a constant villain's banter schtick, which kept the drugged up cast either in stitches or on nervy edge as the stories got wilder and wilder. After shooting one night, Bindon and some of the cast members went on a pub-crawl. Bindon terrified the actors by having three fights in three different pubs. The following morning he arrived on the set carrying a matchbox; grinning he asked if anyone wanted to see what was inside. It was a thumb; in one of the previous evening's fights someone had made the mistake of putting their thumb in Bindon's mouth; foolish, very foolish.

But as much as he was a street fighter, a bully and a braggart, Bindon was also immensely charming with a line in patter that frequently saw him in the centre of a gang of friends at one of his Kings Road bars, either the Man in the Moon, The Roebuck or the Water Rat, regaling them with tall stories. It also saw him in bed with a succession of models, IT girls and pop stars (or their wives) whose jaws would hang slack after they witnessed his party trick (he could hand five pint pots from his erect penis). When boasting about his conquests he would tell his mates that the lucky girls were 'receiving swollen goods'.

His circle of showbiz pals grew; he might be found pub crawling with Richard Harris or playing frisbee with Ryan O'Neal; he attended a Christmas party at David and Angie Bowie's Oakley Street Chelsea home, and stood singing carols with Paul and Linda McCartney wearing a huge red dildo strapped to his forehead.

But having glittering new friends didn't change his ways; in the same year as he was making *Performance*, Bindon was awarded a

Queen's Award for Bravery when he jumped into the Thames to rescue a drowning man. But things were not as they seemed; later it was revealed that it was John who had thrown the man into the river in the first place.

It was in the Water Rat pub that Bindon first met Peter Grant, Led Zeppelin's hulking manager; the band's Swansong label operated from an office just up the road. Bindon had been called upon when the gargantuan Grant, whilst trying to snort a line of cocaine in the pub toilet, had become stuck in the cubicle; He was deployed to take the door off and break down the wall to get Grant out.

In 1977, Grant employed Bindon to help out with Led Zeppelin security on their American tour. He became a major player in one of the nastiest and well-documented scenes of violence in the Led Zeppelin story.

Grant's 11 year-old son Warren accompanied the band to a gig in Oakland; and had been seen attempting to prise a souvenir - a Led Zeppelin sign - from a backstage caravan door. Allegedly, one of the promoter Bill Graham's guards had clipped Warren round the ear but the band's drummer John Bonham had witnessed the event and kicked the guard in the balls. This wasn't sufficient punishment for a raging Grant who demanded big time retribution. While Richard Coles the tour manager kept guard, Grant and Bindon attacked the guard inside a caravan. He was badly beaten.

The incident led to the arrest of Coles, Bindon, Grant and John Bonham who were all charged and led away in handcuffs. It seemed there had been earlier scuffles; in the afternoon Bindon had hit one of

Graham's stage crew causing his head to strike some concrete. Grant had hit another. Incensed, three of the crew issued a civil action for $2 million in damages against the defendants - a case that dragged on for months.

Bill Graham later wrote in his book *Bill Graham Presents: My Life Inside Rock and Out,* of how much he liked the band but not the machine that surrounded them. "I didn't like those people," he said. "I didn't like their influence on society or their power. Back then Zeppelin were kings of the world... They surrounded themselves with physical might and they were ready to kill at the slightest provocation."

Robert Plant later said of the gig, "It was an absolute shambles. It was so sad that I would be expected to go on and sing *Stairway to Heaven*. People know how I feel about that song. I had to sing it in the shadow of the fact that the artillery that we carried with us was prowling around backstage with a hell of an attitude. It was a coming together of these two dark forces which had nothing to do with the songs that Page and I were trying to churn out."

John Bindon would later stand trial for the murder of John Darke a local fence, drug dealer and arsonist. There had been a huge knife fight in the grandly named Ranelagh Yacht Club, which was in fact a run down drinking den in an archway down the Putney end of the King's Road. Darke had stabbed one of Bindon's friends; Bindon had pulled a hunting knife from his snakeskin cowboy boots, attacked Darke and then was in turn stabbed in the back by one of Darke's accomplices. Darke then sat astride Bindon and stabbed him in the neck, head, chest and face. Somehow Bindon struggled free and stabbed Darke while, he alleges, his friend slashed Darke across the spine with a machete. Bindon transferred his attentions to one of Darke's gang, slashed him across the face and severed part of his nose; elsewhere someone was being coshed with a vodka bottle. Darke died on the way to hospital.

Bindon's friends dragged him away from the fracas before the police arrived and left him, bleeding heavily at a pub up the road where some of the drinkers, Bindon's mates, took charge. Back at the Ranelagh, the other customers, about sixty of them, melted away as did the membership book, which contained the signatures of all who had been there that afternoon. As the police arrived, two customers were shovelling multifarious weapons into the Thames.

Bindon called for his girlfriend Vicki Hodge who arrived at the pub with some clothes and money to pay a dodgy doctor. She says that Bindon had been stabbed in the heart, the back, in his eye, in the throat and in his testicles. She and some of his friends bandaged him up, filled him full of tranquilisers and somehow got him up to Heathrow (he was wrapped in a red blanket so that the bloodstains didn't show. Hodge told the ticket staff that Bindon had been injured in a rugby game) and on a plane to southern Ireland where, allegedly, IRA friends hid him. The Republicans had him fixed up by some Irish nuns, telling the sisters that some evil Englishmen from north of the border had stabbed him.

When Bindon recovered a little, he examined his surroundings and began thinking that he was very vulnerable at the hospital and that dark forces back in west London wouldn't have much trouble tracking him down. He concluded that it would be safer if he handed himself in to the authorities and informed the British police that he wanted to go back to London. It was fortunate that he had made arrangements because soon, members of the Guarda arrived to try and establish who was this Englishman with multiple stab wounds that the sisters were caring for.

During the police questioning, Bindon seemed to be either hinting at royal connections or pleading for Princess Margaret's name to be left out of things. The committal hearing took place in a blaze of publicity. It was alleged that Bindon stabbed Darke to death in a contract killing, a contract issued over a drug deal gone wrong; Bindon claimed it was self-defence. Vicki Hodge frequently visited him while he was on remand in Brixton; she made a point of wearing miniskirts and thigh-high boots for the occasions, leaving the other prisoners cat calling and banging on their prison bars. She later boasted that she often wore no knickers on the visits, just to inflame the inmates.

During the resulting trial at the Old Bailey, it was again alleged that, far from being an act of self-defence, the slaying had been a contract killing; Bindon's Brixton cell mate reported that Bindon had told him he had been paid to despatch with Darke for £10,000. He'd also confessed that he had once killed someone else, using a shotgun hidden in a bunch of flowers. Bindon hammed it up for the jury, once apparently fainting complaining of an asthma attack, and once bursting into tears; he said he'd been overwhelmed because of the extent of his injuries and how he felt he had been violated, like he'd been raped. Meantime, Hodge sat in the front row for the duration, wearing her most provocative skirts (with or without lingerie).

Mysteriously two of the four co-defendants, whose evidence may have been detrimental to Bindon's case, disappeared, then unnamed men twice visted one of the trial lawyers and threatened to kill him. There was more hoop-la when Bindon called upon an old friend, the actor Bob Hoskins to provide a character witness; Hoskins, in giving evidence, referred to Bindon as 'a big gentle bear' and as a result the trial swung in favour of the defendant. It was such an affectionate and disarming description of the killer in the dock, and provided as it was by a big Hollywood star, that it cut through all the evidence that the police had painstakingly put together depicting an afternoon of drinking and vicious blood letting culminating in a murder.

The celebrity on show dazzled the jury who were soon eating out of the defence lawyer's hand; at the conclusion they acquitted Bindon while finding that the two co-defendants, unable to call upon the testimonies of film stars, were guilty; they were sentenced to three and four years respectively while Bindon walked free. He didn't walk far beyond the courtroom doors though before he was whisked away for drinks and interviews in a limousine paid for by the Daily Mirror.

However, the public bar beatings, the Led Zeppelin assault case and now a murder rendered Bindon too hot to handle in the entertainment industry and the work dried up. He did a bit of debt collection, laying into people for money, and there were also the many other assaults that he dished out for free. Even the devoted

Vicki Hodge left him and Bindon became alone and broke (although he did reputedly refuse the offer of a fight with gangland figure Lenny (the Guv'nor) McLean, organised by Freddie Foreman, because he considered the £10,000 purse inadequate). He dined out on his story about the killing of Johnny Darke for years but eventually people got bored with that and the free drinks flowed less freely especially when Bindon started to look very sick.

It's said he died of cancer although other reports suggest that he may have been selling his renowned manhood for cash in his later years, and had contracted AIDS as a result.

Bindon was apparently the inspiration for the Vinnie Jones character in *Lock, Stock and Two Smoking Barrels*. That's hard to disbelieve. After all, Bindon's favourite phrase was "I think there must have been a little misunderstanding".

18

Lionel Bart and the Fun Palace

ANOTHER VISITOR to Mustique was Lionel Bart. When, in 1966, his musical *Oliver* became a huge hit Lionel decided to acquire a property that befitted his status as one of Britain's most successful composers and his £8,000 a week wage packet. Number 3A Seymour Walk SW3, was a converted priory, a once pure and sanctified place,

which was quickly sullied by its new landlord. That it had been a priory is supremely ironic considering Bart's chronic alcoholism and drug enthusiasms. The Priory is just where he should have been.

Behind the crumbling walls of the house with the inauspicious address situated just west of fashionable Gilston Road, you might well have found any number of Beatles or Stones or The Who chatting with London's two most eligible bachelors (and flatmates) Michael Caine and Terence Stamp. At one memorable party, the guest list was just about as star-studded an affair as the decade could offer; in attendance were all of the Beatles and all of the Stones who were joined by Cassius Clay (before he adopted the moniker

Mohammed Ali) and, just three days after they had won the 1966 World Cup, the entire England football team.

A failed violinist and screen printer, he had written *Living Doll* for Cliff Richard, in about the length of time it took Cliff to sing it, and the theme for *From Russia With Love* sung by Matt Monro. Then of course there is *Food, Glorious Food, Where Is Love?, Consider Yourself, You've Got To Pick A Pocket Or Two, I'd Do Anything, As Long As He Needs Me* and all the 24-carat others in the musical that everyone knows; Bart had made it across to the posh west of London and was never going back.

That stratospheric level of success, that fawning adulation and that outrageous income naturally went straight to his working class head and he splurged fortunes on the Fun Palace and its legendary decadent parties. The Priory had a statue of a stork on the roof as a landmark for the taxi drivers who all assumed it was an exclusive nightclub, and to some extent they were right, but this club was strictly by invitation and you didn't pay to get in. Instead you might possibly have left with more money than when you entered. Lionel dubbed the house that had once been Aubrey Beardsley's studio, the 'Fun Palace' and it is said that there were two large glass urns in the hallway for those entering or leaving to avail themselves of; one was full of cocaine and the other full of money.

The main room of the house was the size of a grand country house drawing room but of course, Seymour Walk was only yards from the busy and then quite grimy Fulham Road, just behind the old ABC cinema. Above the room was suspended a minstrel's gallery which reminded visitors of the bridge of a great liner. There were candelabra that had been made for the film *Beckett* which were exact replicas of the originals in Canterbury Cathedral. The toilet bowl was a Gothic throne which when you flushed it by pushing on a gold crown, played *Food, Glorious Food.* There was a stone font opposite as a washbasin. A musical staircase played other selections from *Oliver* when you walked up it.

But in truth, Lionel preferred his mews flat behind South Kensington station to the rambling party house pile down the road. The more discreet mews was where he could entertain all the rough trade and rent boys; it was here in his red velvet boudoir that all the two-way mirrors were positioned to enable himself and his friends to witness all the man-on-boy fun – a room that would see almost as much traffic as the nearby tube station.

Unfortunately, the wild life style took its toll on Lionel (one of his directors once called Bart "a homosexual, Jewish, junkie, commie", missing out the word 'alcoholic' from his affectionate aspersion), and he became a regular visitor to the Chelsea branch of Alcoholics Anonymous for many years. 'My name is Lionel Bart; I am one of England's best loved composers and I'm an alcoholic..."

Lionel had an undoubted healthy disrespect for all the money that was pouring through his fingers, founded in the poverty of his childhood and the uselessness of his mug punter father. "I hated money and had no respect for it", he said. "My attitude was to spend it as I got it." And that's exactly what he did; mission accomplished.

But he didn't only ruin himself with self-indulgence, unless you include spending money on failed musicals as an indulgence; not unsurprisingly, everything new he wrote was measured against his masterwork *Oliver* and found wanting by potential investors. More and more desperately, he began subsidising new shows with his own money, a sure-fire way to go broke fast. No doubt about it, his father wasn't the only gambler in the family, except Lionel was punting fortunes.

When it had all gone, he flogged off the rights to *Oliver* for peanuts (he says he sold the score to Max Bygraves for £1,000 but that's probably apocryphal) and missed out on millions as the show returned to the stage time and time again and the royalties from the film continued to pour in, but now sadly all into someone else's coffers. The Fun Palace was long gone and so were his chances of ever duplicating his fantastic success. When he showed the script for a new show, *Quasimodo*, to his friend Noel Coward, the great man looked it over and remarked, "Brilliant dear boy, but were you on drugs when you wrote it?" When he was made bankrupt in 1972, another famous friend Princess Margaret called him a "silly bugger" for making such an awful mess of his finances.

It's a classic tale of rags-to-riches-to-rags worthy of a musical by Bart himself. He had once had homes in London, New York, Malibu and Tangiers. Andrew Loog Oldham remembers hustling Lionel for money when Andrew was working the Riviera and had spotted Bart having lunch with Pablo Picasso. The grand properties were sold and Bart was to die a poor diabetic in an Acton flat. Too late in the day, he had kicked the booze and garnered some sort of regular income. The impresario Cameron Mackintoh, who having once worked as Assistant Stage Manager on *Oliver* was now producing the show observed the parlous state of its wayward geniu creator and gifted him a substantial weekly gratuity for *Oliver*, a show in which Bart could claim no remaining interest apart for the obvious one. He had written it; it had made him; it had broken him (or at least the effort of trying to live up to it had broken him) and now it was providing a living for him once again, though in a far less magnificent fashion.

But no matter how tragic the story is, there is always something impossibly romantic and reckless about those who get to have it all then throw it all away, those who grab life by the scruff of the neck and wring it. The music business has long attracted this kind of adventurer, seemingly sane individuals who carefully weigh up all the options, then say fuck it and toss a dice. For them: far better to have held the pedal to the metal for a minute than to have driven carefully for ever. Why is it no surprise that Bart and Keith Moon were great friends?

19

The Cheyne Gang

IT HAD been Jagger's idea to buy a house in Cheyne Walk. He liked the idea that he would be in one of London's most famous roads; it reeked of style and subversion. He loved the view of the river and wanted to be able to rest his eyes in shades of green, staring out across Battersea Park. He'd always envied Christopher Gibbs' apartment at number 100. That house really was the epitome of Swinging London, or at least the film director Michaelangelo Antonioni thought so when he was scouting locations for the party scene for his film *Blow Up,* whose lead character played by David Hemmings is a photographer loosely based on David Bailey (although others claim that the character was in fact based on filmmaker Peter Whitehead).

The vast wood-panelled first floor apartment was adorned with trappings brought back from the Marrakesh and Tangier souks, lamps, brassware, patterned rugs and richly embroidered cushions scattered all over the floor, Persian carpets (which were good to stare at when you were tripping), wall hangings and leather camel saddles. From the large back windows you could gaze down on a delicious garden set off by a Mulberry tree reputed to be the oldest in the country. Gibbs fitted perfectly into this milieu, an antique-collecting aesthete, always immaculately be-suited unless he was wearing flowing Arab robes about the house, a grand, gay English, aristocratic

decadent who loved the company of exotic pop stars like Mick and Keith, their music, their louche ways and their drugs. The apartment's furnishings were the backdrop to some of the most exclusive parties the 60s were to offer, the Mariannes and Anitas, the Pauls, Keiths and Micks wafting about in kaftans and velvet, admiring the wide river view, looking down on the house boats and their bohemian occupants, listening to Ravi Shankar, high on this that or the other.

How had the Dartford oiks come this far, in eye-to-eye contact with the type of people who lived along Cheyne Walk its mansions peppered with famous person's blue plaques? These were, on the face of it, two utterly polarised groups. On the one side were the young hip aristos, the pleasure seekers, Tara Browne, Sir Mark Palmer, Gibbs, Robert Fraser, the Ormsby-Gores and all the networks that radiated out from them through the old boys and gels of Eton, Roedean, Harrow, Cheltenham Ladies College and Oxford; and on the other were the prancing dandy pop stars ex-the LSE or art school or just off the dole. "It was", says Christopher Gibbs, "a time of tremendous, unequalled social fluidity. Music was one of the levellers, hashish another".

And who had brought the two distinct groups together into debauched union? It was Anita Pallenberg of course; Anita whose one-time boyfriend Mario Schifano, the artist, knew all the toffs while Pallenberg knew all the riff raff. She had blagged her way backstage at a 1965 Stones gig and made Brian Jones fall in love with her; they looked at each other and it was like they were looking in a mirror, the ultimate narcissistic experience (much the same frisson Jagger felt when he first set eyes on Bianca).

Brian's Anita was Mick's Marianne or was it the other way round? In the event Keith had them both. Come to think of it so did Mick. Oh, and so did Brian. It was a tight group the Rolling Stones.

It was Christopher Biggs who had persuaded Brian and Anita to buy the Courtfield Road flat.

Film director Michaelangelo Antonioni, looking for a new *Dolce Vita* in London, was just another in a long list of foreigners packing the planes into Heathrow in a quest to find the 'scene', a mythic place populated by long haired boys and easy girls in kinky boots. His influential film, *Blow-Up* though panned by the British critics, nevertheless won the Palme d'Or at Cannes and was a huge success in Europe; ever more evidence that the Swinging London phenomenon had more to do with the outsider's perceptions than those of the man on the Clapham omnibus.

The French and the Italians were far more interested in the threads and the bare flesh – it was the first British film to portray full frontal nudity - than the threadbare story. Where had the David Bailey/David Hemmings character got those wonderful jeans? Do all London fashion photographers live in loft flats, drive convertible Rolls Royces and get to roll around with a naked Jane Birkin? And, of course, they all wanted to have been invited to the three-day pot party which, although it was just a scene in a movie, was actually the real thing going on in Christopher Biggs's exquisite house by the Thames, the gorgeous and the stoned rolling around on the gigantic bed while the cameras recorded every lick of every Rizla.

It's said that for one scene Antonioni sprayed the grass in Greenwich Park a different shade of green to get it to his liking and maybe even tinted the colour of the marijuana used at the party. As a matter of interest, in the club scene where Jeff Beck smashes up his guitar and amps you can briefly glimpse Michael Palin and Janet Street Porter in the audience although if they made it to the pot party they kept off camera.

Whiffs of decadence were pervading the air; when the Stones recorded *Beggar's Banquet*; the outer sleeve is white; however, on the inner sleeve the band is pictured in debauched splendour at some kind of Bacchanalian feast; Christopher Gibbs gave the record its name.

As soon as he could possibly afford it, Mick bought 48 Cheyne Walk for £50,000. Marianne Faithfull says that the house used to belong to a shipwright and had a wobbly floor and a crooked staircase. Jagger didn't have to think too hard about how he wanted it styled, Moroccan throughout, but with lots of other bits, everything in Gibbs's house - the tapestries, silks, intricately woven rugs, drapes,

 brass lamps, painted furniture; he wanted the 'full of Eastern promise' trip, but he also wanted a proper Regency bed and this amazing Louis XV bath that he'd seen. Luxury. Mick was developing taste by the bucket load as his bank balance grew, not only in his women, his wines, his fast cars and architecture; he also wanted top end interior design. Who better to get all that sorted for him than his friendly antique dealer just up the road whose other house was in Tangier (complete with a pet cockerel). Gibbs subcontracted the job to his high-class interior designer friend David Milnaric who turned the five-storey house into a Moroccan bazaar; Mick and Marianne drove to their new house in his cream-coloured two-door Bentley. When Donald Cammell needed someone to style the Lowndes Square house for *Performance*, Christopher Gibbs was again the obvious choice and he pretty much duplicated what he'd done on Jagger's house. If you wanted decadent ariviste rock star splendour, there was no one else to touch Gibbs.

20

Gender Benders

HAVING BEEN born a boy in Liverpool then sailing the seven seas in the navy; having danced in drag in Paris and then had a sex change in Casablanca; having hung out with Europe's stateless, wandering demi-royals and sleeping with Peter O'Toole *and* Omar Sharif in Marbella, and having spent time in prison in Italy; April Ashley, returned to London in the mid 60s and found herself drinking in the Chelsea Potter in the Kings Road.

The following day, she ventured out for groceries and realised that London had changed quite a bit since she had last visited: "As I veered into the King's Road it was as if I were seeing it for the first time... *Quorum... Alvaro's... Mary Quant... the Casserole... Hung On You... the Pheasantry...* Were they all there on that morning? Mini-skirts, op-art dresses, geometric haircuts (Vidal Sassoon), men with hair over their ears wearing striped blazers, chiffon scarves, white shoes, purple trousers ... *The Picasso Cafe* was full of Mods, boys like dolls, girls with orange lips, white faces, black Dusty Springfield eyes; the Beatles were singing out of boutique doorways and there was an ozone zing that was new, alert - it was the beginning of winter and felt like spring. Diving into the *Chelsea Potter* - Joan and Shura Shivarg, Charlotte Rampling and Jeremy Lloyd, Ozzie Clark; David Bailey lunching with Jean Shrimpton at Alvaro's; Sir Mark Palmer and Catherine Tennant in silver shoes, pea-green stockings; Tara and Nicky Browne chatting to Michael Fish in the middle of the road and handing out sweets to strangers. Anthony Haden-Guest was writing about them, Michael Rainey was selling clothes to them at his shop where, if you knew him, he'd go down into the basement, pull out a brick and roll a marijuana cigarette (later he married Jane Ormsby-Gore and left World's End in a gypsy caravan to look for the Holy Grail in the West Country). It was *a la mode* to go to the opera on the arm of your hairdresser, interior decorator, fashion designer, photographer, plumber. Hairdressers had the shortest vogue of the lot - it lasted about three months - plumbers the longest ... *The Avengers* on TV, Harold Wilson in Downing Street, young boys driving Rolls-Royces, groovy, with it, too much, fab. Lord Snowdon had discovered Carnaby Street, and the King's Road gossiped in its favourite haunt, the Aretusa Club, which heiress was thrown out of the Royal Enclosure at Ascot for wearing trousers, which heiress had eloped with a road-sweeper".

April Ashley Odyssey by Duncan Fallowell & April Ashley

April, Britain's first gender reassignment, was soon the toast of a whole new generation of clubs - Annabel's, George Harrison's Sybilla's, Peter Cook's Establishment Club and Muriel Belcher's

Colony Room Club in Dean Street, which April refers to as a "lair of bohemian alcoholics". The Ad Lib vied with the Scotch to be the trendiest nightspot. It's where she met the Beatles and the Stones. When John Lennon said Rolling Stones to her, she thought he'd said 'Rolling Pins' adding that she thought Mick Jagger was small but had lovely skin. She went to parties where the guests consisted of, she said, "titles clashing with the hit parade and the armed services". One party guest she regularly encountered was the bohemian hostess Viva King who had once been the libidinous Augustus John's personal assistant. King had gone into the great artist's studio one day and seen him beating an erection on his desk, going, "No, no, no, no, no!"

Another Ashley intimate was Sarah Churchill, Winston Churchill's actor daughter, another hedonist who was given to excessive drinking bouts, which often led to outrageous and dangerous behaviour, on which occasions April would be called upon to rescue her; she once found the sozzled femme directing the traffic in her nightie.

April would openly discuss her gender reassignment and was a slightly notorious but exotic figure in the 60s and 70s, popular with gossip columnists and chat shows. When John and Yoko appeared on the *Simon Dee* show talking about bagism and getting in and out of bags, the other guest's seat was occupied by April, who reflected that they were "all clowns together".

She was once a long-term friend of Amanda Lear (they had a falling out and now don't speak); in a recent interview April again alleged that she had affairs with Peter O'Toole and Omar Sharif, as well as Michael Hutchence and the Turner Prize sculptor cross dresser Grayson Perry. She was also a boozing partner of one time *Dr. Who*, John Pertwee and the theatre critic flaggellant Ken Tynan who used to come round to be spanked by April's houseguest.

That paragraph seems to somehow sum Chelsea up.

Amanda Lear – A Norwegian sailor? Salvador Dali's muse

Tara Browne, who had been dancing with Brian Jones in the Le Castel nightclub in Paris one night in 1965, had made the mistake of introducing his girlfriend Amanda Lear to Salvador Dali. Dali's chat up line was suitably singular and spelled the end of the affair for Tara. The great man twirled his moustaches and declared that she was his new muse and that they would be life long soul mates.

It was easy to see the attraction; Amanda was a six-feet tall Eurasian with high cheekbones and a husky, sexy voice. The sensual Dali utilised his nose in his assessment of the extraordinary Lear; he sniffed her and concluded, with some surprise that she didn't smell, something that continued to amaze him and attract him for the fifteen years that they were together.

Amanda is inscrutable about her real origins; her mother, depending on her mood and to whom she was talking, might have been English, French, Vietnamese, Mongolian, Russian and/or Chinese. Her father might have been English, Russian, French or Indonesian; he served in the British Navy, or was it the French? Her place of birth has ranged from Switzerland to Hong Kong via Hanoi or Saigon, and her date of birth anywhere between 1936 and 1946.

April Ashley is having none of this, asserting that the beautiful, long-limbed Amanda was actually born Alain Tapp and that they used to dance together in the Parisian club, Le Carrousel when Lear was known as Peki D'Oslo (there is a suggestion that Alain had once been a Norwegian sailor and that the name Peki D'Oslo combining Peking and Oslo, is a clue to the real Lear's identity). Ossie Clark, in his diaries, talks of meeting Peke D'Oslo and witnessing her whip act at Raymond's Revue Bar in Soho.

Furthermore, Ashley says that they had both visited the famous sex change surgeon Dr. Burou in Casablanca; that she had offered to pay for Amanda's operation, which Lear used to refer to as "Operation Pussycat"; and that a fearful Lear, had declined at first and then accepted a similar offer from Dali himself.

 Lear denies all of this, asserting that one only has to look at the photo session that she did for Playboy magazine to see that she is 100% female. Dali made up all the stories of her trans-sexuality, she says, to help further her career. She told the Daily Telegraph in 1971, "Everything Dali said, I just listened to. He was the genius, who was I? When it came to launching my career, he told me I was a lousy singer and if I wanted to sell records, I'd have to

find something other than the music to attract people to buy them. So we built the Amanda Lear persona into something very intriguing and very ambiguous and it worked". If true, Lear may be one of Dali's strangest creations.

According to Ashley, Lear only became Lear when she and Amanda met a chap (called Lear; first name lost in the mists of time) in a pub, who, for £50, allowed himself to be persuaded to marry her to enable her to get British nationality. The new couple knew each other for precisely the length of the marriage service.

Her relationship with Dali had obviously been an open one. She would only have sex with him - what Dali referred to as "using the sewing machine" - when Dali's wife Gala was either out at the shops or off at the theatre with a young man.

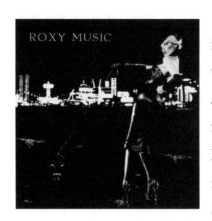

Amanda had retained a small flat in Chelsea, which she used when she was in London on modelling assignments, frequently undertaken for Ossie Clark. As well as the Beatles and the Stones, she was mixing with Yul Bryner, Twiggy, Sacha Distel, Marianne and Anita and David Bailey – all the groovy grandees of the era. Bryan Ferry thought she would look great on the cover of the Roxy Music album *For Your Pleasure* (It's her in the black sheath fetish dress, teetering on those high, high heels, with a black panther on a leash; a panther that looks less dangerous than she does, snarling like a pussycat).

David Bowie thought so too; Ferry was engaged to her and later Bowie had an affair with her. "It was the first time I went out with a man who wore more make-up than I did", she said. She was also linked romantically, inevitably to Brian Jones.

A curio is the story that on the night Brian Jones died; instead of there being only his girlfriend and a few staff in the house as the police were informed, there had actually been a party going on with a large number of guests - guests who have for various reasons evaporated into the night. Amanda says that Brian invited her down for the shindig and had sent a car for her but that somewhere on the way, on a whim she decided to go to Paris to see Salvador Dali instead and got the car to drop her off at Gatwick airport. She has since said how much she regrets not going to the party, that maybe she could have done something. However, in the light of the unreliability of the rest of Amanda's account of her life, caution should be taken with that tale.

Despite the Playboy session, the stories of her once being a man persist. Simon Napier-Bell, one time manager of the Yardbirds and Wham says on his web site, "My publishers sent me off to Paris to make a record with Amanda Lear, someone I'd known years before as a young Asian-looking guy called Peki who hung out in the Gigolo, a gay bar in London in the 60s. Now that Peki had become Amanda, I wasn't interested anymore".

Joanna Lumley's character Patsy, in *Absolutely Fabulous*, bears more than a passing resemblance to Amanda Lear; the low voice being only one of a number of similarities. This is no coincidence;

Joanna was herself a model in the mid 60s and has said in interviews that Patsy was to some extent based on the mysterious story of A. Lear. Indeed, in the Morocco episode (series 2, episode 3), it is suggested that Patsy used to be a man. When Lumley spoke to *Advocate* magazine in 1996, she mentioned, "Amanda Lear and people. They were so famously beautiful and so famously Norwegian sailors".

In 2001, a French version of *Absolutely Fabulous*, called *Absolument Fabuleux* was made and Amanda Lear was intended to take the Patsy role. She apparently turned the offer down, saying, "I've already lived it".

Whoever she really is, Amanda Lear is an enduring (gay) icon, particularly in Italy, France and Germany where she has had a successful pop career for over thirty years (she speaks four languages). In 2000, she was in the news when her husband and a family friend died in a house fire that also destroyed some of her Dali sketches. More recently she has been a TV presenter, where she gets to display her scathing wit. Lear has written a book about the Dali years (*My Life With Dali*), which a Hollywood producer had optioned, with a plan to cast Claudia Schiffer in the Lear role. "I ran into Claudia at a restaurant," Lear recalled. "She said, 'I love your book! Who wrote it for you?' I said, 'I did, darling. Who read it to you?' So that was the end of that. They never made the movie."

21

Ossie Clark - designer, scandalous diarist

SHE'S A pallid-faced, panda-eyed beauty; dead straight foot-long hair and a fuck-me fringe hanging over coke and kohl-a eyes shot with glitter dust that shines on Saturday nights in Tramps. She's got thigh-high boots and paper knickers; she likes things that glitter. She's a Chelsea girl, the Kings Road's Queen, swinging down the street so fancy free; her faux innocence hides the truth; her formidable self-possession; her child-like naiveté, her sexual availability.

Come-and-get-me.

She's a dolly bird with a need to be desired, to be dominated, yet free, an individuality that hides interchange-ability. You're never alone with a clone. She's having lots of sex but 'look at me mummy; no pushchair mummy like you had at nineteen'. She shows that off by not 'showing' a thing. No bump when she grinds; she's as thin as thin; she's on the pill. On her wall, swathes of colour, clips from the magazines – her idols? The Shrimptons, Chrissie and Jean.

Who dressed the dolly birds? Who made the minis apart from Mary Q and Alec Issigonis? It was Ossie Clark that's who; and it was Clark's friend, drug buddy and favourite model Chelita Secunda,

Marc Bolan's PR, who had first sprinkled the glitter on to those elfin cheeks and launched a thousand glam bands.

Those habitués of the Kings Road boutique and the disco got their posh togs from *Hung on You, Granny Takes a Trip,* Mary Quant's *Bazaar* and *Ossie Clark's Quorum.* Ossie was another seemingly ordinary lad who was made extraordinary by art school, in Ossie's case, Manchester Regional Art College. Among his group of friends were Celia Birtwell, the actor Ben Kingsley and Anthony Price who had a lot to do with styling Roxy Music (as well as the Stones, Bowie and later Duran Duran). Spotted as a prodigious talent, he passed an entrance exam to the Royal College where his circle of friends expanded rapidly; David Hockney became both friend and briefly lover. Ossie graduated, the only one in his year with a first-class degree and went to America with Hockney, where he met Bette Davis and Dennis Hopper, and where, when he went to a concert at the Hollywood Bowl, he was mistaken for George Harrison and mobbed.

On his return he met Alice Pollock who had a shop called *Quorum,* originally in Ansdell Street near Kensington High Street and later at 52 Radnor Walk, just south of the Kings Road. In the pre-Pink Floyd years, Dave Gilmour doubled as the shop's van driver and provider of music for the fashion shows. Ossie and Celia Birtwell started supplying designs and fabrics for the beautiful people by the beautiful people; a good looking boy himself, his partner Alice Pollock was a stunner and when on one occasion Celia went to Paris, Ossie described how les Parisiens stopped in their tracks open-mouthed to stare at this 'sex kitten in sailor pants'. Obviously gay, Ossie was nevertheless hopelessly in love with Celia. It was a productive but doomed relationship.

The buzz in the Kings Road in the spring of 1966 was palpable to the extent that Mary Quant commented that there seemed to be American TV crews filming on both sides of the street at the same time; the Radnor Walk shop became mini-skirt central and the ever prurient press were soon beating a path to the door to snap the thigh-flashing models. Brian Jones lived above the shop with Suki Poitier for a short while (the building behind housed the *English Boy* model agency run by Sir Mark Palmer before he hit the road in his gipsy caravan) and Ossie sent a steady supply of floral shirts upstairs to his discriminating, trend-setting neighbour. Brian told Keith; Keith told Mick and when Ossie happened upon a warehouse full of snakeskin and saw the potential for close fitting jackets for rock stars, his credentials were solid gold. He said that he knew he'd arrived when Marianne Faithfull ordered a suede suit trimmed in python skin from him and didn't even query the price. For Mick, Ossie was the perfect partner. Clark knew exactly what Jumping Jack Flash should look like and made for him many costumes including the devil's black cape Mick wore at Altamont.

Previously Britain had held a reputation for Tweed, cashmere and raincoats. Now Faye Dunaway and Liz Taylor were photographed in Ossie's mini skirts; Sharon Tate bought a full-length snakeskin coat with mink lining. Warren Beatty was buying tight satin trousers, Brigitte Bardot spent £350 on a pair crepe pants and Liza Minelli's saucy costumes for *Cabaret* were made by Quorum.

The list of models that suddenly wanted to be associated with all things Ossie is a parade of the beauties of the era: Patti Boyd (soon to be Harrison and later Clapton), Marianne Faithfull and Chelita Secunda (who had married Tony Secunda, manager of The Move and the Moody Blues). His favourites were, Gala Mitchell, Kari Anne Muller, who later became Kari Anne Jagger when she married Mick Jagger's brother Chris (Muller was the inspiration for the Hollies hit *Carrie Anne* and the pin up beauty that adorns the cover of the first Roxy Music album), Amanda Lear, Lady Carina Fitzalan-Howard, now Mrs. David Frost and sister to Marsha Fitzalan who played opposite Rik Mayall in *The New Statesman* as Sarah B'stard. There was also the American beauty Penelope Tree, one-time girlfriend of David Bailey, and Alice Ormesby-Gore soon to be Eric Clapton's girlfriend and fellow junkie, her brother Julian Ormesby-Gore who put a bullet in his brain, Linda Keith, Keith Richard's girlfriend and a powerful ally of Jimi Hendrix before he was famous, Jane Asher and Suki Poitier. Eartha Kitt just loved her snakeskin dress.

The list of customers was an astonishing array of pop talent, aristos and socialites. 'Oh look there's Paul and Linda; there's Bianca. Jimi! Hi! Mick, Yoko, Andy.' It was pretty clear that Ossie possessed the same kind of pop star charisma as his customers and he was treated as an equal, partying hard in all the glamour spots. When he was in London, Ossie would spend every evening in the Aretusa or the Speakeasy or Tramps or (much to the consternation of Celia) the gay club *Yours or Mine*. He spent holidays with the Gettys at the Marrakesh palace; he designed Bianca's wedding dress; he'd bump into Brian Epstein in gay haunts; he spent a vacation in Marbella with Suki Poitier (they went to a bullfight on acid). He was invited to Mick's 30th and Ronnie Wood's 27th; he hitched rides in the Atlantic Records jet with the company's founder and friend to the Stones, Ahmet Ertegun. Dave Gilmour, Mick Jagger and George Harrison would all provide finance for Ossie's shows. Ossie was in the groove.

The names of the rich, famous (and well-dressed) pepper his diaries: Nikki Waymouth, one-time wife of Nigel Waymouth of *Granny Takes a Trip* and *Hapshash*, daughter of Samuels the jeweller; Jeremy Fry, heir to the Fry's Chocolate company who gave James Dyson the vacuum cleaner designer his first break; Kit Lambert who managed The Who and who haunted some of the same gay clubs as Ossie, including the *Yours or Mine* where Lambert may have been beaten up by drug dealers on the night he died of a brain haemorrhage, Wayne Sleep, the star dancer from the Royal Ballet; Steve O'Rourke, racing driver and manager of Pink Floyd, Phil May, singer with the Pretty Things and husband of Electra Nemon whose father Oscar made the Winston Churchill statue in Parliament Square, fashion designer Manolo Blahnik, and Jimi Hendrix who once told Ossie "I believe I'm a prophet from outer space and I won't be here very long". He even sheathed the hot legs of Rod Stewart; sometimes it seemed as if everyone in the room was wearing an Ossie creation, including Ossie.

And there are marvellous bits of trivia; how when he was staying in Hockney's spare room, Ossie managed to let the bath overflow, flood the Powis Terrace flat and infuriate his landlord; on one occasion he popped round to see Hockney and catching him dying his hair with a bag on his head. Later he discusses picking up men with the late broadcaster Ned Sherrin who remarked that the first time he picked up a guardsman, he rewarded the young man with ten shillings and a squeaky toy.

That level of success had its consequences. The non-stop partying necessitated a large cocaine input that caused fractures in Ossie's personality; the day after he'd married Celia Birtwell (David Hockney was one of the two guests), he went off to Barbados on a honeymoon – on his own. Understandably, his homosexuality was already putting a strain on his relationship. He wasn't around for the birth of either of his sons, Albert and George; he had taken to giving Celia a clout every now and then. He would give interviews and then just grunt answers to questions; he wouldn't turn up for business appointments and would be found in his bed hiding under the covers. Celia was fully aware of his desire for men; it manifested itself in coldness toward her. However, he wanted it both ways (no pun intended); when she sought affection elsewhere and had a brief affair, Ossie found out and broke her nose.

David Hockney saw all this and sympathised with Celia; the two spent a lot of time together and she became his confidant at a time when he was having problems of the heart himself. In gratitude he bought her an expensive ring, an act which drove Ossie into a Hockney-hate campaign; he started referring to David as 'Mr. McGoo'. When Ossie needed £7,000 to buy a house, he sold the portrait that Hockney had done of Celia, Ossie and the cat 'Percy' (the cat's real name was Blanche), to the Tate Gallery where it is now

its most popular exhibit; the picture had been a wedding present.

Another in a long list of terrible drivers of the era, Ossie crashed a silver Buick Riviera three minutes after the insurance cover was arranged and turned over Eddie Grant's Mini Moke on a holiday at Eddie's plantation house in Barbados; later he reversed into a car with a policeman sitting in it. He was frequently breathalysed and banned.

His diaries are a litany of celebrity drug takers and Clark, realising this, comments: "The idea of this book in the hands of the police is terrifying".

His inevitable bitter split with Celia meant a split with his children, which plagued him for years until they reached a rapprochement. Sexually, it was boys, boys, boys, but there were also occasional girls. However, he had lost the woman he loved and tormented by his sexuality, sought solace in sordid liaisons on Hampstead Heath. There were financial crashes and changes of address. He spent some happy times living with Marianne Faithfull in Danvers Street, Chelsea at a time when she was being very 'naughty' as she would say and bad influences both, they were very naughty together.

By the early 80s, with the exception of a few loyal regulars and debt collectors, Ossie's phone stopped ringing. Fashion is by its nature ephemeral and unless the designer has the energy and élan to stay literally at the cutting edge then he passes with it. Two other notable clothiers to the rock chic, Bill Gibb and Thea Porter were suffering similar problems. Financially Clark's life was in chaos; he faced personal bankruptcy and was forced to sign on the dole, spending some years living in a Warwick Gardens house owned by Chelita Secunda who had been battling with a heroin addiction herself and had suffered several drug busts. However, he had found a regular boyfriend, Nick Balaban, who Ossie dominated but who in retaliation gave Ossie the run-around with other men. There were several violent incidents between them. It was a schizophrenic existence that might on one night see Ossie shoplifting food from a supermarket for dinner, and on another drinking in the Colony Club in Soho next to Francis Bacon and Lucien Freud, who regularly feigned not to recognise him; then invariably there followed a trip to Hampstead Heath for rough sex with a stranger.

At the same time be making dresses for Michael Caine's wife Shakira and Angie Bowie and despite the remaining powerful and rich friends, he was totally dependant on Social Security cheques, broke to the extent he had to sell his remaining David Hockney etchings to pay a gas bill, but at the same time Pete Townshend and his family might pop round for tea. Letters from his lawyers about income tax liabilities alternated with visits to the 'clap' clinic. Although fully aware of the dangers of HIV/AIDS he continued to be recklessly driven into having sex with strange men on the Heath. "Why, I wonder, do I gamble with death?" he mused.

Years of drinking, smoking, cruising for boys, shoplifting, loneliness, depression, self-loathing, thoughts of suicide, only sporadic work, changes of address and begging letters to Hockney, who he sometimes saw as a saviour but then who at others, it seemed to Clark's fevered mind, was making off with Ossie's wife and kids, resulted in much bitching. It was clearly the oddest of relationships since later in his tell-all saga, Ossie reveals that he was in love with Hockney.

One day it would be champagne and cocaine, another day five tins of Special Brew and a snort of heroin. One night he had to borrow a fiver for dog food and cigarettes and the next, he is visiting Paul Getty, one of the richest men in the world. He has to claim supplementary benefit in order to pay his rent (and then doesn't pay it anyway) but the new flat he is staying in at that time is one of the great stucco houses in Powis Terrace, Notting Hill. On another occasion, he wrote, he hadn't eaten for a week – too poor – and then attended a dinner for Christian Lacroix who had been a lifelong admirer of Clark. He was a fully paid up speed freak by then and was seeing a psychiatrist. Around him AIDS victims dropped like their flies; his friend Derek Jarman, the film director, his ex-boyfriend Nick Balaban, Hockney's long-term partner Peter Schlesinger and many, many more from the pop and fashion worlds. In those terrible times, it seemed like if the drugs didn't get them then the drink would and that AIDS would decimate any survivors. 'Do you shoot to kill?' was the graffiti on the contraceptive machine. "Death comes knocking every day", he wrote. Even taking to Buddhism didn't help the depressions.

But hope in the shape of a loan of £15,000 from Dave Gilmour spurred him into a new venture, his own studio again. Not for Ossie a trip to the bank for a business loan: it would have been a fruitless journey anyway since he remained an undischarged bankrupt. With Gilmour's cash in the bag, he figured, he could get the rest of the finance in packages and tackled Pink Floyd's manager Steve O'Rourke and Linda his wife. Then he mused that Jagger might need some new clothes and if he can get Jagger, then all the others will follow; Michael Caine, David Frost, Paul Getty, Eric Clapton and Floyd keyboard player Rick Wright were in his sights.

His plans came to nought however and a while later, one of the coolest designers in British fashion history was reduced to stealing coins from the wishing well in Holland Park to buy cigarettes.

In 1995, Clark had a fateful meeting with an Italian washer upper called Diego Cogolato. Their relationship was a stormy one; Diego had a problem with drink and violence. One evening on a garage forecourt, Cogolato nudged a car with the car he and Ossie were using; unfortunately the driver of the other car was an off duty policewoman who called for back up because the stroppy duo had aggressively argued with her. Diego and Ossie were convicted of common assault and sentenced to community service and probation respectively. A short while later, Diego, apparently deranged by Prozac and amphetamines stabbed Ossie thirty seven times and then beat his head in with a terracotta pot. Cogolato was sentenced to only six years for manslaughter.

Apart from perhaps Kenneth Tynan, Ossie was the bitchiest Pepys of the era and like so many from that time of hope, he fell into bitterness, disillusionment and suffered a tragic death. He had been the man most likely to, so close to the Beatles that he knew their inside leg measurements, drank with them and was once even mistaken for one of them, but then he was forgotten. It must have been so hard for him, having once been so instrumental in that great decade and then becoming a junkie on the dole living in squalor. And while he languished in poverty, the whole razzamatazz was still going on around him: the glamorous shows, the gigs, the wild parties, the sex, the drugs and the champagne. But the bands weren't wearing his clothes any more and no one would front up the money for another fashion parade yet he still had all their phone numbers; their details were all in his book. Oh yes, they were in his book all right.

It was the end of Ossie's torment; it had been a savage end to be sure, but if he hadn't been murdered, given his reckless sex life he was on borrowed time anyway; undoubtedly the virus would have dragged him down before he'd lived much longer. At least he escaped that indignity.

It could have all been so different.

22

Back on the Cheyne Gang

MICK STOOD looking out over the river from the huge window at 48 Cheyne Walk. "Look at that bloke in that canoe Keith; he can't get his paddle out of the mud. He's gonna go over in a minute; up shit creek without a paddle… It was really misty the other night. Did you see it? All along the river; very late; right over Battersea Bridge.

"You can see right into the park can't you. I'm gonna get a telescope I reckon, so I can look at all the girls. We're at the centre of it all here Keith. Cheyne Walk. This is the best street in London, well if it weren't for all the cars. It's a bit noisy; I'll have to get double-glazing. Do you remember doing that photo session on the corner down there? A couple of years back. I remember looking up at this house. I never thought I'd ever own it.

"John and Paul haven't got a river view have they? McCartney said he loved this house but he can't move here because it would look like he was copying us, and he wouldn't like that would he? We should insist; get them both to move down here as well; all live in a row, a street of the stars, a stella street.

"Marianne bought this enormous chandelier the other day; six thousand quid; six thousand quid! Just for a light for the hallway. That's a year's wages for an accountant; well a normal accountant anyway, not our accountant; six thousand quid would get you about half an hour with our accountant. It's seventeenth century though, the chandlier. Cut crystal. French I think. You can't put candles in it. You'd burn the house down. I expect you'll be doing that Keith, joint in the ashtray; have you got any insurance?

"I like those trousers man. Are they Ossie's? He was here the other night; chopping out coke on my mantelpiece. I said, 'that's a Georgian fireplace Ossie' and he just grinned at me; razor blade marks all over it. Got this amazing python skin bolero jacket off him though".

Usually, Mick kept the blinds down at all times and only one lamp illuminated the Georgian fireplace from which, Ossie Clark says in his diaries, he snorted cocaine. It's said that Jagger liked to pad around in the gloom wearing women's slippers, or mascara, or one of Marianne's dresses… or all three.

Almost the same day that Mick bought his Cheyne Walk Queen Anne town house; Keith bought *his* Victorian Cheyne Walk house, 100 yards up the road. Number three, otherwise known as River House, had belonged to an ex-Conservative minister Anthony Nutting, erstwhile a stanchion of the establishment, who had swallowed his principles and without a trace of embarrassment announced that he saw no reason why he shouldn't sell his mansion to a long haired degenerate; not when he realised there was no chain or purchaser's mortgage to impede a quick sale; especially not when Keith produced a banker's draft for £55,000, which rankled the Stones' singer.

Five thousand pounds more; why did he have to try and outdo Mick all the time? The extra £5,000 had bought Keith an extra floor. Keith's place was *six* storeys tall, considerably bigger and far grander than Mick's. Keith protested that he wasn't trying to outdo Jagger at all; that the six-storey house was the only one on the market at that time; the only one he could find. He'd had no choice but to get a bigger, better house than Jagger; all with that half smile on his face. Number 3 Cheyne Walk, grand as it was didn't seem to boast many illustrious former residents, although George Eliot had briefly stayed at and died next door at number four.

Jagger's garden was sufficiently large to build a studio down there. Only the best for Mick who, when he wanted to start guitar lessons phoned his mate Eric Clapton who'd trot round the corner from his place at 36A Old Church Street whenever he was beckoned. Eric had good reason to accommodate the budding guitarist singer from the Stones; Mick and Keith were conspiring to boot Brian out of the band, Cream was breaking up and there was an outside chance that

Clapton would get Brian's job; he figured he might be able to ease from one super group into another; 'er that's an 'A' chord Mick'.

And let's face it; there was no way Mick was going to ask Keith to teach him anything. He'd take guitar lessons from Keith on the day Keith asked him for a lesson on the harmonica. Still it was good having Keith just up the road. They'd lived together for years one way or another and he didn't really want to cut the umbilical yet. Any time they felt like recording, he could just pop down the yard rather than having to go and make phone calls and get cars to take them to Olympic Studios down in Barnes; a helluva lot cheaper as well.

 Idyllic at first, Faithfull reckons that after a couple of years in Cheyne Walk, the magic had started to seep out of their relationship, that their sex life was all but over; that far from tearing into steamy nights of passion in the great bed, she and Mick would sit propped up on Moroccan cushions reading ghost stories to each other; although the bed *did* get used carnally from time to time. One night while Mick was in the studio, Marianne was sitting in the big bed all on her own; Prince Stanislaus Klossowski de Rola (Stash) did a Romeo routine; driven by a need for company or just plain lust he climbed the wisteria growing up the front wall of the house to the balcony and was rewarded with a night of love making. She states she felt OK about cheating because Mick was doing it too and that it was boredom that had driven her into a heroin addiction. Soon she started falling down in the street and passing out in restaurants and dinner parties. Jagger came home one

night and she was unconscious on the bathroom floor. He wouldn't leave her though and it wasn't until 1970 that she split, with her child under one arm and a Turkish rug under the other. The chandelier was left hanging.

Getting a period town house down by the river had always been pretty difficult in central London; there actually aren't that many when you consider the length of the embankment, especially enormous ones with gardens; so the Cheyne Walk houses had always been at a premium and had always boasted a disproportionate number of well-heeled, famous occupants. Ralph Vaughan Williams lived at number 13 from 1905 to 1928. There he wrote many of his most famous works including *The Sea Symphony, The Lark Ascending,* and *The London Symphony,* which features the cries of street traders. Among those who visited him there were his good friends Maurice Ravel and Gustav Holst (who had through Vaughan Williams' recommendation been given a job as a singing teacher at James Allen School in Dulwich).

Dante Gabriel Rossetti lived at number 16 with a whole menagerie of creatures (he was banned from keeping peacocks owing to complaints fom the neighbours about the noise). Sir Marc Brunel who designed the Thames Tunnel lived at number 98 as did his son Isambard Kingdom Brunel who nearly died when the tunnel flooded. Bram Stoker, the creator of *Dracula*, resided at number 27 for a short time. Jane Asher and Gerald Scarfe now live at number 10, where David Lloyd George had earlier lived. J. M. W. Turner died at 119 Cheyne Walk in 1851. James McNeill Whistler liked the river views so much he lived at three different addresses 21, 96 and 101 when he was painting them. Elizabeth Gaskell, who wrote the biography of Charlotte Bronte, lived at 93. Henry James lived at 21 some years after Whistler. Hilaire Belloc, perhaps best known for his children's poems but also an MP and political writer lived at 104.

London was entering a psychedelic period in the late 1960s but J. M. W. Turner had experienced one of his own over a century earlier. When a prospective buyer, staring at one of his seascapes complained (possibly in an effort to get the price reduced), "After all Mr. Turner, cliffs are only chalk and stone and grass. I can't see those wonderful blues and reds and yellows in the combination". "Hmm", pondered Turner, "but don't you wish you could?"

Turner was in hiding in Cheyne Walk; his house in Queen Anne Street in Marylebone, with a large gallery at the rear, was generally accepted to be his official abode. However there was much gossip about his relationship with the twice-widowed Sophia Booth, so Turner secretly acquired the Cheyne Walk address and adopted the name Booth to ensure that he and his partner could live a quiet life in obscurity. The local boatmen, who had no idea of his real identity, called him 'The Admiral', because he often carried a telescope, and Turner didn't disabuse them of the notion that he was indeed a retired seafarer.

Turner's health was failing when he lived in Cheyne Walk; at nights, his sleep was disturbed by vivid and alarming images of pictures that he hadn't yet painted. By day he experienced constant aching in his legs and indigestion brought on by the lack of strategic chewing teeth, but he kept painting almost every day, right to the end of his life in his Chelsea sanctuary.

Curiously another famous Cheyne Walk resident was also trying to hide. When the Pre-Raphaelite painter Dante Gabriel Rossetti bought Tudor House at number 16, his long-term model and short-term wife Lizzie Siddal had just died of an overdose of laudanum. The Pre-Raphaelite supermodel may well have contracted tuberculosis after spending hours laying in a bath of either tepid or cold water when she'd modelled for Millais' famous picture of *Ophelia*. In fact Siddal's father pursued Millais for compensation after her death.

Rossetti, his poet friend Algernon Swinburne, Lizzie, Millais, the designer William Morris and his wife Janie were a close-knit group of friends and the beautiful people of their time. They jumped in and out of each other's beds with the same gusto as those around the Rolling Stones. Millais' friend John Ruskin the critic who was an evangelist of the Brotherhood introduced Millais to his wife; she sat for Millais and he fell in love with her. Her marriage to Ruskin was annulled because she was (humiliatingly) able to prove that she was still a virgin even after years of marriage, (it was rumoured that Ruskin was disgusted by his wife and possibly by women altogether, although he went on to marry a 17 year-old when he was 46 thus scandalising society again). Surviving this, they went on to have eight children.

Rossetti painted his friend William Morris's wife Jane and it is assumed that they had an affair. His paintings reflect the fertility of the age. Pre-Raphaelite art with its intense colours, exquisite detail and its preoccupation with the myths and legends and medieval romance could at a stretch be compared with the posters that Hapshash and the Coloured Coat were producing just up the road one hundred years later. And during that period when Bohemian Chelsea was at the centre of an artistic revolution, outrageous styles of dress, decadence, casual sex, drinking and drug taking were almost as prevalent as they would be in the 60s.

The ethereal Lizzie modelled for Rossetti for ten years and became the first 'face' of the Pre-Raphaelite brotherhood. He eventually married her but she was becoming more ill and when she gave birth to a stillborn child, Rossetti's eye began to wander. Driven mad by illness, jealousy and a life-long melancholy, Lizzie overdosed on laudanum and died. There is speculation that there may have been more to the 'accidental' death than was at first assumed. At the graveside, Rossetti tortured by grief, remorse and possibly guilt suddenly thrust a book of his unpublished poems into her coffin and wrapped it in her flowing red hair. Eight years later in 1869, he had become crazed with drink and drugs himself. Convinced he was going blind, he stopped painting, resumed writing poetry and became obsessed with the small book of poems he had put into the coffin. After lobbying the Home Secretary, he was granted permission to exhume the body but declined to be present when a great bonfire was lit at Highgate Cemetery and the grisly task was undertaken.

The volume, which had been eaten through by worms, was retrieved but was hardly legible and when the poems were finally published, they were badly received and criticised for their erotic content. Whatever the state of the volume, it's said that Lizzie's body seemed like it had only just been interred and had strangely defied the ravages of time; maybe the laudanum had served to preserve it but Rossetti was haunted by the exhumation for the remainder of his life.

Some months after the funeral, Rossetti moved into the great house on the embankment with the young poet Algernon Swinburne, an alcoholic who had developed a penchant for flagellation; he used to make frequent visits to a discreet salon in St. John's Wood where he met many other high society fans of the whip. Swinburne's masochistic desires, needless to say, may have had their origins at Eton where he was flogged on several occasions and had subsequently, as was the custom, been ordered to thank his beater for his efforts. Perhaps the thrashings became part of his muse because he is commonly considered to be one of the best English language poets, despite his somewhat unfashionable flowery style. Algernon was certainly an interesting and excitable character whose drink-fuelled rantings would be, in the brief moments before he became incoherent, and he did every evening, terrifically entertaining. He was prone to popping down to visit the guests or talk to the staff, stark naked, then wandering around the house reciting.

Despite the high regard in which his work was held, the mercurial poet had a physical and mental breakdown and had to be looked after for the rest of his life – another resonance of the 1960s and 70s when drug burn outs and acid casualties were bunging up the mental wards. Plus ça change plus c'est la même chose.

Rossetti was enjoying great success but only little by little; there is no doubt he was becoming more eccentric, shattered as he was by Lizzie's death, leaving us compelled to speculate about his part in it. The house was badly run; rats could be seen in his studio. He was probably making £4,000 a year from his paintings but had no bank account and would stuff money into a dresser drawer from where the staff would just as quickly remove it. Consequently there was always a household crisis in the offing. He was plagued with insomnia and would beg his friends to stay up drinking and smoking with him to all hours. He would only venture out of the house when there was insufficient light to continue painting and was given to wearing a dark cloak and wide brimmed hat, which unsettled the local children who used to call him 'the bat man'.

Then there was the menagerie. Rossetti acquired a rotund wombat, which would sit on his lap drinking milk out of a cup. Indeed there is a drawing in the Tate Britain gallery of this very scene. The wombat once devoured a sitter's straw hat. When the Reverend C. L. Dodgson (Lewis Carroll) visited Rossetti to take some photographs in the beautiful garden (which had once been part of the gardens of King Henry the VIII's riverside Chelsea Palace), he was introduced to the wombat. It is said that the creature, which used to sit in the centre of the dinner table when Rossetti was entertaining - often his near neighbour Whistler was a guest - was the inspiration for the dormouse, which slept in the middle of the table at the mad tea party in *Alice in Wonderland*.

The garden was crowded with peacocks, armadillos, kangaroos, squirrels, mice, a raccoon and two owls called Jessie and Bobbie. The raccoon proved to be the most difficult tenant in the Chelsea zoo because it would constantly gnaw its way out of its pen and make a meal of the neighbour's chicken eggs. Another difficult tenant was a white bull that Rossetti staked out on the lawn whereupon it devoured the grass and all the bushes it could reach before kicking the outhouses down.

It was bedlam: one of the young kangaroos murdered its mother and was in turn eaten itself (or perhaps executed) by the raccoon; a white peacock was released into the living room and immediately dived under a chair where it stayed until it was dragged out dead several days later. The armadillos burrowed their ways along the gardens, leaving mounds of earth and destroying carefully laid out flowerbeds. One of them burrowed right under the foundations of a neighbour's house and came up through the kitchen floor, surprising the cook who screamed blue murder. A fallow deer that Rossetti had purchased chased one of the peacocks, standing on its tail feathers until they all came out when the denuded bird flapped up into a tree and started screeching wildly. The long suffering neighbours overcame their awe of the superstar artist in their midst and complained to Rossetti's landlords, the Cadogan Estate, who issued an edict that peacocks were never to be kept in Cheyne Walk, a rule that unfortunately prevails and prevents peacock farming in Chelsea to this day.

The house fell into disrepair and the master of the house fell with it. He became even more of a recluse and began reckless experiments with a new drug known as chloral hydrate, a depressant which when administered with alcohol acted like a sleeping pill and was the 'Mickey Finn' of Victorian body snatcher legend. However Rossetti, tormented by failed love affairs, enraged and frustrated by the plans of the Cadogan estate to build in the back garden of 16 Cheyne Walk and hounded by outspoken critics of his work, unsurpringly declined in health. The immense amount of chloral he took every day coupled with a diet of rum and milk saw him into the ground aged only fifty-four.

A fountain featuring a bronze bust of Rossetti was constructed in front of the house but in 1970 the bust was stolen and melted down. Almost a hundred years later, the house would again serve as a hideaway for an illustrious tenant when, haunted by the death of his beautiful wife Talitha, yet another victim of the remorseless heroin scourge that was sweeping London, Paul Getty, one of the richest 28 year-olds in the world, went home, pulled his heavy curtains closed, locked fair daylight out and made for himself an artificial night. A recluse, he lived for years in the gloom. In an eerie echo of the tragedy of Rossetti and Lizzie, it seemed that yet another resident of number 16 Cheyne Walk would be wracked by guilt caused by the death of a lover. In fact, it is not inconceivable that the aesthete Getty, well acquainted as he was with the history of the house, may have decided that whatsoever he felt about the apartment in Rome, the palace in Marrakesh or any of the other Getty residences that encircled the globe, his Cheyne Walk town house, the finest house on the embankment it has to be said, was the best place for him to do his mourning; that precisely because of Rossetti's experiences there, Getty saw it as an appropriate house of pain.

23

'Spanish' Tony Sanchez

THE USE and abuse of drugs on the Thames-side boulevard continued apace. A regular visitor to Keith's number 3 and an occasional visitor to Mick's number 48 was 'Spanish' Tony Sanchez who had his own pad in Palmerston Road in Kilburn (although sometimes, when he wanted to impress one of the Beatles perhaps, he would tweak the geography a bit and say that his flat was in the more fashionable Maida Vale).

'Spanish' frequently stayed up all night with Keith doing heroin and listening to Stanley Holloway tapes, laughing when Keith laughed – that is if he wasn't driving around town looking for Keith's heroin. He became Keith's minder, driver, dealer (Keith's addictions dictated that he keep his supplier close), and, if you take any notice of Tony's version of events in his book *Up and Down with The Rolling Stones*; his friend. Keith figured he needed a bodyguard since he had started spending a lot of time hanging around dodgy houses with extremely heavy dudes doing heroin deals; these were the days before he started carrying a gun, at a time when he was probably in the top ten of most recognisable faces in the world.

He needed a driver; by God he needed a driver.

Like Keith Moon, Keith Richard had never ever bothered to have a driving lesson let alone take a test and stories of his appalling driving skills abounded. So, after a couple of bad experiences involving considerable damage to himself and others, Keith wisely decided that careering around London in a Bentley full of class 'A' drugs was something he should avoid doing. But he had this problem; he was a junkie and he needed a regular supplier as well as a driver and Sanchez fitted the bill on all counts.

Spanish was omnipresent, he was there when the folks shot up and he was there when the shit went down. He says he once arrived at Brian Jones's flat and that Anita was passed out on the bed with "bruises all over her face", and it was obvious to him that Brian had "beaten her savagely". To try and bring her round, Sanchez, according to his book, shook her and "then slapped her face", thus adding to the bruise count no doubt, before taking her to hospital to have her stomach pumped. Apart from the slapping business, that all seems quite caring and sympathetic until you consider why the girl was passed out in the first place; quite possibly as the result of taking too many of Tony's drugs.

But before he met the Stones, in an attempt to avoid the world of the major villains in his family, Spanish had originally attempted a career and trained as a croupier in a small Mayfair club called Le Chat Noire where he couldn't help but meet even bigger villains than his relatives, like Albert Dimes, a Soho enforcer who was into bookmaking and loan sharking in the 40s and 50s. He says in his ghost-written book that he met Robert Fraser in the 'Bar Italian' in

Frith Street - which is presumably the Bar Italia – and that they discussed high-minded things like the Spanish civil war (in Spanish) for an hour. However, when they met again it was to "score some hash", so perhaps their conversation had at some point strayed away from the complexities of 1930s Spanish politics and had lapsed into the vernacular of dope deals.

The relationship deepened when Spanish persuaded Reggie Kray to stop threatening Fraser over a £20,000 gambling debt he'd run up at the twins' club, Esmeralda's Barn in Knightsbridge. When Robert had needed a bit of cash in a hurry, Spanish rigged a game of chemin de fer so that Robert won it. That was his entrée to the glittering world that surrounded the Fraser gallery; Spanish was invited back to the Mount Street flat where he met some of the Moody Blues and smoked a joint for the first time in his life.

Fraser was the matrix; through him Sanchez met Marianne and then her husband John Dunbar; from there he was into the Stones and, after she'd moved on to live with Jagger, he says he was into Marianne's bed. She admits she had affairs with Spanish over the years but that the drugs were the only attraction and she has little good to say about her former lover/provider: "I was getting deeper and deeper into drugs, much to the despair of Mick. I was also getting involved in a long affair with Tony Sanchez, Spanish Tony, dealer by appointment to the Stones…. He gave me all the drugs I wanted….

"He was a dreadful person. You only had to see him eat to know how loathsome he was. He was a lowlife, a small time spiv, but a weakling at the same time… It's an odd feeling when you realise that somebody who you've been sleeping with is there only because you're Mick Jagger's girlfriend. Or were. He was a star-fucker". And of course a drug dealer; soon he was scuttling all around town in his Alfa Romeo picking up grass for people – usually famous people. Then came the cocaine, which for some reason Spanish refers to as "non-addictive". But, according to his book, when Brian and Keith asked him to get it for them he refused because he didn't want to be "labelled as a dangerous drug dealer". Then came the LSD. Fraser had asked Spanish to go to Redlands on the occasion of the bust but Tony refused because "the thought of taking any kind of hallucinogenic drug frightened me", but he did get Fraser the heroin he had in his possession when he was busted. Tony's attempts to pay off a bent copper to influence the case failed; whatever happened to the money, only Spanish knows.

But he still had his uses: Keith was in car mode; he'd just bought a magnificent S3 Bentley but considered it a bit demure; not quite the right vehicle for a young rebel-rouser Rolling Stone. Then he came across an eighteen-foot long Mercedes Nazi staff car complete with a folding hood at the back just like in the war films. When Keith had taken it for a spin with Spanish beside him, he'd jumped two sets of traffic lights by the Westway flyover and squarely rammed a car sitting at a third set of lights. Leaping from the car, Keith hailed a cab and split, leaving his new friend to pick up the pieces. It wouldn't be the only time Spanish was left to do Keith's dirty work.

Tony's star-studded list of customers increased. John Lennon became almost a daily caller but Sanchez maintains, he didn't want to be considered a dealer and so gave John crushed up aspirin instead of the pills or powders Lennon was really after, in the hope he might go away. However, an undeterred Lennon came back for more drugs, real or imagined, the very next day and, Sanchez says, they remained "good friends". Brian Jones was disappearing into his sad drug oblivion and despite the fact he was "deeply concerned" about Jones he continued to supply him too.

The evidence mounts against poor old Tony.

With so many rich and famous clients, or should that be friends, clamouring for his attentions (and presumably in an effort to try and get rid of some of the ready money that was bulging his pockets), Sanchez opened the Vesuvio Club in Tottenham Court Road and decked it out in the de rigueur Moroccan style, the walls decorated with Inca sunbursts. Each of its twelve cubicles, discreetly screened by tapestries, had a hubble-bubble opium pipe on its table. At the opening party, the punch had been spiked with Methedrine, there were plates of hash cakes and Spanish had thoughtfully provided a hash stash by each pipe.

London's finest bohemians turned out: Charlie Watts, Jagger and John Lennon and, in the carefree years before her death, Talitha Getty and husband Paul. Mick had arrived with the latest pressing of

Beggars Banquet under his arm and the guests were dancing to it when, the story goes, McCartney produced, hot from the presses, a copy of the Beatles' latest single *Hey Jude* which, once played to the awed crowd, was played again… and again. Once again the Stones were relegated into second place by their masters the Beatles, a real humiliation for poor Mick who'd had his nose put out of joint in a club he considered to be the Stones' home turf.

The drug mill ground on. Sanchez disingenuously states, "I woke up one morning early in 1969 to the realisation that I was a heroin addict. And so, it seemed, was everyone around me. Keith Anita, Marianne, Eric Clapton…" His presence is ubiquitous. Just days after Brian's death, the Stones (and Sanchez) are in an armoured car which is creeping towards their Hyde Park stage for the famous free gig. Spanish says he was in the back with the band in the capacity of photographer, but Michael Cooper, a professional was also there, so it's hard to know why they would need Tony. Perhaps Sanchez's camera was only a prop; when one of the band wanted a cocaine booster, he conveniently had an available phial of powder to hand.

On one of the occasions when Anita was in a clinic supposedly taking the cure, it was Spanish's flat she ran to when the shivering terrors became too much; he'd administered the medicine she craved and she returned for more of the same the next day, and the day after, thus rendering her treatment useless. The doctor told Keith there was no point Anita going on with the course; that she had more heroin in her blood now than she had done when she was admitted to clean up.

Mick and his new wife Bianca were in the habit, so to speak, on occasional evenings, of taking the air down the embankment and popping in to visit the Gettys who had, according to Tony, become their coke-sorting buddies. He said; "the four of them would go on and on snorting until they were so wired that I had to give them heroin to calm them down again". When, on one occasion, Getty had wanted Sanchez to provide some more drugs, he insists he demurred, "I still refused to sell dope", he said. "I had no desire to become a drug peddler to the aristocracy". This seems to be slightly at odds with the name of his book, originally and innocuously called *Up and Down with the Rolling Stones*, which when it was reissued became less ambiguously entitled *I Was Keith Richards' Drug Dealer*.

St. Tropez was the chosen venue for Mick and Bianca's wedding and Mick insisted Spanish bring some cocaine down with him for his guests. A private jet left Gatwick; on board were Paul and Linda McCartney, Ringo, Eric Clapton and Alice Ormsby-Gore, Keith Moon, Peter Frampton, Robert Fraser, and Spanish who brought a friend who he had paid to be the mule. At the airport in the south of France, all the A-listers were herded onto a coach together while Spanish and his mate, curiously favoured among all the VIPs, got to ride in Mick's limo.

It was further down the coast in Villefranche that Keith and Anita, a short time after the wedding, set up in their tax exile on main street, a palatial and infamous house called Nellcote. Again Spanish is present, flitting backwards and forwards to Chelsea carrying this and that. A procession of junkies, coke heads and stoners seemed to arrive with every flight, Eric Clapton, Marshall Chess, the boss of Rolling Stones Records, Gram Parsons the musician and *Performance* actor Michele Breton, all joined Keith and Anita in the heroin club. The *Sergeant Pepper* sleeve photographer Michael Cooper arrived swigging methadone, trying to kick the habit. His girlfriend had just committed suicide in rehab and within 18 months he was dead too – another suicide; an overdose of Mandrax washed down with a bottle of whisky.

The glamorous Tommy Weber, while not a junkie, arrived bearing gifts; his two young children each had half a kilo of cocaine tied to their waists in money belts. Weber, a one time racing driver, had once managed the jazz-rock band Osibisa and was apparently irresistible to beautiful women including, it's said, Charlotte Rampling. His business, post car racing, was hashish smuggling.

Count Jean de Breteuil, a playboy dope dealer also did not arrive empty handed; he brought his connections. It's said that he used to employ a chauffeur at the French consulate to smuggle his gear and as back up introduced the resident smack users to some heavy-duty dealers from Corsica who would ensure the house's drug larder was always stocked up.

Leaving Nellcote, de Breteuil went to stay in Keith's Cheyne Walk House and have an affair with Talitha Getty during the short period that she was separated from her husband. When she went back to Paul in Rome, de Breteuil went to Paris with Marianne Faithfull; there he administered the last bit of heroin that Jim Morrison would ever ingest. When Morrison's body was discovered, it was de Breteuil who was the first to hear about it when he received a call from Pamela Courson, Morrison's drug-using girlfriend who had been two-timing him with de Breteuil (keep your friends close but your dealers closer).

It's generally understood that Jim took the hefty dose in his apartment and then died in the bath but more recntly it's been alleged that a couple of dealers working for de Breteuil sold Morrison the gear in a club. It was 90% pure and Morrison who hadn't been warned to cut it to make it less lethal, was found slumped over-dosed in a toilet cubicle in the club. The club's owner called upon a doctor friend to check Morrison over and the medic pronounced that Jim was dead, whereupon the two dealers turned up, suggested that Jim had just passed out and lugged the corpse down the street to a car then on to his apartment where they plopped him in the bath tub.

De Breteuil, the high-society low-rent dealer rushed to Morrison's apartment, established that Morrison really was dead and panicked. When he got back to Marianne in a highly agitated state, perhaps because she couldn't quite grasp the gravity of the situation, he smacked her about, and then made her pack their bags; they both made a run for the airport and caught the first plane to Tangier. Killing rock stars had become something of a speciality for him: it was de Breteuil who, only a few months earlier, had sold the pure heroin to Janis Joplin that overloaded her system and killed her. We may never know what really happened to Morrison, although Marianne Faithfull probably knows, and for all sorts of reasons will probably take the secret to the grave with her.

Faithfull later described de Breteuil as "a horrible guy, someone who had crawled out from under a stone… He was just slightly higher on the evolutionary scale than Spanish Tony… but he had a lot of drugs". Perhaps unsurprisingly, Spanish and de Breteuil were friends. Tony used to call him 'Johnny Braces'.

Tony's own girlfriend Madeleine d'Arcy arrived at Nellcote; a beautiful blonde dancer who although heroin free at the time, would, within a couple of years, become a hooker doing tricks for fifteen pounds a night to support a habit that eventually killed her. She too met a gruesome end, even more gruesome than the other casualties;

Spanish discovered her alone in her flat, dead, beaten bloody - injuries that she had somehow inflicted on herself.

Prince Stash wafted into the villa with amazing stories of Far East travel, spouting on about the *Tibetan Book of the Dead*, *Tannhäuser* and carrying a variety of percussion instruments that he played for the assembly; a soundtrack for the long, balmy, smacked out nights. Everybody had a project, or just a packet of powder; Stash waffled on about getting a movie made called *Moonchild*, based on a 1917 Aleister Crowley novel, the man dubbed by Lord Beaverbrook, "the wickedest man in the world".

The Polish Prince Stanislas Klossowski had first met the Stones in 1964 when he had been playing percussion with Vince Taylor, a British Elvis clone and a major player in French rock 'n' roll who was an influence on David Bowie's *Ziggy Stardust* character and is best known for the track *Brand New Cadillac* which appeared on the Clash album *London Calling*.

When Stash came into the picture, Taylor and his band the Playboys were opening for the Stones at the Olympia in Paris (that night Mick met Donald Cammell for the first time and Keith met Stash). Vince got the gig with the Stones on the back of the brilliant career he'd had in Europe – sold out concerts, record deals and miles of press with the attendant jump up drugs and worshipping girls; Mick loved the sound of all that, the way Andrew Oldham sold it to them; the Stones would have to try and keep up with Vince, try and rise to the occasion.

Perhaps because of the adulation Vince's gigs aroused, Taylor was having a few problems, losing a grip on reality; it was all too much: too many late nights, too much bantering, too much to drink, too many pills and too many girls. Vince was mates with Bob Dylan, Nico, and all the other intrigued exotics that littered groovy Europe at the time and it went to his head; one night he and his band, including Stash, were playing in London; Taylor was full of drink and chemicals and proceeded to have a live mental breakdown. He ranted on about being the prophet Matthew in front of his bemused band, then he wrapped his head in a towel, mumbled through a couple of songs, announced he was giving up rock 'n' roll then demolished all the equipment. His touring musicians thought it was time to break up the band and Vince joined a religious movement. Taylor released a few records after his conversion, but died in 1991 aged only 52.

Stash was considered great company but unfortunately had a special talent for being in the wrong places at the wrong time; a few years prior to *Exile on Main Street* he'd been busted with Brian Jones in Courtfield Road, after that he'd had the misfortune to get busted at the other celebrity drug house 101 Cromwell Road where Syd Barrett and

John Esam were losing their minds on LSD; years later he was busted at Keith's house at 3 Cheyne Walk, but third time lucky, this time he was acquitted.

Villa Nellcote was acting as a magnet for heroin, cocaine and grass traders who were now arriving from all over. How Europe's ordinary, regular, narcotic starved drug users were coping during this period when all its first division dealers were humming around Nellcote to serve Keith's extraordinary coterie is hard to imagine.

Yet despite the constant influx of drug smugglers, the gargantuan demand in the house was outstripping local supply and Sanchez was despatched to London to locate a hidden cocaine cache in Cheyne Walk. Not keen to courier the stuff down to the south of France himself, he rather ingeniously, bought a toy piano at Hamleys and hid the packet inside it, giving it to an unwitting delivery driver to take down to the villa for him, along with a consignment of carpets, records and all the other knick-knacks that tax exiled pop stars need. Keith swiftly searched the van on its arrival and then called Spanish demanding to know where his gear was. Told it was inside the piano, Keith's fingers fumbled at the expensive little toy, trying to prise it open, then he lost patience and smashed it to pieces.

And so it goes on, the vicious circle; drugs, the acquisition of them, the taking of them; the talking about them; then start all over again.

The relentless sick, dull, selfish tales of drug smuggling, payoffs and OD's in Sanchez's book and other accounts of the Rolling Stones' *Exile on Main St.* period and beyond, do nothing to enhance the reputations of any of the participants and the decadent end of the decade leaves a dead taste in the mouth. What they do however, is make the survival of Anita, Marianne and above all Keith Richards, given his addictions to guns, knives and smack, all the more miraculous, as so many of his courtiers dropped like flies. As Sanchez (or perhaps his ghost writer) says, "Satan's wings were flapping awfully close to the Rolling Stones".

Jean de Breteuil (Johnny Braces) went to Paris and gave Jim Morrison the huge dose of heroin that killed him. Then Talitha Getty was found unconscious in her husband Paul's Rome apartment. She had also received a massive heroin injection. Talitha had briefly been de Breteuil's lover in Cheyne Walk. Three days later she was dead. Short chronology; just four weeks later de Breteuil himself was dead; cause of death? His own produce. Warhol's muse Edie Sedgwick died four months later; Hendrix died the same year. The beautiful people were checking out in an altogether ugly way.

Things got too heavy and Spanish ducked out of sight. He put himself into rehab after his girlfriend's death but is now presumed dead.

But consider this: if Keith had needed to put real effort into getting his smack instead of just shouting down the corridor for his live-in dealer, could it have been a different band? Might the music have been better if it weren't for the presence of Spanish Tony? Were their finest moments lost? Of course we'll never know. The tortuous recording of *Exile on Main St.* in the south of France, when weeks would pass without a single note being played, is hard evidence of the debilitating effects of hard drugs. Heroin sends you to into torpor then sleep and cocaine makes you an unimaginative, opinionated bore. It's not called 'dumb dust' for no reason.

Bill Wyman confirmed that view when he wrote, "Whatever people tell you about the creative relationship of hard drugs and the making of rock 'n' roll records, forget it. Believe you me, they are much more a hindrance than a help".

So just how good might the Stones have been if Keith hadn't been whacked out of his head for ten years? Could they have risen to dizzier heights? If heroin hadn't been spilling out of stash boxes and cupboards, might even Anita and Marianne have got off it? That's maybe unlikely since they were extremely resourceful users, but it's hard to forget that they both lost babies; could those twin tragedies have been averted? Maybe the appalling 60s/70s body count could have been reduced.

Spanish Tony and his friend Johnny Braces, dead or not, have a lot to answer for.

24

The Gettys

TALITHA POL was one of the most exotic examples of the beautiful people; she was one of the earliest adopters of the 'boho-chic' and 'hippie-chic' look. When she married Paul Getty in 1966, the couple became the most golden of the jeunesses d'oree, as they wandered the world sampling all of its delights, including high-grade heroin. As Kevin West put it in a 2001 article about Talitha, "the young Gettys-with their dazzling combination of beauty, charm, money, style and notoriety-blew across Europe as the freest spirits in an age of free spirits".

Hippie deluxe.

She was born in Java of Dutch parents and was the step grand daughter of Augustus John and his muse, Dorothy "Dorelia" McNeil, both leading lights in the turn of the 20th century Chelsea bohemian culture. Her early years were spent in a Japanese prison of war camp and when the war ended she moved with her mother to London. The broadcaster and writer Jonathan Meades had occasion to meet Talitha when he was attending RADA and said that he thought her "the most beautiful young woman I had ever seen... I gaped, unable to dissemble my amazement"

Talitha dabbled in film work playing in a number of small roles and even had an un-credited bit part in *Barbarella* (which also featured

Anita Pallenberg) but most of her short life was dedicated to jetsetting with the likes of Yves Saint-Laurent and Rudolf Nureyev. The Getty's Marrakesh palace (dubbed the 'Pleasure Palace') was a regular haunt of the beautiful people where there were parties of all the earthly delights, leading San Laurent to invoke the F. Scott Fitzgerald book title *The Beautiful and the Damned* when he talked of the Gettys and their crowd. "I knew the youthfulness of the Sixties," Saint Laurent said in 1984. "Talitha and Paul Getty lying on a starlit terrace in Marrakesh, beautiful and damned, and a whole generation assembled as if for eternity where the curtain of the past seemed to lift before an extraordinary future."

By day, Talitha would search the souk for objets d'art and exquisite knick-knacks; at night she would bring home trunks stuffed with trinkets as well as entertainers: musicians, conjurors, dancers, acrobats and storytellers to amuse their top-drawer guests.

It's said that her husband Paul (along with Brian Jones and with maybe a soupcon of Andrew Loog Oldham) was one of the inspirations for Jagger's Turner character in *Performance*. However, their wealth, the glittering parties and their attractiveness masked the reality; Paul Getty was a deeply unhappy man who got his kicks from fast cars, booze, heroin and bedding starlets.

He was the third of five sons of the oil billionaire John Paul Getty, once the richest man in the world. His mother, who had only lived with the oil baron for three years (they had met when she was 14 and he was 40) tried to commit suicide when she found out she was carrying him – a traumatic event for the boy when he learned of it. After they were divorced, mum and the young Getty, who was perhaps understandably, a little unstable, lived in California while the old man eventually settled in the UK. Getty senior had very little to do with the raising of Paul, except to occasionally correct errors in the letters that the boy wrote to his father and mail them back.

Paul's first job was working at one of the old man's petrol stations, pumping gas and making $100 a week. After a spell in the army where he served in Korea, young Getty joined the family company as a manager in Italy. Federico Fellini was filming *La Dolce Vita* (figuring Nico) in Rome at that time and there were many distractions for Paul who, disillusioned with corporate life, started running with the international set and dabbling in drugs, to the disapproval of his father who all but cut him out of his will. As a consequence, Getty is said to have inherited only $500,000 (other reports say more) from an estate worth billions. His eventual great fortune was apparently derived from a number of trusts set up by his grandmother.

In 1965 Getty met the almond-eyed Talitha, at the London home of his father's personal assistant, Claus von Bülow, a trusted servant. Von Bülow notoriously stood trial for the attempted murder of his wife Sunny in 1982; he was found guilty and sentenced to thirty years imprisonment but was then declared not guilty on appeal. Sunny remained in a coma until late 2008. The affair was made into a movie, *Reversal of Fortune*, starring Glenn Close and Jeremy Irons.

Getty divorced his then wife and married Talitha who he called his 'wild bird'. At the ceremony, he wore a psychedelic tie and she wore a white velvet hooded mini-dress with mink trimmings; they lived together in a sumptuous roof top apartment in the Piazza d'Araceoli, next door to Carlo Ponti (*War and Peace, Dr. Zhivago*) and his wife Sophia Loren (*The Millionairess, The Fall of the Roman Empire*), in a fashionable part of Rome, the broad terrace of which she turned into a facsimile of the Moroccan palace. Talitha's extraordinary, exotic appearance shocked the provincial Romans and while she was just one of the set in London, she became 'the one' in Rome, frequently in the newspapers and photographed outside exclusive restaurants by the nascent paparazzi. Then the heroin usage began and they both became addicted.

In 1968, Talitha gave birth to Tara Gabriel Gramophone Galaxy Getty who triumphed over his extraordinary parentage and extravagant moniker to grow up relatively normal, and has become a conservationist working in Africa. But despite the sobering influence of a new child, mother began to more and more live up to her nickname, once holding a party in a pigsty in Rome and hanging out with the druggies on Rome's Spanish Steps with the baby hanging papoose-style on her back.

Paul had four children from his first marriage, Aileen, Mark, Ariadne and the eldest J. Paul Getty III who was kidnapped in Italy and a ransom of $17 million was demanded. While he was chained to a stake in a cave for five months, Getty senior, the grandfather, refused to pay up because he feared that it would set a precedent and thus endanger the safety of his other fourteen grandchildren.

The old man was scorned as an uncaring miser, however his stand made some sense in that if kidnapping Gettys had caught on then it might have turned out to be a highly expensive affair even for him. In addition, perhaps the old man placed some credence in the theory that was then circulating that his grandson might somehow be complicit in the kidnap plot in a bid to extract some money for himself from the billionaire. Getty senior was sending out the wrong signals though; it was said that while he kept the kidnappers waiting for a response to their demands, he had been spotted spending $6 million on art in a single morning at Christie's. This must have infuriated the criminals who hacked off part of one of the boy's ears and mailed it to a newspaper (the ear was stuck in the mail for three weeks because of a postal strike) then the old man relented and paid a ransom of $3.4 million. But it was only to be a loan he stressed; Paul the father had to had to pay all the money back to John Paul the grandfather from his trust with four per cent interest. Disgusted, he never made contact with his father again.

Some time after his release, the grandson J. Paul Getty III took an overdose of prescription drugs mixed with alcohol and went into a coma for six weeks. He recovered consciousness but was left paralysed and nearly blind.

The Getty tragedies continued and have often caused speculation that their fantastic wealth carried with it a curse. In 1971, Getty embarked on an affair and Talitha departed the Rome apartment for the London house by the Thames. Count Jean de Breteuil happened to be staying a few doors down in Keith's house in Cheyne Walk and presumably on the lookout for heroin and on the rebound from her husband, she had a brief affair with the dealer to the stars. She returned to Rome to try and patch things up with Paul (meanwhile the Count went to Paris with Marianne Faithfull), but it seems she was rebuffed and on a night that has never been explained, was whisked away to a private clinic where it was said she had died of a barbiturate overdose. Six months later it was revealed that she had in fact taken a lethal dose of heroin described by the inquest as 'massive'.

A guilt stricken Paul Getty was cleared of contributory negligence but fled the country fearing that sooner or later he would be arrested and charged with some sort of offence in connection with her death and the drugs. He hid away in his Georgian fortress at 16 Cheyne

Walk and entered into a twenty-year depression that was fuelled by rum and heroin. Eating little, his body endured a tremendous battering; he developed circulatory problems, and for a long time could walk only a few yards with great difficulty. He also had cirrhosis of the liver and signs of diabetes.

During this dreadful period Kenneth Tynan the raconteur and critic had been trying to raise $150,000 finance for a film project. At a meeting Getty enthusiastically offered him the cash. His people would send a cheque straight away he said, but it never arrived. Then months went by when he was un-contactable or made yet further promises that he failed to keep. Tynan, driven frantic by the process, the endless calls, the fruitless visits, started to talk of suicide although he realised that Getty's state of mind (he referred to his friend as "a well meaning junkie"), was the problem rather than it being merely a case of broken promises. Part of Getty's difficulties stemmed from his heroin addiction (number 16 has seen its share of substance abuse), the cure for which, required him to be unconscious for a lot of the day. Suddenly he was whisked into a Harley Street clinic suffering from priapism – he had a permanent erection, which, at first, he found hugely amusing but later when he developed a blood clot, the pain became unbearable, the rare condition became life-threatening and his humour deserted him.

Despite his various tribulations, Getty somehow found the strength to get out of the house and seek an efficacious addiction cure, booking in to the London Clinic for a course of treatment that in the end lasted 500 days at a cost of $500 a day. But despite the expense, he had hauled himself back from the edge and was extremely grateful for his second chance. It was at the clinic that he resolved to start giving some of his great wealth away, for as much as the cost of the clinic was a fortune for mere mortals, for Getty it was petty cash and wouldn't inflict a dent on earnings of around $750,000 a week from investments that may have totalled $3 billion.

Redemption came with the aid of a new girlfriend Victoria Holdsworth, the daughter of a Suffolk farmer whom he later married. Getty made the transformation from philanderer to philanthropist. He contributed £50m to the National Gallery in 1985, £20 million to the British Film Institute who have used the money to restore their prints of old films (they have a print of every film released in the UK many of which were disintegrating). St Paul's Cathedral received £5m for the cleaning of the West Front, the Conservative Party received £5m after it lost the 2001 general election, Canova's Three Graces was purchased for the nation with £1m; the Churchill Papers were kept in this country at a cost of £1m and The Oldie magazine was bailed out (Getty eventually bought it).

But there were thousands of other smaller donations. Hearing the story that a concert pianist John Ogdon had fallen on hard times and needed to sell his piano, Getty sent him instructions to go and buy a new one and send him the bill for it. During the miners' strike, despite the fact Getty supported the Conservatives, he contributed towards the welfare of many of their families.

Through Mick Jagger, Getty developed an interest in cricket (perhaps uniquely for an American) and he gave away millions to help develop Lords and the Oval as well as a number of village cricket grounds. Via his J. Paul Getty Jr. Charitable Trust which advertises itself as "Supporting Unpopular Causes", he favoured donations to organisations in the north of the UK rather than the south and small projects over big ones; he helped to rehabilitate prison inmates and young offenders, preserve dilapidated churches and offered assistance to women driven to self-mutilation. The dissolute wastrel had become an angel.

During the London Clinic phase of his life, Margaret Thatcher visited him to thank him for his contribution to the National Gallery. She sat by his bedside and said, "My dear Mr. Getty, we mustn't let things get us down, must we? We'll have you out of here as soon as possible".

Despite the visit he was eventually released from the clinic and bought the 2,500-acre Wormsley estate, built a knapped-flint library; in it Getty stored a collection of rare bindings and illuminated manuscripts that constitute the finest collection of its sort in a private library in the country. In the collection are the earliest English manuscript, the seventh-century *Historia Ecclesiastica* by the Bishop of Caesarea Eusebius Pamphili, four leaves from the only remaining medieval illustrated biography of St Thomas à Becket and a number of rare British and continental 20th-century bindings. Elsewhere on the estate, Getty constructed a perfect oval cricket ground with a mock-Tudor pavilion set against the hillside, When the ground was inaugurated in 1992, John Major and the Queen Mother were in attendance. Paul was given the honorary title of Knight

Commander of the Most Excellent Order of the British Empire in 1986 for services to charity but couldn't be addressed as Sir Paul because of his American citizenship, which he finally renounced in 1998 (despite the US embassy trying to talk him out of it), when he received full honours.

Friends speak of a kindly, soft-spoken man who despite every conceivable benefit in life struggled to find happiness but who eventually achieved some sort of solace by becoming a rather eccentric English gentleman. Aged 70 when he died, it was a miracle he got anywhere near his three score years and ten given his dissipated lifestyle, however, the family curse, if such things exist, reared its ugly head yet again when his daughter Aileen was diagnosed as having AIDS.

25

The Young Americans

THERE have always been planeloads of Americans arriving and leaving the UK. That's what Heathrow is surely, the USA's most easterly airport. However, during the 60s it seemed like they were everywhere, dropping in to London airport and dropping out in London clubs.

Britain's two big bands, the Stones and the Beatles, naturally, drew them like wasps to a jam jar; talented musicians like Gram Parsons, Jimmy Miller and Jack Nitzsche arrived in the UK full of great ideas and hope, and burned out junkies and alcoholics like er... Gram Parsons, Jimmy Miller and Jack Nitzsche returned to the US, disillusioned and full of dope.

Parsons, who arguably wrote *Honky Tonk Women* had only limited success after his spell working with the Stones and in his last days would often disappear into the desert around Joshua Tree in California where he would consume LSD and magic mushrooms and go looking for UFOs. He eventually died, aged 26 of a morphine and alcohol cocktail and his body was taken to the airport to be shipped home to Louisiana, however two friends stole the cadaver from the airport, returned it to Joshua Tree and cremated it in the desert as part of a longstanding pact. The friends were eventually found guilty and fined for the theft and the cremation but curiously only of the coffin since, at that time, stealing a body was not considered a crime.

Jimmy Miller who had produced Spencer Davis albums and co-written *I'm a Man* with Stevie Winwood went on to produce *Beggars Banquet, Let it Bleed, Sticky Fingers, Exile on Main Street* and *Goat's Head Soup* for the Stones, directing proceedings during their finest hours. Although he went on to work with Motorhead and Johnny Thunders, it seemed to many that somehow the life had been sucked out of him when the needle went into him. 'Mr. Jitters' as Marianne Faithfull called him, died of liver disease. Richards later told Crawdaddy magazine, "Jimmy went in like a lion and came out like a lamb. We wore him out completely; same with Andrew Loog Oldham, burned out like a light bulb". Of Gram Parsons, he remarked, 'Gram was one of my closest friends. Unfortunately, many of my closest friends have died suddenly".

Jack Nitzsche had co-written *Needles and Pins* with Sonny Bono that was a hit for the Searchers. He contributed many 'bricks' to Phil Spector's 'wall of sound', which reached its apotheosis with Ike and Tina Turner's *River Deep Mountain High* and he would contribute keyboard parts to *Paint it Black, You Can't Always Get What You Want* and *Ruby Tuesday*. When hanging out with the Stones, he naturally ran into Marianne Faithfull and started working on *Sister Morphine* with her, telling her stories of an unhappy marriage and revealing an obsession with the San Andreas fault in California and how someday everybody was going to fall down the hole when the earthquake struck. Nevertheless, moth-like he moved back there.

While it's true to say Nieztsche had a continuing occasionally glittering career, which peaked with him getting an Oscar for *Up Where We Belong* for the movie *An Officer and a Gentleman*, it was a career plagued by alcoholism and substance abuse (he had also been arrested for violently assaulting his girlfriend), bad habits that more likely than not stemmed from the London years. Before he died, he was filmed on the reality TV show *Cops*, being arrested for pointing a gun at some youths who had stolen his hat. He can clearly be heard pathetically telling the cops that they shouldn't arrest him; didn't they know he had an academy award?

Another American who frequently commuted the Atlantic was Phil Spector, who was a long-term mentor to Andrew Loog Oldham. The Beatles (sans Paul McCartney) had of course, used Spector on *Let it Be*; he produced *Bangla-Desh* with George Harrison and Lennon used him on various solo singles. He was even A&R director of Apple Records for about a year. However, it was while recording the *Rock 'n' Roll* sessions with Lennon that, some accounts suggest, Spector seemed to experience some kind of breakdown in the studio, pulled a gun, fired a shot and made off with the tapes. Others say that it was Lennon's aberrant, drunken behaviour that inspired the incident. However, things were never quite the same for Phil thereafter; he had a terrible car accident and became a virtual recluse.

Spector eventually emerged from his seclusion and could be seen drinking on Sunset Strip and flirting with cocktail waitresses, one of whom, Lana Clarkson, went back to his house and wound up shot to death. Just weeks before the shooting, Spector told the Daily Telegraph that he had bipolar disorder and that he considered himself "relatively insane". He is in prison pending an appeal.

Another young American, the Boston born Joe Boyd came, saw and conquered. He ran the UFO Club with John Hopkins; he produced *Arnold Layne* for Pink Floyd; he produced Fairport Convention and Nick Drake and although he has had his skirmishes with drugs and the concomitant excesses of being involved with the pop world of 60s London; he has so far lived to tell the tale in his book called *White Bicycles*. Perhaps because he wisely stayed outside the Rolling Stones' inclusion zone, Joe has survived but unfortunately his protégée Nick Drake hasn't.

Some got out alive; there were exceptions like Joe but generally the rate of attrition among the musicians and their hangers on was appalling. The flower of youth was going down the plughole, flushed away, usually by its own hand.

Lucifer Rising, Kenneth Anger and Bobby Beausoleil

Drifting in and out of the Jagger, Richards, Robert Fraser axis, American filmmaker and self-confessed warlock, Kenneth Anger held for many an otherworldly quality. Someone spoke of being at a party and seeing Anger across the room but on attempting to cross to talk to him, suddenly he was gone. Others swore they'd seen him there too but also couldn't locate him to talk with. Only later did they find out that the omnipresent Anger had actually been in Paris that night.

When Anger, who was a devotee of Aleister Crowley, the Satanist who had been called "the wickedest man in the world", made the short film *Lucifer Rising*, the gang was all there. Shot in the Egyptian desert (and in Robert Fraser's apartment), Donald Cammell is Osiris and his stunning girlfriend Myriam Gibril is Isis. Marianne Faithfull plays Lilith, and Jimmy Page, also a Crowley fan, provided 23 minutes of soundtrack music, as well as making a split second appearance in the film looking at a picture of Crowley. That indulgent rock stars and avant-garde film directors should be fascinated by Crowley and his cult of Thelema is not difficult to explain. One of its doctrines, 'There is no Law beyond Do what thou wilt' seems to be a licence to do anything you damned well please; it's the ultimate libertine credo.

Lucifer was originally played by Jagger's brother Chris (Mick wouldn't do it) but after arguments on the set, Chris Jagger flew home and Anger took the lead role himself. Anger cast Cammell as the Lord of the Dead because of Cammell's supposed obsession with death. He was well cast. In 1996, Cammell shot himself in the head. There is a story that after the suicide attempt, Cammell survived for

45 minutes and that he asked his wife to prop him up with cushions and get a mirror so that he could watch himself die, although this has been repudiated by Rebecca and Sam Umland in their authoritative book *Donald Cammell: A Life on the Wild Side*.

Bobby Beausoleil had been the original star of the first version of *Lucifer*. A musician from Santa Barbara, he had talked his way into a job playing rhythm guitar with a band called Grass Roots, an early incarnation of Arthur Lee's Love, and knocked around with Frank Zappa in LA. He was a good-looking boy, which may be why Arthur wanted him in the band, to attract the girls and, Bobby reckons, the guys too since the band frequently played in gay bars. Beausoleil also claims that Arthur Lee called the band Love after him because his nickname at the time was Cupid. However, he used to get angry when anyone referred to him or those around him as hippies, preferring to call himself a 'barbarian'.

It was when he was playing in another band, the Orkustra, that Kenneth Anger spotted him and asked him to appear in *Lucifer Rising*. Beausoleil listened to this strange character going on about him appearing in his new movie, about the occult and about Crowley. He listened to the story of Isis and Osiris and about the dawn of the age of Aquarius and was justifiably dubious but then Anger started his seduction. He began saying things that turned the aspirant young pop star's head; he said he knew the Rolling Stones: better than that, he knew the Beatles.

Beausoleil moved into Anger's house, an old Russian embassy building that he had leased and which had a magickal circle that was already painted on the floor before Anger moved in. They shot some material together and then had a bust up, apparently over some marijuana, Anger alleging that Bobby had made off with his film and his car; Bobby counter-alleging that there hadn't been a film to steal – just scraps of test footage - and that maybe Anger was trying to avoid admitting to his backers that he hadn't made a film yet. Anger's response was to put the 'curse of the frog' on him.

Rejected by Anger, Beausoleil drifted around LA for a bit and then ran into Charles Manson playing the guitar on Malibu beach. It was a fateful meeting. They stayed in touch; Beausoleil was drifting up and down the Pacific Coast highway between LA and San Francisco while Charlie and his harem were similarly bumming around the coast and the desert in a school bus. Every now and again, one or the other would acquire a house and they would meet and play music. They both knew Dennis Wilson from the Beach Boys who had allowed the Manson 'family' to stay on his estate; he and Wilson got Manson into the studio to record him.

How did Manson meet a Beach Boy? Wilson had one day stopped to pick up two girls hitchhiking and taken them back to his house in the Pacific Palisades. It turned out they were from Manson's family. When Wilson came home one night, the whole Family had moved in. It was a pretty sick relationship; Manson and Wilson would play guitar together and be waited on by female slaves but there was a price to pay. The Family ran up bills of thousands of dollars for this that and the other in the few months they stayed, including $21,000 for a wrecked motorcar. Wilson paid out.

At other times, Manson stayed at the Spahn ranch. It was on an old film set of a western town that had been used for episodes of the *Lone Ranger*, a cowboy programme featuring a masked man, a horse called Silver and an Indian called Tonto.

The Spahn ranch (and Charlie's girlfriends) proved an irresistible draw to local motorcycle gangs, the Straight Satans and Satan's Slaves who hung out or lived there alongside the Manson gang. Bobby met up with the motorcycle outlaws there and when one day they wanted drugs, he told them he could get them some, no problem. He took $1,000 of their money and visited an acquaintance, Gary Hinman, a revolutionary communist and musician with a mescaline factory in his basement, who sold him some drugs, which Bobby gave to the bikers.

The following day, one of the bikers put a knife to Bobby's throat and told him that the mescaline had been no good and they wanted their money back. Worse, the stuff had been sitting around for so long it had turned to strychnine and they had all been poisoned by it. One of the bikers offered him a gun to assist the debt collection and Beausoleil went back to see the dealer with two of the Manson girls riding alongside.

When Hinman told Bobby he couldn't pay, Bobby whacked him with the gun a couple of times. Then the story gets murky; Bobby says he left one of the girls with the gun covering Hinman while he was walking around the house looking for valuables. Supposedly the girl allowed herself to be overpowered and Hinman took the gun. Bobby returned and the two men struggled; the gun went off, its bullet going through the side of the kitchen sink; eventually Bobby regained the gun. At some point, Hinman was slashed across the face and ear with Beausoleil's knife. Another account says that one of the girls had called Charlie Manson saying that things had got out of hand and that when Manson arrived, he walked in the door, slashed Hinman across the face with a sword and then left.

Beausoleil says that he calmed Hinman down and they agreed that Bobby should take possession of two vehicles that belonged to Hinman as recompense; then he treated the injured man and stitched up his ear with some dental floss - he couldn't let him go to hospital because of the anticipated repercussions – but Hinman insisted on seeing a doctor and threatened to go the police. In a panic, Bobby stabbed him and killed him. Then they daubed 'Political piggy' on the wall in the dead man's blood to make it look as if some heavyweight local revolutionaries might have been the perpetrators.

At first the police had no leads and assumed the case would remain unsolved – just another hippie weirdo killing; then they got a break. Stupidly, Beausoleil had made off in one of the victim's 'repossessed' cars and ten days later was apprehended by the police sleeping inside it at the roadside where it had broken down. He had no driver's licence and had a knife in a sheath on his belt. He was arrested.

A day or so later Manson's Family killed a preganant Sharon Tate, the actress wife of film director Roman Polanski, and others in what became known as the Tate-La Bianca murders. One of the Manson women wrote 'PIG' in Tate's blood on the front door of the house and 'Death to the pigs' on a refrigerator – an echo of the Hinman murder. Also daubed on the wall was 'Helter Skelter'; Manson was obsessed with the Beatles, especially with a selection of tracks from the 'White' album: *Blackbird, Revolution* and *Piggies,* but *Helter Skelter* in particular. He regarded the raging rock song as his licence to kill.

The gang murdered another couple the following night; there was a suggestion that Manson had ordered the murders in an effort to manipulate the police into thinking that Beausoleil was innocent and that the real murderers were activists – perhaps black activists. It was further suggested that Beausoleil was a fully paid up member of the Family and had performed the first murder on Manson's orders – something he denies. If that was the plan it failed.

Bobby was tried, found guilty and sentenced to death. After sitting on death row for three years, the law was changed, the death sentence repealed and Bobby was put into the main prison system while he planned a series of appeals. They all failed too and he is still in prison after 38 years.

At some point, Beausoleil got back in touch with Kenneth Anger who had finished *Lucifer Rising.* At this point, Anger and Jimmy Page had fallen out over the film score, which Page had taken three years to complete and which Anger didn't like (Page was given a curse as well). Bobby convinced Anger that *he* should be allowed to put together a score and with the aid of a few thousand dollars from Kenneth he started building instruments and recruiting a band from within the prison. With a makeshift studio knocked up in a cell, the cons recorded the soundtrack, which is on the final version of the film.

Once so sweet looking that he was nicknamed 'Cupid', Beausoleil later developed a far more devilish demeanour. Bearded and heavily tattooed with cartoon nymphets and occult designs, he has the word 'Lucifer' emblazoned across his chest (as does Kenneth Anger). It took him years to complete the tattoo with black ink and the broken end of a guitar string.

Kenneth Anger became obsessed with the Stones, according to Marianne Faithfull. He alleged that Mick, Keith, Anita and Brian Jones had 'Witch's tits', that is to say, they each had nipples in addition to the two traditional nipples on other parts of their bodies. It was said that witches would suckle their familiars or even the devil himself from these hidden, unholy marks and it was marks like these that the Witchfinder General of 17th century England and other witch hunters of the era would look for. Those suspected would be stripped, shaved and their bodies minutely examined for any blemish that could be regarded as diabolical. Once found, the victim's fate was assured.

Anger said that Brian Jones had a witch's tit on his leg and that he (Anger) had seen it. Jagger went along with these tales for a while, indulging Anger, who clearly adored Mick, but then when Mick tired of the stories of the black arts, Anger was given to hurling copies of William Blake's books through the window of the Cheyne Walk house. Jagger collected all the black magic books and burned them all in the great fireplace. Kenneth then had a contretemps with Robert Fraser, but Fraser was spared a curse; instead a little package containing a razor blade was posted to him with a note saying 'A cure for your stutter'.

Kenneth's first short film, made when he was 17; is about a young man, played by Kenneth, who dreams he is raped by some American sailors – racy stuff for the immediate post war years. French filmmaker Jean Cocteau, himself gay and a campaigner against homophobia invited Anger to Paris where through his twenties Anger was the avant-gardistes' toast of the town, sitting at pavement cafes talking strangeness with the likes of Frederico Fellini and Paul Getty. When funds became scarce, Anger wrote two books *Hollywood Babylon I* and *II*, exposés of the more wicked stars and starlets of Tinsel Town, from silent film stars Lillian and Dorothy Gish (were they incestuous lesbian lovers?) to Judy Garland (dead of a barbiturate overdose sitting on the toilet in her Chelsea house).

His film *Scorpio Rising*, often assessed as his best, is all bikes, bikers and bulging crotches but it, and *Lucifer Rising*, were enormous influences on the likes of Gus Van Zandt and Martin Scorsese who, despite the slim portfolio of Anger's finished work puts him right up there with the greats. The third significant short Anger made was *Invocation of My Demon Brother*, crammed with occult symbols and featuring a monotone soundtrack written and performed by Mick Jagger on an early Moog synthesizer, not dissimilar to the one seen in

Performance (the unreliable device was later bought by Tangerine Dream).

Quick to promote his relationship with the Rolling Stones (as he is to say that he was a child star when evidence of such is hard to find), Anger claims it was he who inspired Jagger to write *Sympathy for the Devil*. That is quite possibly true. Since then, Anger has turned on his idol, bitchily referring to the Stones as a "ragtag band of senior citizens".

These days, the steam has gone out of Anger's career; his output remains limited and he lives alone, a chronic insomniac, with few possessions in a tiny apartment in a seedy area of LA, but he may yet have one last grand moment when, if ever, the third instalment of *Hollywood Babylon* comes out. It threatens to dish the dirt on some more modern household names and is so potentially libellous that the publishers may have to wait for its subjects to die before they put it out. Perhaps there are lurid stories in it about some of the three-in-a-bed activities of Donald Cammell.

26

Donald Cammell –

Performance director, libertine

HAVING 'the wickedest man in the world', Aleister Crowley around the house when you were a kid might not have been the healthiest influence on Donald, the director of *Performance* and a whole lot more. And the family home wasn't really a house so much as a tower on the Royal Mile opposite Edinburgh Castle. Known as the Outlook Tower, on its roof it has a camera obscura, an optical device, which projects a view of Edinburgh on to a table. Perhaps Donald's obscure view of the world was seeded here. The tower is now open to tourists as part of a world of illusions show.

The family were the Cammells of Cammell-Laird, the ship builders, although the family fortune had long been lost in the Wall Street crash. Donald's father Charles had been a great fan of Dante Gabriel Rossetti, which must have given Donald a charge later in life when he spent so much time hanging out in Paul Getty's house in Cheyne Walk where Rossetti had lived with peacocks and a wombat. Cammel senior had also written a book about the old Satanist Crowley.

Donald's prodigious artistic talents were spotted at an early age; it's said he could appreciate perspective at the age of only three. He was educated in a Scottish monastery and then in London where he won numerous art prizes before going off to Italy to study with Pietro Annigoni, later famous for painting some of the most accomplished pictures of HRH Queen Elizabeth. After a row with Annigoni, Cammell returned to London, gained a scholarship to the Royal Academy and moved in to flat 2, Chelsea Manor Studios in Flood Street next door to the studio where the Sergeant Pepper sleeve was photographed and up the road from Maggie Thatcher's house.

As well as studying, he set himself up as a portrait painter and this allowed him to indulge in his other great passion, seducing women. Two of his notable conquests were Barbara Steele the actress best known for her horror movie roles and cat woman Eartha Kitt. Another was Jill Ireland, David (*The Man From Uncle*) McCallum's wife. He was mixing in exulted circles now and was photographed at his easel by the society photographer Antony Armstrong Jones, later Lord Snowdon, one-time husband of Princess Margaret. Donald painted a portrait for Margaret.

Plagued by dark depressions, which he tried to combat by taking lithium and amyl nitrate, Cammell was, when not in a gloom, generally cheerful and quite fit; he used to train with weights and was apparently an accomplished Scottish dancer. A contemporary of his observed that Mick Jagger had intently watched Donald dancing one day, with his head held erect and arched back, hands on his hips and taken more than a little of that stance on board when practicing his own dance steps.

Cammell abandoned the Royal Academy early, much to his father's consternation; they rowed about the matter over dinner and precocious Donald showed an early sign of his fiery nature by throwing a glass of wine in his father's face. The film business beckoned; he had been a lifelong movie devotee and a great fan of Marlon Brando whom he had hero worshipped since his school days. An encounter with his idol Brando in Paris had a profound effect on Donald, despite the curious circumstances of their meeting. Brando was being treated for second-degree burns to the testicles after spilling a pot of hot water into his lap in a restaurant. Cammell sat by the hospital bed where Brando lay, his body shaved, wearing a diaper.

When he married one time Greek beauty queen Maria Andipa his moods lifted for a while but when she discovered she was pregnant everything changed. Donald didn't want a child in his life. Maybe it was selfishness or possibly it was because he thought he was carrying a damaged gene (one of his films was entitled *The Demon Seed*) and didn't want to curse the child with it, In the event, it caused the end of the marriage and Cammell had little to do with the unfortunate child and rarely mentioned him ever again. Many of his friends never knew he even had a son.

Two months after the birth, Cammell had fled to New York. It was here he met Deborah Dixon, a model, who became his companion for the next eight years during which time he started talking about suicide, often quoting an Aleister Crowley document given to them by Kenneth Anger, "Man has the right to live by his own law… to die when and how he will". Dixon's income allowed Donald to live the rich bohemian lifestyle he craved so perhaps as a tonic they moved to Paris. Roman Polanski recalled seeing Donald sitting in a café with Amanda Lear, Salvador Dali's mistress and biographer. Nico, also modelling, was a friend. Perhaps because of the beautiful women he found there, Cammell decided that Paris was his spiritual home and took French citizenship.

Another encounter with a Euro wanderer happened in 1961, or 1962, when Donald met Stash, Prince Stanislas Klossowski, son of Balthus the painter who despite his pedigree was on his uppers and contemplating suicide. Cammell took the homeless young Pole under his wing and helped him straighten out. That he needed money was obvious and it may be just a coincidence but during those early 60s years when they were closely associated, a number of what appeared to be Balthus's trademark risque works started appearing in Paris. It has been alleged that Stash had stolen the pictures from his father's studio, that

Cammell had touched them up a bit and then they had been put on the market.

In an unmade film *El Paso* that Cammell had written, he has his lead character voice an opinion on Cammell's favourite artist Caravaggio, "who risked a life of solid respectability to descend into the twilight world, to consort with thieves and murderers, to put his life on the line. Because only then did he feel that he could paint the truth".

Was Donald getting some thrills by defrauding galleries and making himself some cash into the bargain?

Another beautiful model, Anita Pallenberg, appeared on the Paris

scene and she was recruited into the group that came to be the nucleus of the Stones' Chelsea set (Cammell met the Stones at one of the Paris shows). There was, of course, much flitting off to Morocco the rich hippie hangout where Cammell met Kenneth Anger: the two hit it off; of course they did; they had Aleister Crowley in common.

Making movies became Donald's main preoccupation and he wrote a number of screenplays and treatments including: *Avec Avec*, a heist caper which became *Duffy* starring James Coburn, Susannah Yorke, James Mason and James Fox and *The Touchables*, about four dolly birds who live in a pleasure dome and kidnap a rock star (based on Brian Jones) as a sex toy. Through his career, his films have contained references from his own life and *Duffy* is a case in point; in it a wealthy shipping magnate has sons from two marriages but the reference could end there; the father is shown as manipulative and unscrupulous, traits that could not easily be attributed to Donald's father despite the fact the two did violently argue about Donald's decision to give up painting. In the film, both father and son are exotic dandies in dress and personality and they share a girlfriend. Cammell it's said was a big fan of the ménage a trois, though he had not, as far as we know, indulged in such a practice with his father. The girl they share is amoral, sadistic even and is treated as a sex object; a commodity.

In The *Touchables*, four women share one man; in *Performance* Turner (Jagger) has Anita Pallenberg and Michele Breton at the same time. In a later film *The Wild Side* he uses the ménage a trois device on two occasions. In *Duffy*, James Mason talks of having sex on a plane and of a girl lifting her skirt to show him a tattoo on her thigh; in *The Wild Side*, Anne Heche has sex on a plane. In *White of the Eye*, one of Donald's last efforts, a character lifts her negligee to show a tattoo on her thigh. Sexual fantasies. Obsessions.

Given these clues by his films, it's not hard to see where the plot for *Performance* came from. In *Duffy*, the lead character is a thief and a collector of modern art (Cammell had known a retired jewel thief who had inspired the story). He himself was an aesthete who hung around with gangsters – David Litvinoff and later John Bindon – in fact, if he had been touching up Balthus' paintings for money then he'd dabbled in a bit of criminality himself. In *Performance*, Turner the burned out rock musician invites James Fox the violent criminal into his house. In a later film *El Paso* there are two key figures, the gangster and the film director. The magician Kenneth Anger also had some claim to be responsible for the feel of the film. Anger was, Cammell said, "the major influence at the time I made *Performance*", adding that the film was "directly attributable to him".

In the years after *Performance*, Cammell wrote scripts and tried to get finance for this and that but his films rarely got made and the reputation that *Performance* had given him was beginning to fade. His co-director Nic Roeg had since directed the highly regarded *Walkabout* and *Don't Look Now* and was soon to direct *The Man Who Fell to Earth* with David Bowie. Roeg was now regarded as an auteur, while a frustrated Donald, eager for something to happen, began to look less like the hot London director who'd once worked with Mick Jagger just looking for a bit of finance and more and more like a desperate hustler. It's a fine line.

The talk of suicide recommenced when he returned to New York; one day his then girlfriend Myriam couldn't find him. Cammell eventually turned up saying he'd been on the roof and that he had been considering jumping. According to his brother David, Donald had been preoccupied by suicide and talked about it before his eleventh birthday. These were obvious cries for attention but in

Donald's case, cries that should perhaps have been taken more seriously.

However, his pursuit of the beauties of the age was unremitting. Patti D'Arbanville, (who inspired the Cat Stevens songs *Lady D'Arbanville* and *Wild World*), and actresses Faye Dunaway and Jacqueline Bisset were all said to have liaised with the driven, dissipated Donald.

He married Patty Kong whom he renamed China, because, he stated with typical arrogance, it sounded less ordinary, when she was just 18 and he was 44. He'd known her since she had been 11. Kong's mother was a long-term friend of Marlon Brando who was disgusted by the relationship and as a protest dropped out of Cammell's film *The Demon Seed*, which should have starred him playing opposite Julie Christie. He also threatened to get Cammell deported; there was even talk of getting Cammell charged with statutory rape. During the shooting of the film, 'China' exacerbated the problem by walking around the set in sheer dresses with nothing on underneath which only served to further alienate the film's conservative backers.

Time passed and Cammell's great hero Marlon Brando got over his distaste for the sexually driven Englishman and together they started to write *Fan Tan*, sitting together for months on Brando's Tahitian island drafting and redrafting the script but in the end, Brando's interest waned and he bailed out on the project, leaving Cammell staring at another failure. In desperation Donald tried to turn the project into a book but the capricious Brando wouldn't assent to its publication. Cammell resolved to simply wait until Brando died and then publish the work but of course, Brando,  bloody-minded to the end, survived him. The book is available now and is highly regarded; the Washington Post wrote that Cammell "had the makings of a fine novelist". Donald would never know of the accolade.

Although the film business may have been forgetting about *Performance*, the music business hadn't, or at least U2 hadn't forgotten it, or its director Donald Cammell. To them he represented a truly exotic figure; the man who had made what is undoubtedly Britain's best gangster movie, which is also possibly Britain's best pop movie. To them Cammell was an authentic voice from the 60s; after all he had been one of the inner set, who'd sat cross-legged on the Persian rugs smoking dope with the likes of Brian, Mick and Keith, Paul, George and John. Donald directed their *Pride (In the Name of Love)* video. That song appeared on the album *The Unforgettable Fire,* the album that propelled U2 into the world arena.

But it was a temporary triumph and soon Donald was back on his lifelong project, to get Marlon Brando on screen, the two names side by side on the poster: 'Brando and Cammell'. And it has to be said Brando was sufficiently enamoured of Cammell to devote weeks and months to their so far fruitless collaborations. They worked together on a movie script for something tentatively called *Jericho* in which

Brando would play a burned out CIA agent on a vengeance trail. The end scenes were to be "unbelievably bloody", as Cammell put it. During the writing process, Brando went off to make another movie and when he returned he was, yet again, utterly disillusioned with the movie business. He told his partner that basically he loathed making films, which spelt the end of the *Jericho* project. Donald realised finally that his dreams of a co-production with Marlon Brando were never going to happen and that further attempts to make it happen would only lead to yet more crushing disappointment and frustration. Worried for his own sanity, he never attempted to work with the capricious Brando again.

The nearly movies continued as did the suicide threats; Cammell was being relentlessly minced by the movie machine as have so many Hollywood dreamers before and after him. A year before he finally successfully killed himself, his wife China left him for a younger man and this was a fatal blow. He spent a year in misery and although she returned just before his suicide it is thought it was only a visit while she finalised plans to leave him for good.

Cammell opted to despatch with himself with a gun, going out with a bang as it were; these were after all the last few frames of the movie of his life. When he shot himself in the head, with a .38 Smith and Wesson Special, he didn't aim the gun at his temple like in Russian roulette but instead pointed it at the top dead centre of his forehead - execution style. This was reminiscent of the way that Chas shoots Turner in *Performance*. When the pathologist did a toxicology report, he reported that there were no drugs or alcohol traces in Donald's body; the man who, according to David Litvinoff, had tried every drug known to man was, at the moment of his suicide, as clean as a whistle.

In searching for reason for his suicide, Rebecca and Sam Umland in their book *A Life On The Wild Side* suggest that quite apart from his exceedingly patchy film career and the failure of his marriage, there is circumstantial evidence that Donald may have been sexually assaulted while he was a boarder at a monastery in the 40s. Certainly someone who chattered about suicide at such a young age would seem to have suffered some sort of trauma early in life, a life, which, in his youth at least, had otherwise ostensibly been happy.

Undoubtedly he was one of the most prominent libertines in that decadent period, a fan of group sex and dabbling with homosexuality. He even suggested he'd had an affair with Mick Jagger during the filming of *Performance*. However since Jagger was supposed to be having it off with Anita Pallenberg at this time, the suggestion has to be taken with a pinch of salt otherwise with all that libidinous behaviour going on, when did they do any filming? At other times Cammell denied he was gay but then a TV documentary about him, *Donald Cammell: The Ultimate Performance* dug up a couple of pictures, one showing Cammell and David Litvinoff (a well known homosexual) standing naked together, and another showing Litvinoff holding Cammell's not insubstantial knob in his hand.

Given to explosive rages, often towards women and a reckless driver, the Umlands conclude (in meticulous detail) that Cammell suffered from a borderline personality disorder. Whether this condition bestowed him with the power to be the exciting avant-garde film director he was or whether conversely it held him back from scaling much greater heights, we can only speculate about. His death, by his own hand, ended any chance of our finding out. The long talked of suicide finally happened. "I predicted Donald Cammell's suicide", said Kenneth Anger at the *Tampere International Short Film Festival* in 1998. "He was in love with death".

One associate said of him, "he was the kind of guy who would fuck the producer's wife and then wonder why the film didn't get made". Roman Polanski said, "I loved Donald but he was wicked. He was a wicked guy".

27

Apple Turnover – Who Let the Dogs In?

SOMETHING happened at the end of the Summer of Love and before what has been called 'the Winter of Disillusionment' – the music, the drugs, the Beatles all changed. Quite possibly the Beatles had taken hippie-dom as far as it could go. With Apple they had experimented with an open door, open arms policy; they had tried to set up an edifice which would take music, electronics, film, the spoken word - all brought to them by a set of dreamers - and try and make those dreams come true. In its brief life, it was the least cynical multi-million pound organisation on the face of the earth. With its on-site cordon bleu chefs and its young eccentric owners, a proto-Google, it was a philanthropic, straight-from-the-heart, full-of-soul, chancer's paradise.

One of the fundamental problems was that with the exception of Mary Hopkin and the Beatles, none of the artists could sell records. After Apple's demise, Lennon complained to his chronicler Miles, "Apple was a manifestation of Beatle naiveté, collective naiveté, and we said we're going to do this and help everybody and all that. And we got conned just on the subtlest and the most gross level. We didn't really get approached by the best artists, or any of the recording thing;

we got all the bums from everywhere - they'd been thrown out from everywhere else. And the other people who were really groovy wouldn't approach us because they're too proud... I tried... to see everyone, like we said "You don't have to get down on your knees" - I saw everyone day in day out and there wasn't anybody with anything to offer to society or me or anything. There was just 'I want, I want'"

It couldn't keep going.

Richard deLillo (Apple's resident House Hippie) in his book about the rise and fall of Apple: *The Longest Cocktail Party* described the lobby of the Apple HQ, "the place looked a bit like the waiting room of a VD clinic in Haight Ashbury in 1967. And sometimes like the casting office for extras in a spaghetti Western..."

The sofas groaned under the weight of deluded, kaftan-wearing shirkers and soi-disant entrepreneurs. There was a chap who wanted to do Punch and Judy shows on Brighton beach, an Irish tramp who wanted to burn dolls with Napalm as an anti-war protest, a Canadian furniture salesman who wanted the Beatles to finance his new shop; a family moved into the offices, the mother breast fed her baby in reception while her other children, all naked, ran screaming from room to room; they wanted John and Yoko to set up a home with them on an island in Fiji. There were some Californian Hells Angels (who also moved into the offices), who'd arrived with the Merry Prankster Ken Kesey, there was a girl who wanted the Beatles to pay for her to have her teeth capped; there were loons and messiahs and devil worshippers, some of whom arrived penniless at Heathrow and just offered the names of John and Paul up as sponsors. They were all, on the orders of Derek Taylor, Apple PR and the Beatles' representative on earth, given a scotch and coke, a puff on a joint, some words of encouragement and sometimes even some money. The Canadian furniture salesman started blustering and was just shown the way out.

Taylor was, in many ways, the embodiment of the whole hippie dream, resolutely refusing to become cynical about the layabouts cluttering up the reception of the Beatles' offices, until the last possible moment, until financial ruin was staring them all in the face. In one two week period, his office went through 600 packs of Benson and Hedges, the favoured cigarettes for joint rolling, four bottles of Courvoisier brandy, three bottles of vodka, two cases of J&B scotch, plus cases of bitter lemon, tomatao juice, lime, tonic water, ginger ale, four cases of lager and god knows how much marijuana. Then, the day's work complete, he and some journalists would go off to check out the clubs.

When Derek wasn't drinking scotch and Coke with mad people, he would be beating off the newspapers or spending an inordinate amount of time trying to get the increasingly remote Beatles all together in one room at the same time to sign papers or chat to the press or for this or that or any other reason. It was almost impossible. However, something he did succeed at was the legendary Monterey Festival, which was basically put together by him, a couple of Mamas and Papas and Paul McCartney's address book. It was the event that saw Swinging London up sticks and go on holiday to the west coast of America, Taylor remarked: "We decided to hold a festival to celebrate all that was being achieved. The idea was to spread music and love and peace and turn everyone on; turn them on to the good life and the colourful life and to give money away as fast as we could because we seemed to have plenty of money. If we wanted 100,000 flowers flown in from Hawaii, we did, if it seemed like a good idea at the time…"

To our modern ears and our hardened hearts in the land of the ticket scalper and the *Dragon's Den* this all sounds ultra naïve, profligate and downright stupid but the sweet sentiment encapsulates the era, ephemeral as it was, and whispers to us over the years, of a time of hope.

At Monterey, Brian Jones got up on stage to introduce Hendrix, then Otis Redding stole the show; The Who smashed everything to pieces, but what everyone wanted to know was, 'where are the Beatles?'

Taylor spoke about the frenzied speculation among the crowd that the band was actually in attendance at Monterey, hiding behind disguises, and that at any moment they would spring on to the stage and play a set. "The Beatles were there of course at Monterey", he said, "but only in spirit because without them none of this would have happened".

The Beatles had sent a film crew with boxes of equipment, but permission to film the show was refused; the band turned rejection into an opportunity for a bit of drug smuggling; the film crew filled the air tight camera lenses with liquid acid and shipped them back to London. The acid was the incredibly potent STP variety that at the festival had incapacitated David Crosby, Andrew Loog Oldham and Pete Townshend; they talked of how just a drop of it could strip your personality away and of how the terrifying effects lasted many long hours and days. Now there were pints of the stuff on Lennon's shelf in Weybridge.

Despite the inevitable brain damage that would follow Lennon's adventures with STP and the sense that the dream was nearly at an end, Taylor remained undisillusioned: one of his great talents was to find the essential beauty in all that his golden friends were trying to achieve. Romantically he refelected on a time before powerful drugs were ripping people's minds apart: "The Beatles, those faces, that time, that music... they represented hope, optimism, wit, lack of pretension; that anyone can do it. Their capacity for survival impressed people. They just seemed unstoppable. Without anyone getting hurt or dying; it was really the longest running story since the second world war".

But the succession of freeloaders and nutcases that washed up against the doors of 3 Saville Row began to wear everyone down, not least the footman who, dressed in a Tommy Nutter suit, doubled as the office bouncer; it convinced all inside, starting with McCartney that this was all becoming a joke. In the eyes of the press, he perceived that the Beatles were becoming a laughing stock. Through their generosity and high-minded, freethinking ideals, they were becoming figures of fun – a band whose reputation and credibility had until then been inviolable. And they wouldn't stand for that.

Outside the microcosm of the band, many others also perceived that the vibe was changing, that there were a whole bunch of new people on the scene without quite the same stance, the same wide-eyed innocence and expectation, who weren't breathing the warm air of love. They *looked* like the first wave of hippies, dressed the same, used the same kind of language, man; but they seemed coarser, less idealistic, more selfish; they had a bad attitude. It was like the barbarians had entered the gates. Instead of sharing a sleeping bag with a friend, it seemed like they were waiting for their friend to go to sleep so they could steal their stash, their cash, their clothes, or their woman. The word for shoplifting was replaced by the word 'liberating'; it wasn't downright theft any more, it was 'liberation'. 'Hey man, I'm just 'liberating' these vegetables, this packet of cigs, this dole cheque, your stash'. Dreamers who wouldn't work 'for the man' had become unemployable layabouts; the unemployment statistics soared; the old men from the shires started grumbing about reintroducing conscription.

Pop music, up to that point, had somehow maintained, especially under the auspices of the Beatles, a connection with art, freethinking and expression. Money had been a kind of accidental by-product, and was considered by many to be a vulgar and corrupting ingredient in the 60s stew. Pop artists that were deemed to have gone for the pound or the dollar rather than some higher ideal were considered to have 'sold out'. 'Sell out' was a pejorative term; it was yelled at Dylan by an audience bemused by the fact that he produced an electric guitar on stage when before he had been strictly acoustic. The Who, ironically released their *Sell Out* album which featured adverts and jingles; Frank Zappa released *We're Only in it for the Money* with a parody of the *Sergeant Pepper* cover art on its sleeve.

There had been a new egality, but it wasn't communism. Those that weren't politically minded or jealous were for some reason rather proud that the Beatles and the Stones were becoming immensely rich. Their fans wanted them to have mansions and Aston Martins; they wanted them to have more money than their parents and your parents so they could humiliate adulthood by going abroad and driving Ferraris without doing a *proper* job. The kind of young man who could drive a sports car, have hair over his collar and a gorgeous girl in the passenger seat just drove your dad into blind, spluttering rage and that was great.

The Beatles and the Stones were of the people after all; they were the paragons of the age. It was all part of the new assertiveness of youth. In the main teenagers didn't want to be tractor engineers on a kibbutz, earning the same five quid a week as everyone else (although some did that); instead they were going to wear bright colours, smoke dope and go on foreign holidays. They wanted a hi-fi, a Mini Cooper and a dolly bird of their own; just like Paul McCartney; just like the picture of silent movie star Theda Bara on the masthead of his International Times (IT), who was quite literally an 'it' girl (The original intention was to put a picture of Clara Bow on the masthead. Clara was the definitive 'it' girl but a picture of Theda had been used by mistake and that spaced out, curiously contemporary look made her an icon). And if they couldn't actually live the pop star life in reality then they would live it vicariously through their idols and heroes. Put on the record, close your eyes and picture yourself in a boat on a river…

And toward the end of the long couple of summers of love, despite  the decadence, the dope and the anticipation of unlimited available sex there were still wafts of purity in the air cut, as they were, with the smell of rotting fruit.

But at Apple in Savile Row, the house where Lord Nelson's lover Lady Hamilton had once lived and where Derek Taylor tenuously remained the guardian of the vibe, when people started stealing the nick-nacks, the records, the ashtrays, the fan heaters, the televisions, the cones out of the loudspeakers; that was very irritating and reduced his faith in human nature. But when they started taking the lead from the office roof that was quite another thing; that meant the barbarians hadn't so much scaled the gates of the city, they'd unbolted them and loaded them on the lorry ready to be melted down. They were literally dismantling the dream.

Allen Klein was bought in to stem the losses, to halt the ridicule, to streamline the Apple organisation, to restore the credibility of its artists – the Fabs especially – and to find out who was stealing all their money.

28

A Very British Revolution

THE MARCH 1968 Grosvenor Square riot, in the gardens directly in front of the American Embassy, where Tariq Ali and Vanessa Redgrave led the assault and where Jagger tried to join in, until he was recognised and harassed for his autograph by fans who failed to grasp the seriousness of Jagger's (radical chic) intent, didn't halt the  Vietnam War. The May 1968 demos, sit-ins and blockades at Essex University had failed to produce a revolution. The Paris student riots had also failed to produce the partnership between the students and the workers that looked as if for a moment it might bring about a change of government. In fact it had the reverse effect and strengthened De Gaulle's grip on power. Then later in the year, the Chicago police charged peace demonstrators with truncheons and tear gas and continued to pound and kick the gassed youngsters as they lay on the floor trying to shield their heads, their eyes streaming until the blood flowed onto the concrete. The youth of the western world had got too uppity with their beads and their hair and their flowers and their fucking little bells, their spirit, their goddam opinions and their… youth! They had to be punished. Punished for being… for being young. Vague thoughts of revolution turned to revulsion for the system. The state and its agents became the enemy; bobbies became pigs.

One dark night, John and Yoko, who had been staying at Ringo's Montagu Square apartment, received a delegation of seven policemen and one policewoman, with a search warrant and two sniffer dogs, Yogi and Boo Boo. Before the cops unearthed some cannabis they were, via the letterbox, on the receiving end of a bit of lip from Lennon who at first refused to let them in while he tried to contact his lawyer, and who ended up being charged with obstruction. It had all been the handiwork of Detective Sergeant Norman Pilcher, the doyen of the celebrity drug bust. He had already targeted Eric Clapton, Brian Jones, Donovan, and Mick Jagger; now he had reached his pinnacle, he had bagged a Beatle. Some complained that he was picking on pop stars because he liked being in the tabloids, some said it was just envy; that the plodding police officers on £30 a week couldn't stand the sight of pop stars, yobos who'd never done an honest day's work in their lives sweeping past in their chauffeur-driven Bentleys. Others said that Pilcher was merely acting on the instructions of a paranoid Establishment to make an example of one of the 'vile bodies', to retard, if not snuff out the nascent 'youth' culture or 'alternative' culture or the 'underground' – call it what you will.

What dark forces of the Establishment may have given such orders we will never know but it didn't seem that it was the Labour government for when the Home Secretary Jim Callaghan read the morning papers, he'd carpeted the Detective Sergeant and asked him to explain why he had needed so many officers for such a relatively minor matter and how was it that the press had turned up at the Montagu Square house only a couple of minutes after the police? Odds on Lennon didn't call them (John's aversion to London's finest and the police generally is perhaps understandable; quite apart from the fact that they were trying hard to bust him, his mother had been killed by a car driven by an off duty policeman. The villains in the Beatles' animated film *Yellow Submarine* were dubbed 'the blue meanies').

Yellow Submarine

A few hours after the arrest, Yoko almost had a miscarriage, was taken to hospital and the baby died a few days later. Having been warned by doctors that it was going to die Lennon recorded the baby's fading heartbeat using a stethescopic microphone.

There is a story that a sixteen year-old Richard Branson, who was just out of school and running a magazine called Student had been pestering Derek Taylor to ask John and Yoko for a song to put on a flexidisc that he was going to cover mount as a giveaway on his next issue. The couple were struggling with the upcoming court case and the loss of the baby and, it seems may never have got the message, however when Branson threatened Apple with legal action, Lennon phoned the mini magnate saying he had a recording for him, asked Richard into the offices and played him the tape of the dying baby's heartbeat; a few seconds into the recording, Yoko burst into tears; Branson never used it.

On the drugs charge John was fined £150, a big enough amount for an average worker on £20 a week but not a lot for a Beatle. However the reverberations from the case echoed on for years; it led to the US authorities issuing a deportation order against him in 1971 and may have led to Yoko losing a custody claim for her child Kyoko.

But an over zealous Pilcher had attracted too much attention to himself; perhaps there were Beatles fans at the Home Office meticulously going through the records of his past busts because a year later he was to experience standing in the dock himself when he was arrested for conspiracy to pervert the course of justice; it was alleged he had committed perjury. He was convicted and sentenced to four years imprisonment. Perhaps there were other Beatles fans among the inmates of the prison ready to greet him. Instant Karma.

This affair echoed the aftermath of the Oz trial, to the extent that it directly gave rise to a corruption enquiry launched to find out why 'alternative society' magazines run from dingy basements by shabby proprietors who always seemed to be broke, were being singled out for prosecution under obscenity laws, while in Soho bloated pornographers were operating in the open with impunity and raking it in. The answer was obvious, a large number of police officers were on the take.

After due investigations, Detective Chief Inspector George Fenwick, then in charge of the "dirty" squad was imprisoned for ten years and around 400 other police officers were prosecuted and sacked for a variety of related offences. It was the Lord Chief Justice, Lord Widgery who made direct comparisons between the 'obscenity' depicted in Oz with the material available in the shops in the Soho red light district. He directed his clerk, a former merchant seaman, to pop up the road to Soho during a court recess to buy £20 worth of the hardest porn he could lay his hands on. Widgery pored over the material in his chambers; his reaction to the unwholesome products is unrecorded but he probably blanched at what he saw. Oz magazine looked like an illuminated hymnbook in comparison.

Lennon had his own brush with obscenity allegations when in 1970, the Mayfair London Arts Gallery exhibited a series of lithographs he had made of himself and Yoko. Among them were some graphic illustrations of the couple having oral sex. The blunt instrument of the law in this case was a camel hair-coated Detective Inspector Luff who raided the gallery and seized eight of the prints. Luff declared that in his view, they were the work of a 'sick mind', adding that 'many toilet walls depict work of similar merit'; he felt that the gallery should be prosecuted for obscenity on the basis of the 'great influence of John Lennon as a Beatle". The court later dismissed the charges against the gallery and its owner. Papers released thirty years later by the Public Record Office show that the police could only find two individuals of the forty or so in the gallery at the time of the raid, who were prepared to complain about the pictures.

29

The Death and disposal of Judy Garland

BLAISES Club at the Kensington Imperial Hotel, 121 Queen's Gate, SW7, was just a short limo ride from Brian Jones's Courtfield Road flat; it was in Blaises he and Judy Garland struck up an exotic boozing buddy thing; they lived so close he could drop her off on the way home to her glass-roofed Chelsea mews house round the corner at 4 Cadogan Lane. Judy had recently been married at the groovy quick-o drive-by Registry Office on Chelsea's Kings Road just half a mile away, where she got hitched to Mickey Deans aka Michael DeVinko, a New York disco manager who'd first met *The Wizard of Oz* star when he was doing a pharmaceuticals home delivery service and had dropped off a private prescription to her hotel room. They had their wedding reception at Quaglinos restaurant. He was gay but that didn't stop Judy announcing to the world: "This is it. For the first time in my life, I am really happy. Finally, finally, I am loved". Just over two months later, she was falling out of Blaises with Brian, both of them bombed; so far gone in fact that they were holding each other up. Two weeks later she was dead; two weeks after that, he was dead.

Judy was found by Mickey Deans bent double on the toilet. How long she'd been there was anybody's guess because rigor mortis had set in and the slight crooked body was quite rigid. She was only 47; on the death certificate it said, "Barbituate Poisoning (quinalbarbitone), incautious self-overdosage; accidental".

Apparently the press got wind of her death before the auhorities could remove the body; in minutes the mews street was staked out with photographers. Big problem: how to get rid of the body without being snapped; Judy was tiny and weightless; it was obvious really, the small stiff, still folded figure was hung over a policeman's strong arm like a folded coat and a blanket was draped over the top of her. The big cop smiled for the cameras as he departed with Ms Garland hung over his arm and the news hounds never suspected a thing.

The day Judy died there was apparently a tornado in Kansas (the location of the farmhouse she lived in as Dorothy in *The Wizard of Oz).*

After the autopsy, her body was flown to New York City; it lay in an open casket in a chapel where visitors could say their farewells. The blue velvet-lined coffin had a clear plastic snot catcher over it to protect Judy's corpse from sneezes, like you'd see in front of a salad bar in a Harvester steakhouse. Twenty one thousand people filed past to pay their respects and James Mason delivered an eulogy; among the many mourners was Dean Martin, Frank Sinatra, Lauren Bacall, Burt Lancaster Katherine Hepburn, Sammy Davis Jr., Cary Grant, Jack Benny and Lana Turner.

A week later, there was a mini wake for the mini gay icon in a gay bar called the Stonewall, in Manhattan. *Somewhere Over the Rainbow* was playing as the police entered to make a routine raid; when they tried to arrest some drag queens, the mood turned nasty and there was a mini riot. Disturbances continued over the next few nights and it has been said that this was the moment when thoughts of a gay rights movement was crystallised; a month later, the Gay Liberation Front was formed. Later when another gay campaigning group was formed, it was called Stonewall after the bar.

30

Lennon and the Island he gave away

HENDRIX looked at Lennon quizzically over the bottle of Johnnie Walker Red label.

"Whadya doin' ownin' an island?"

"Escape. There's nowhere in the world I can go where they can't find me man".

"There must be an escape place warmer than Ireland man. That coast is on the Atlantic right? I hear it's got the wind tearin' over it".

"Yeah, I should've checked that out a bit better. When we went to see it, the sun was out and I just kind of said, 'I'll buy it'".

"Those Irish must've thought you were crazy man".

"It was a crazy day. We were walkin' around with this boat builder bloke called Quinn who'd taken us over there in his boat and I was filming with me camera and he kept staring at me. Then we went to his house and I was wearing me fur coat and his dog kept barkin' at it. But it was good. They all thought we were weird people from London but the man Quinn didn't really know who I was so I thought, 'Great' – somewhere where they haven't got Beatlemania".

"Cool".

"Yeah, very cool. It was then I decided to buy it. When we walked through the village there were kids shouting out 'John' and that. Some shouted 'Paul'. But I get that all the time. I even get 'Ringo'".

"That's funny man. They don't shout Noel or Mitch at me".

"Do they shout 'Ringo'?"

"Nooo. Ringo's not as black as me man".

"Anyway, they said later... so the Irish solicitor guy was telling us... that they reckoned I was tripping when I bought it. They must think I'm on drugs all the time".

"You are on drugs all the time".

"You can fookin' talk".

"So what's gone wrong then?"

"Well I got loads of soil samples done to see if it was OK to build a house there and then I sent me caravan over - I've got a gypsy caravan that I bought for my kid Julian. I got the boat builder guy to build a special raft to float the caravan over on, and the idea was that I would stay in it, in the caravan from time to time, while the house was being built. Cos it's empty; there's nothing on it, no buildings, nothing. That was the idea; I'd be the fookin' king".

"And she'd be your gypsy queen".

"Right. Queen Yoko of Ono. Well Dorinish actually. That's what it's called, Dorinish island. She'd have been Queen Yoko of Ono Dorinish. But she didn't see it till a year after I'd bought it. We went over there in a helicopter. That freaked the fookin' locals out I'll tell you. We went over with Robert Shaw, the actor bloke, and Ronan, the guy who owns Radio Caroline – he's Irish. I thought it might help".

"And did the Caroline man help?"

"Apart from the seagulls dive bombing Yoko, it was great. We sat in the caravan and had a picnic that we took with us, and it all looked groovy you know? The sea looked beautiful and it was totally silent. Then I noticed my arse was all wet and there was like fungus growing on the walls. Then the wind started blowing and the fookin' caravan nearly fookin' blew over so we jumped in the helicopter quick and fooked off, didn't even pack up the plates and stuff. Left it like the Marie Celeste".

"The Marie what?"

"The wind cries Marie".

"I don't quite geddit man".

"No. It was an abandoned ship".

"Right. So now you're gonna give the place away? You Beatles have got more money than sense".

"You'll be rich enough soon".

"Not with the thieving son-of-a-bitch manager I've got. I'll never get an island of my own".

"Do you want one?"

"Sure I want one. But maybe down near Morocco or Mexico way, somewhere where the sun shines. Anyway, tell me why you're giving your kingdom away".

"I've found these guys; they're squatting these houses in Camden and around the place. They figure all property is theft; all that stuff. They're like gypsies but they're radical, part of the revolution".

"The revolution is in your head. They'll just rip you off like those guys who used to live in the Apple offices".

"What's to rip off? I'm not giving them any money. They're gonna put some tents on the island and start a community, an alternative community. Bring up kids there; go fishing, weave their own clothes; start a school. Sit round the fire and tell stories, sing songs. They're not bread heads. They really want to give it a try. It'll be like Swiss Family fookin' Robinson… without the ostriches".

"Yeah, don't forget Disney made that movie man. It's just a movie. And the sun was shining down there".

"Wouldn't you like to do that though? Sit around the campfire with your wife and kids and play the guitar and sing to them?"

"Yeah, one day, I've got a bit of living to do first. I've got to make some albums. Don't forgit, when you were cutting your first records, I was jumping out of aeroplanes with the 101st Airborne".

"I'd like to have seen that. It must have taken balls".

"I can think of better things to do with my balls… So you're gonna let all these gypsies live on your island?"

"Yeah. I might even drop in on them when they get established. Sit round their fire and play some songs with them".

"A band of gypsies huh?"

"Right".

The Utopian visions talked up in the dope-smoke fug-filled living rooms of Chelsea and Notting proved to be too difficult to realise in practice and remained only visions. When Lennon sang 'Nothing's gonna change my world' in *Across the Universe*, he should perhaps have sang, Nothing's gonna change *the* world. There may have been a groundswell of constantly evolving liberalism in the UK, the USA and thereafter the world but it was all incremental and for many, it was progressing at glacial speed. There had been no revolution, no insurrection, and no guillotine. The unions hadn't marched down Whitehall arm-in-arm with the young radicals, the flags of Che fluttering overhead. The army hadn't turned on its masters.

Escape from the smother of the modern world seemed to be the only remaining option for those intent on a restructured society. Perhaps, they thought, it might be possible to establish safe communal havens from where the fight could continue and in that spirit a lot of the London hippies hit the road.

The Beatles, under the influence of Magic Alex, considered buying a small group of Greek islands, a sun drenched little archipelago only a few hours from London where they could escape Pilcher and his ilk, a mini kingdom in the Mediterranean presided over by four Scousers, where they could occasionally step out of the media spotlight, get out of the spin drier and relax. There might even be tax advantages if they could only persuade the cash-strapped Labour government that they had a reasonable case for taking money out of the country. After much lobbying by the Apple big brains, Jim Callaghan conceded they could invest £90,000 abroad, on the basis that the Beatles had contributed so much to the Exchequer, that they were a special case. However by the time the government had reached its decision; Lennon had reached one of his own. "Forget the island", he told his minions. "I've lost interest".

He hadn't, however lost all interest in an island kingdom. Lennon had read that there was a small scrap of land in Clew Bay in western Ireland. He paid around £1,700 for Dorinish in 1968. From then on the locals called it 'Beatle Island'. After he abandoned his plans to build a house there, Lennon granted Sid Rawle (known as the King of the Hippies) to start a settlement there. Sid, who had once been a park attendant in Slough, now found himself the master of an empire. He sent out fliers around the flower children of London advertising for aspirant drop out settlers and moved on to the island with a party of 25 pioneers, including one child, where they reactivated an old well and erected a number of tents to house them and their supplies.

They grew vegetables, lit bonfires in the evenings and would shop in the village store once a fortnight, signalling with flags to a local oyster fisherman whenever they needed to be picked up. Dolphins scudded in and out of the bay.

However, they were soon to be made rudely aware of the terrific winds that frequently rushed across the 19-acre island, which would often dislodge boulders that clattered up and down the beach day and night. The gales would also dislodge the tents, which frequently blew into the sea and were lost, so the intrepid settlers had no alternative but to take down the smaller tents and pack boulders on top of them whenever a gale was forecast. There were many nights when they would be forced to take refuge in the main tent where they would stay huddled through the night while the savage wind raged around them, sitting on the bottom edges of the tent's wall in an effort to keep the structure on the ground.

On one particularly windy night, everyone was gathered in the main tent; it was raining heavily and the wind was sufficient to knock the settlers to the ground if they were foolish enough to venture outside. At around four a.m., figuring the last remaining tent was about to go, they took down the centre pole and heaped rocks on the canvas, then lay on the ground with the weighted wet material covering them. In the morning the sodden settlers emerged from under the canvas to a beautiful sunny day and gazed at a stricken ship that had run aground during the night. The vicious and capricious weather had beaten them. It was the end for Sid Rawle's gallant band.

Sid went back to the mainland. He joined a number of like minds in a tipi settlement in west Wales and became famous as the leader of a 'crusty' convoy and organiser of a number of Stonehenge festivals. Lennon and Yoko still harboured plans to build a house on Dorinish though and they revisited it before he was murdered. They stayed in a local hotel where there is now a bedroom called the 'John Lennon suite'. After John's death, Ono sold the island for £30,000 and gave the money to a local children's charity. Dorinish is now used for sheep grazing and is occasionally visited by the more intrepid Beatles' fans.

31

Mods, Meaden and Captain Beefheart

AT A time when all the ex-art school students (Lennon, Ron Wood, Pete Townshend, Keith Richards, Eric Clapton), were bouncing around in front of the wardrobe mirror plucking away at their tennis racquets and trying to recreate rock 'n' roll; there was a movement swiftly growing.

Mods. Modernists. In 1959, there were probably ten Mods in London. By 1964, massed scooter-riding armies were invading beach resorts like locusts on Lambrettas. The first few originals wore Italian suits, often dark blue, with button-down collar shirts and Italian or French shoes. Their natural environment was the West End's coffee bars where they made a cup of capuccino last all night while they smoked copious cigarettes and shot glances at each other's hair and clobber. The hairstyles were as Italian as the Gaggia coffee machines; kids that had for years suffered the indignity of having their fathers, sloshing British Brylcreem on their heads now wanted a 'dry' look, short and neat without quiffs. The 'French cut' was a crew cut – two inches long all over. The 'clobber', Fred Perry polo-style short-sleeved shirts, often worn with Levis; and the Harrington jacket (as worn by Ryan O'Neil in his role as Rodney Harrington in Peyton Place), became popular.

The first big time Mods: Brian Jones, Andrew Oldham, Eric Clapton or Rod 'the Mod' Stewart... and Peter Meaden.

The poor old rockers never knew what hit them. There they were, a bunch of burn up bike boys – knights of the road – just your average tearaways – Levis and leathers, handy with spanners, and all of a sudden, there they were in the middle of a style war. They didn't object to Brylcreem on their hair; why should they? Crash helmets made your hair greasy anyway. And what does a biker need to know about modernism?

Rockers liked bikes, be they BSA, Triumph, Norton, Ariel, Matchless, AJS, Royal Enfield, Vincent; they had to be British and they had to be bikes, the bigger the better. Never mind the oil and the grease; the very speed of the machines meant that your face was perpetually blackened by road grit, soot and dead flies; bikes were loud, fast and bloody dangerous and that's why they liked them.

A rocker, though he may have been able to wash up and wear casual trousers and a jacket for a wedding, still looked as if he would have preferred to be wearing a Lewis leather jacket, jeans and leather boots with white fisherman's socks folded over the top, and heading for Beachy Head to light a bonfire and drink cider. Clothes held little importance for rockers who were basically anti-fashion and couldn't give a damn if you were wearing a Tonik jacket and chisels or a duffel coat and a beard; if you didn't have a Beezah you didn't rock.

Many Rockers came from small towns and villages in the provinces while the Mods, in the main came from the city; but the Rockers didn't mind city boys; it was the scooters that the rockers objected to; scooters were anathema; the scooters and the drugs. Mods took Purple Hearts (Drynamil), couldn't pass a mirror without performing some personal grooming and were cissy. But mainly it was the scooters that were the problem.

 Mods rode Vespas and Lambrettas, or the bus if they couldn't afford a scooter – imported machines from Italy (like the coffee machines and the haircuts), which, compared to bikes, were underpowered and, if you believed the news reels and *La Dolce Vita*, often ridden by women. Scooters had brightly coloured side panels that covered the workings; that was the thing the Rockers despised most; Rockers worshipped their engines – engines that were at least twice the size of scooter engines. They spent endless hours fixing them and polishing them and souping them up, so they had to be on display; and where nasal scooter engines revved, whined and farted – wwaaaaahhhhhene-ne-ne-ne-ne-ne-ne-ne; bikes thumped, slowly, ponderously - DON, DOM, DUB, DUB, DIB, BOM, BOM; Zen and art, and motorcycle maintenance.

Then these scooters with all their unnecessary spotlights and whippy aerials with stupid tiger's tails on the top (why did they have an aerial; they didn't have a radio?) started intruding on to the new arterial roads that had previously been the domain of lorries, family Ford Anglias and the bikes. Sewing machines, the Rockers used to call scooters, ridden by inexperienced little twerps, cluttering the place up. They weren't necessarily homosexuals the Mods, but they certainly looked that way to the Rockers; poncy hipster trousers, backcombed hair, bum freezer jackets and Parkas. Some of them even wore berets. What they weren't wearing was leathers and boots and they didn't ride bikes, therefore they had to be queers and resisted.

The Rockers were right to think defensively, because the Mods were very much on the attack and the establishment was their target. Unfortunately for the poor old Rockers, they had somehow, fallen into the role of society's storm troopers, defending something they thought was essentially the status quo, when all the time they were unwittingly defending the prevailing unemployment and apprenticeship slavery – the very kind of thing that drove them on to the road every weekend in the first place - to feel fear, freedom and have a bit of fun, to escape the tedium, to flash the cash.

And, although the Rockers demonstrated a commendable evolving sense of violence to deal with the Mod threat, involving head butts, helmet swipes and lethal whirling bike chains, they were fundamentally overwhelmed by Parka-clad hordes of earnest little townies, for very many of whom, on their odyssey to the coast, it was the first time they'd ever seen the sea.

One was a club, the other a movement.

The Mods won the seaside wars hands down (one Mod weapon was the aluminium comb with tapered handle that so many of them carried in their back pockets. It was easy to sharpen the handles up with a file and voila – the comb became a stilleto. The girls carried these as well as the boys and were quick to use them to gory effect. But stabbings apart, basically the odds were against them and there are many grainy black and whites of heavily outnumbered leather boys being thrown over promenade walls or being kicked around on the beaches. However the wars were just a phase, just British tribes letting off a bit of steam.

But the original Mods couldn't identify with the influx to their own tribe; the swarms of latecomers who, they perceived, all looked and acted the same; they'd moved on; they resented the newcomers more than they resented the Rockers, and to set themselves apart, had started called themselves 'Individualists' or 'Stylists'.

The Who weren't Mods, not when they started, but Marc Bolan (of whom it was said, couldn't pass a mirror without inspecting his hair and mascara) was. Way back in 1962 when he was interviewed by *Teen* magazine, he was moaning about how hard it was to find a good tailor, but in the process did endorse John Stephen as, "Very good on trousers". Bolan became something of a spokesman for the well-dressed, youthful sect, or certainly the Stamford Hill faction of it that he seemed to occasionally lead, and was often interviewed, long before becoming a pop star. In an Observer article written in the mid 60s which already speaks of the Mod phenomenon in the past tense, Nik Cohn wrote, "Marc the Mod... used to change his clothes maybe four times each day. He was very image then, arrogant and cold and he couldn't even nod to anyone who wasn't hip. By any standards, he had style and he had cool". He was cool OK, until he went home to his parent's new house, a prefab bungalow slum situated next to the greyhound-racing track in Wimbledon. Marc didn't take girls home there, or boys or anyone.

The John Stephen's shop in Carnaby Street to which Marc alluded, was one of the first to stock Tonik mohair suits; Stephen was the first to import Levis; he prodced kilts for men, elephant cord hipsters, double breasted velvet jackets and kaftans for men; 40 years before David Beckham's sarong. You could try the clothes on without having a salesman 'helping' you. The staff was young; there was good music. John Stephen himself called you 'Sir' despite the fact he knew and you knew he knew that in reality you were working in Woolworths and this was your lunch break. The Yardbirds, the Kinks, the Stones and the Beatles using your shops didn't hinder business; Carnaby Street was invaded by camera crews; through newsreels, the world sucked up the myth.

As a consequence of his on-the-button style and unpatronising, refreshing retailing sense, Stephen made a lot of money; one shop had by 1961 become five and as soon as a new branch opened it was instantly mobbed. Apart from the London shops, he developed a chain that spread through the USA, Canada, Norway, Sweden, Germany and Italy. At the age of 20, Stephen bought the first in a succession of Rolls Royces, becoming one of the youngest Rolls Royce owners in the country and growing accustomed to the question: 'Nice motor. Is it your dad's?" He bought houses in France and Spain; you'd see him in the Mirabelle and the Ivy dressed in

Savile Row suits - not for him the flamboyant clothes he sold to the Mods – and on the chair opposite would sit his only companion, a white German Shepherd called Prince, eating coq au vin.

Another longhaired musician who was originally a Mod was Cat Stevens, more recently known as Yusuf Islam in his third carnation. Islamists and fans of the *Morning Has Broken* period of his career both, would be shocked to see the be-suited, clean shaven Cat, with back combed hair, looking every inch the Ace face and singing *I'm Gonna Get Me A Gun* on *Top of the Pops*.

Ossie Clark, designer to the new rock royalty was boasting a distinctly mod look in early photos as was his then girlfriend Celia Birtwell. They certainly had the haircuts.

It was Peter Meaden who had turned The Who (known then as The High Numbers) into Mods. He believed in that whole idea of a Mod 'movement' with its own music, style, literature, stimulants, art, films and even its own exclusive language; and, he believed that the Who should be its standard bearers. He explained the ethos to a journalist, "Modism, Mod living, is an aphorism for clean living under difficult circumstances."

Meaden was everywhere, getting the band's hair cut, supervising what they wore, trying to drum up deals, gathering gigs, getting their name in the music press, going to the gigs and proselytising; all the time chewing up 'blues' pills and clicking his fingers along to some inner raging rhythm. The Scene Club in Ham Yard was his nighttime HQ, where Guy Stevens, who was reputed to have the best rhythm and blues record collections in the country, was the regular DJ. Stevens' day job was running the Sue label for Chris Blackwell's Island label; he would import tunes from the USA like Inez Fox's *Mockingbird* and Russell Byrd's *Hitch Hike* and was the first to bring Chuck Berry to the UK.

Itinerant musicians lurked around the club on Mondays and Fridays. There they would run into all the pluggers and fixers who would be handing out tickets for recording jobs or sessions in backing bands.

The Scene also throbbed with pop star clients despite the fact they couldn't get a drink there. It had no licence and a Coca Cola was as hard as it got. But if you knew what you were doing, you could get a shot of Scotch poured into your Coke bottle; just drink a bit off to make some room, drop the guy behind the bar a 'tanner' (6d) and swig it down, and if you knew who to talk to, you could get Black Bombers or Purple Hearts as well.

When Meaden was in a pub, explaining the whole damn thing to Pete Townshend yet again, he'd usually have a Scotch and Coke, but then the words would start falling from his lips in a torrent, so fast that he never seemed to have the time to put the glass between them; an hour and 20,000 words later he'd take his first sip. In this intense milieu, he knew everyone and they all knew him. "Hi there baby. How ye doin' baby? Great. Yeah. Keep cool", talking like an American DJ, like Wolfman Jack or Alan Freed. He was one of those characters that London occasionally throws up, a super-slick pop-operator who would have been successful either side of the Atlantic.

Meaden realised that Mods didn't listen to any music in the pop charts and that there was huge potential for a band styled in the Mod image. The High Numbers already played a wide range of black music and Meaden turned them on to even more: Tamla Motown, Smokey Robinson and Curtis Mayfield. That he hung out with Andrew Oldham, the other Ace Face super-spieler, who had just got the Rolling Stones to sign on the dotted line, gave him even greater credibility and magnified his allure. All the nippers buzzed around him. But despite their fame, both Meaden and Oldham were still broke; neither of their two bands were making much more than enough to cover expenses and although Meaden was always magnificently turned out in all the latest jackets and shoes, always two steps ahead; he actually lived in his tiny office, sleeping (did he ever sleep?) underneath the desk. The only other furniture in the room was a chair, a filing cabinet and an ironing board.

He did his business in The Scene or in the De Hems bar in Macclesfield Street, Soho. It was here that the music business promoters and pluggers met up, the bandits of the business, paid richly for success and summarily sacked for failure; one bullshitter trying to impress another, the air thick with lies and desperation, with much talk of buying records into the charts. Meaden had just one mantra, "The High Numbers – get them here".

When they did put out a single, *I'm the Face*; the B-side of which was *Zoot Suit*, both tracks were written by him, such was his determination to do it the right way; his way. The record made by the band not yet called The Who only sold a few hundred copies and

Meaden had bought all of them himself in a failed effort to hype a chart position.

Nobody could keep up with him in business or in pleasure though; he pushed it to the limits, although he thought he was keeping a balance. "That's what mod living is all about", he said. "It's a continuous party, sustain it for as long as you can without doing too much damage to your body. You mustn't damage yourself too much, but take it right out on the rim". He'd obviously seen some of the casualties that had started appearing in the Soho streets and bars; slope-shouldered amphetamine addicts with sucked in cheeks, putty-like skin and rotting teeth. You crossed the road because you could smell them a block away; they'd stopped washing and their clothes were dirty. 'Speed Kills' was the message on the bog walls.

When the super-sharp duo Kit Lambert and Chris Stamp crashed in and muscled Meaden aside with a few measly quid as a pay off, everyone was amazed; Meaden turned up his toes then rallied, contemplated a come back but didn't have the resources to fight the drink-crazed, drug-fuelled Stamp/Lambert Action Management operation. His band was stolen, re-dubbed The Who in front of his eyes and hauled off to the top; there was nothing he could do about it, he was on the scrap heap.

Latterly Meaden tried to get in to see The Who at the Aquarium ballroom in Brighton, but wasn't allowed in because the place was already crammed with other Mods – Mods who showed no respect for one of the leaders of the movement because they didn't even know who Meaden was. It must have been a supreme moment of regret and also of vindication for him. 'I told you bastards they'd be big!' He'd lost his band but his band had rapidly become huge in his absence but only because it had stuck to Meaden's manual. The Who was made in his image.

Undiminished, the boy bounced back and took on the soul R&B act Jimmy James and the Vagabonds, who had occasionally supported the Who and who under his auspices, became the virtual resident band at the Marquee in the mid 60s.

He reappeared looking less like a Mod (all traces of the 'real' Mods had by now vanished) when in 1968 he'd somehow got involved with bringing Captain Beefheart and his band into the country to play in some London clubs. HM Immigration collectively freaked when it saw the assemblage of wackos that fell from a plane from Hanover, Germany and the band was held while enquiries were made.

Below is an extract from the official transcript of the refusal to land statement:

REFUSAL OF LEAVE TO LAND

Mr. VLIET is the leader of an American "pop group" known as Captain Beefheart's Magic Band, which specialises in so-called psychedelic music and is currently very popular with a certain section of the population of the West Coast of the United States. The group arrived together and presented a very strange appearance, being attired in clothes ranging from "jeans" to purple trousers, with shirts of various hues, and wearing headgear varying from conical witches' hats to a brilliant yellow safety helmet of the type worn by construction engineers. Like some of his friends, Mr. VLIET sported a bushy beard. The other members of the group whose refusal of leave to land is reported separately are:

FRENCH, John Stephen born 29.9.48 American

HANDLEY, Gerald Wayne born 9.2.46 American

SNOUFFER, Alexis Clair born 14.9.41 American

COTTON, Jeffrey Ralph born 31.5.40 American

Officers on the control were given ample opportunity to form an initial assessment of the group, as they took fully ten minutes to complete the relatively simple operation of filling in their landing cards. When they eventually approached the desks, it proved somewhat difficult to interview them, as they appeared to think on a completely different mental plane and found it difficult to grasp the rudiments of a passport control. However, it was eventually established that they had gone to Hanover from the United States to attend a musical convention and that they were now en route to a similar festival in Nice. All five members of the group possessed tickets from London to Nice and on to Los Angeles and they said that they merely wished to spend up to a week in this country on the way to France. None of them appeared very certain what the purpose of the visit to this country was, some saying it was purely for a rest, and others saying that they were to meet representatives of the press.

However, all of them denied emphatically that they had any intention of taking any form of employment during their stay.

Examination of the funds carried by the group showed that they had very little money, Mr. VLIET having two pounds 10 shillings and twenty marks (two pounds).

At this stage, a gentleman dressed in the American style, with long unkempt hair and with a cigarette dangling from his lower lip, approached the control and introduced himself as Mr. Peter Alexander Edwin MEADEN, born 11.11.41, British and described in his passport as an Artistes Manager. Mr. MEADEN said that he represented New Wave Records Ltd., 17-19 Stratford Place, LONDON, W.1., which firm was sponsoring the group's visit to the United Kingdom, in conjunction with the group's American recording company, Kama Sutra Buddha Records Ltd., New York. He offered to give any guarantees that might be required to facilitate the group's entry into the country but when asked to establish his authority to do so, he was unable to prove his connection with these companies beyond producing a press handout and some blank headed notepaper. Mr. MEADEN denied vehemently that the group would be taking any form of work during their stay here and said that he had only brought them over for press appearances.

At this stage, all five members of the group were escorted to the baggage hall, where their luggage was examined by H.M. Customs.

However, despite the fact that one member of the group had a large number of patent medicines in his case, nothing of interest was found. A search of the group's instruments and their cases was also negative.

On return to the Arrivals Hall, I was informed by a member of the Special Branch that Mr. MEADEN was known to have convictions for illegal possession of a Bren gun, taking and driving away a motor vehicle and selling intoxicating liquor without a licence. In view of this, it was felt that any assurances given by the gentleman would have to be treated with considerable reservations.

It was strongly suspected that the group were going to take engagements in this country and reference to the New Musical Express showed that they were billed to appear at two establishments the next weekend, namely the Middle Earth Club and the Speakeasy Club, both in the West End of London. These clubs were telephoned and confirmed that the group would be playing on stage as a professional engagement. Reference to the Ministry of Labour showed that Mr MEADEN had applied for Ministry of Labour Permits for the Middle Earth Club engagement but that none had been issued, as he had claimed that the group were only to meet the Press at the club and would not be playing - denied by the club who were expecting a full show. Faced with this Mr. MEADEN at first protested his innocence but finally both he and the group admitted that the engagements had been arranged. Mr. MEADEN then pleaded for clemency on the grounds of his own stupidity, a plea which was rejected.

The case was referred to the Chief Immigration Officer, Mr Armstrong, who directed that the group be refused leave to land on the grounds that they had come to this country to take unauthorised employment and with insufficient funds. They were informed that they were at liberty to contact whomsoever they wished and spent some time on the telephone before going to the Detention Suite, where they were given a meal.

Mr. Noreiko, Chief Immigration Officer, Headquarters, was informed of the case, lest there should be any representations. These soon materialised, from Mr. MEADEN's solicitors, who asked that the group be admitted for a visit. This proposal was rejected.

Later in the afternoon, H. M. Assistant Chief Inspector, Mr. T. W. E. Roche telephoned for details of the case, as the Press Officer had approached him for information.

Despite all their efforts, which were considerable, Mr. Ripp and Mr. Wise were unable to secure the issue of Ministry of Labour Permits and the group were therefore returned to Hanover as directed.

Mr. MEADEN, on whose shoulders the blame for the whole incident must rest, was told by Mr. Ripp that his association with Kama Sutra ceased forthwith and he was a dejected man as he finally departed, muttering under his breath. Landing Card attached. An extra copy of this report is attached for the Ministry of Labour.

24th January 1968

Quadrophenia, the archetypical Mod tale of Jimmy Cooper, a London Mod with multiple personalities brought Pete Townshend and Pete Meaden back together, when in 1972, they collaborated on the themes of the record and again in 1978 when Meaden helped with the film; he drew on his own Mod experiences to advise on locations and story lines and was convinced that the whole thing was all about him. He was given to saying "Townshend's writing about me, man, this is the story of my life".

In the film, Cooper takes a handful of amphetamines and drives a scooter over a cliff edge. There hangs the question; did he die or didn't he? In fact, he didn't and the trashing of the scooter was intended as the symbolic destruction of Mod as an ideal. Jimmy walks away into the mainstream of life. Unfortunately Pete Meaden, who had been working with the Steve Gibbons band, didn't. He had a mental breakdown then died at the age of 29 after taking an overdose of barbiturates; a bright point of light extinguished. He never saw the film completed, a film he regarded as about him.

Curiously, the launch of *Quadrophenia* happened at about the same time as a Mod revival swept the UK, which had as its progenitor and figurehead Paul Weller. The Jam became the best selling singles band in the UK since the Beatles.

All 'scenes' are over with as soon as they begin though. As soon as you get wind of a night out or a club, a collar design, a drug or a diet, it's over. And who starts these things, these crazes and styles? How would you know if you'd been there day one, right at the start of something; would you ever realise that? How many does it take to make a scene? More than one, that's for sure. You can't do it on your own.

32

And in the End

OF COURSE it could never last; no city ever gets to keep the crown. It's impossible to be the place of ultimate grooviness for eternity, and eventually even London's lustre tarnished. The Beatles imploded at the end of the decade and Britain's other big bands, the Stones, the Who, Floyd and Led Zeppelin had all gone global. The pop stars were all living in country mansions now; only passing through the capital for press interviews, business meetings or en route to the airport.

But still they came: while the locals had declared that the scene was all over, the word was still spreading to the outer fringes. The next generation, those only recently aware that there was a Swinging London in the first place, were packing their bags to make the pilgrimage to what they perceived to be this marvellous happening place. For them, it was only just the beginning and as much as the suddenly bored London elite resented the barbarian immigrants with their backpacks, anoraks and traveller's cheques, they could do little to stop the hordes.

Carnaby Street was given over to shoddy tat, Union Jacks and plastic policemen's helmets. It got so shabby that in 1973, the council invested £50,000 in a garishly coloured rubberised surface for the road, but even despite the municipal ersatz psychedelia, the tourists still came in search of the swinging city. London had lost its buzz and wouldn't hit the headlines again till the punks sprang spitting and snarling from Chelsea and Notting Hill but the coach loads of day trippers didn't care.

The in crowd moved on; the early 70s were trash glam and hard rock; the mid 70s were the cocaine and disco years and Manhattan was the place to dance till dawn with Bianca and Mick, Andy and Truman. Since then there have been many vibrant cities that aspire to the accolade of the world's hippest. Now kids get their kicks in Barcelona, Tokyo, Rio de Janeiro, Milan, Toronto, Sydney and Dubai. How long before Mumbai, Cairo and Hanoi start attracting the world's hip young gunslingers?

What's for sure is that, in that brief period, London seemed to have harnessed lightning. It had witnessed a youth quake; the music, fashion, art and design worlds exploded. There was unbridled optimism, sex and the whiff of revolution; there was the birth pill and other drugs, mind expansion and cash in the hip pocket. When all these planets aligned and then England won the football World Cup, down fell the fairy dust and a wave of creativity and euphoria spread out across the world from London's mighty heart. The Union Jack became a style icon; the world watched in wonder.

The Legacy of the 60s

The 60s is the decade that won't go away, ever there but forty years gone. Surely there must have been more to it than a small band of people having a really, really good time. How do you quantify a legacy? How did that indefinable 60s thing change the world? Some say that everything has changed; that it's all around, that 60s thinking permeates every strand of life, so vast is its effect that it's like standing directly under the London BT tower, you're just yards away but yet you can't see it. The 60s effect has been so all encompassing that some deny there was any effect at all, that the decade should be dismissed as just a lot of self-indulgent poncing around in crushed velvet and chiffon.

Growing up in the bloodiest century mankind has ever known, overshadowed by two world wars and at least a hundred other smaller ones, where hatred and death were the prevalent themes; is it any wonder that the 60's kids yearned for love and life? Is it any wonder that no matter how naively, they'd try to turn those themes into a new moral philosophy?

A lot of the key players in 60s London, were just out of college or not long out of school when the decade arrived. Many of their parents, uncles - brothers even - had been called up. For the others the great escape was the end of conscription, a terrifyingly brutal time when you had to wear uniforms; get your hair cut, and quite possibly someone was trying to kill you. That's quite apart from the parade ground drilling, routine sadism and shit food that constituted the late teenage years of the post war period for nearly everyone until 1960. By the skin of their teeth and accident of birth Mick Jagger and Keith, Charlie, John, Paul, George and Ringo had escaped the military although Bill Wyman didn't, serving two years with the RAF.

A relieved generation put another coin in the jukebox overjoyed that the drums of war had given way to dance beats. Up went the heat. People began to dream; they started looking forward, straining at the leash, hungry for the future, all turned on.

Isn't it obvious that those dreams, ambitions and ideals would be hitched to the potent, powerful pop bandwagon, the medium of the age; that it would be via the pop song that they sought to effect change? Those pop tunes, from the loudest most bombastic thumper down to the most delicate torch song were en masse the battle cry of the era, the sound of subversion. "It's extraordinary how potent cheap music is", Noel Coward keenly observed.

The late 50s early 60s world was a sick and violent place of looming apocalypse; back then it looked like a third conflagration was imminent and that this one would be the big one, the war to end all wars and for all the wrong reasons, a war that might possibly achieve what the other two had failed to do: annihilate the species; no one would be saved.

The Beatles and their snappy, bittersweet melodies offered an antidote to all that; they lit up the world with optimism, youthful ambition and not a little insolence, directed entirely towards the establishment.

We had manifestly failed to build a country fit for heroes after the second war yet still the populace was expected to go to work, to pay its taxes and to keep its mouth shut. It was time to speak up.

Then some bright spark invented the electric guitar and amplifiers; suddenly young people were able to make an incredible racket. With only a modest stack of Marshall speakers, Jeff Beck could drown out the entire Duke Ellington orchestra or even Adolf Hitler at Nuremberg. And although early pop tunes were pretty innocent fare consisting of nursery melodies and fey lyrics; they also concealed sly hints at sex, discreet messages that only the young could hear. By the mid part of the decade, Dylan was telling us the times were changing, Barry McGuire was warning us we were on *The Eve of Destruction* and Hedgehoppers Anonymous were singing *It's Good News Week* with a lyric about dropping bombs, rotting flesh and contaminated atmospheres; heavy stuff and terribly affecting to an open minded teenager. The sounds of protest became a shriek of anger. Push the button? Why is there a button to push? How could it be moral degeneracy to poke a daisy down the barrel of a rifle?

The strands were being pulled together; the revolting young got it into their heads that with their noise, their underground press, their peacock clothes, their demonstrations and their ban the bomb, that they could actually restructure society. All we've got to do, they said, is march on Downing Street/the Pentagon/the Élysée Palace/the Berlin Wall; all we've got to do is stand together, join hands and the winds of change will blow. Power to the people.

And who will the generals be? Who would lead youth's army into the new sunrise? Who else could it be but The Beatles of course… and maybe the Rolling Stones and the Who, Sergeant Pepper and the Lonely Hearts Club Band leading legions of brightly hued teenagers into battle against the blue meanies. Of course, decades on, it seems the most naïve, stupid, cockamamie idea conceivable. These weren't military generals or revolutionaries; they weren't Fidel and Che; they were pop groups, mere entertainers, nightclub singers, musicians, effeminate, effete, ineffective and irrelevant. What the hell had they all been thinking a cynic could muse?

Poor beleaguered McCartney, time and time again, when asked to explain why the revolution never happened, as if it was somehow the fault of the Beatles or his fault *personally*, just responded, "I really don't think that we thought that we were going to change the world as much as *you* thought we were going to change the world… I mean we wanted 'business with pleasure' for ourselves and if we could get it for everyone else, great, we'd score it for them too. But I don't think changing the world was really in our minds. I think it came as a surprise to find that people thought we were changing the world".

Of course there was a lot more to it than 'business with pleasure' but it's a long time ago now and no one these days can quite put it into words. There was certainly something in the air and a lot of it had a hard edge; Lennon may have been bankrolling the IRA; he certainly financed the British black power movement.

It's easy to knock the silly hippies then and now; the perceived vacuity of the peace and love message, the rag bag peace movements, the Greenham Common 'wimmin', the empty slogans, the happenings and communes, the Krishnas in plimsolls, the bells and the beads, the dirt and the dole scrounging. It's easy to dismiss the 60s as irrelevant, just something that happened between the 50s and the 70s – or more accurately something that happened between about 1956 and 1973; that view has currency; where are your heroes now, now that Janis sells Mercedes and Jimi sells Pepsi? Time and a less anti capitalist vibe has put paid to all of them. No more heroes any more. Even the Beatles are for sale, their precious songs cast into jingles. The malls are the churches; the world is a market and we are all happy shoppers. The hippies/bohemians/mods/youth, whatever the tag, knew that they wanted society disassembled in the 60s, early 70s and they imagined that if it couldn't be anarchism or communism then at least it would be a liberal-led affair; what they hadn't figured was that it would be the political right that changed British society; that even after all the demos and peace marches, that despite all that sound and fury; the forces that did radically change the UK, would be led by Margaret Thatcher.

Yet despite McCartney's protestations and monstrous Maggie, there was a revolution; a few hippie students and their ilk were just the expressive front end of the sweeping desire of youth (and not just a few 'grown-ups') to have a new deal. There was a great groundswell of discontent, which when mixed with energy and optimism effected profound change in the mid 60s and onward; change that resonates today. In the USSR, the Beatles ignited a spark that set a fire, which brought down the Berlin Wall.

As that pivotal figure of the period, the artist, journalist, political activist and one-time manager of the Clash, Caroline Coon once excitedly pronounced: "We won".

There is of course the theory that, if nothing else, without the counterculture, things would now be considerably worse. Who knows how much the world has benefited from that particular injection of the *zeitgeist*? It's of course immeasurable. But the rebellion of the 60s undeniably planted seeds in many minds. The people will take to the streets if they think their basic human rights are being breached; they might need a bit of pushing but they will stir. London does riots.

On the downside we've come close to the nightmare vision of Aldous Huxley's *Brave New World*. We have genetic manipulation, the relentless pursuit of eternal adolescence, sexual liberation and the leisure society, all sorts of opium for the masses, the Age of Aquarius live on satellite. Anti-abortion campaigners blame the libertarians of that time for what they consider to be a licence to commit murder.

But the plusses abound; on the world stage, the efforts of 60s agitators to change the mind-sets of traditionally conservative politicians were largely successful. It looked nasty there for a while as the bomb dangled precariously over our heads but having opted not to destroy the world in the Cuba missile crisis, the super powers were only ever going one way, major disarmament and détente. They saw the madness of mutually assured destruction (MAD) and although it is still maintained, they have at least abandoned most of its overkill capacity, and the concept of using a nuclear weapon is now considered beyond the pale even for the most rabid US Republican.

Like the poor, small scale conventional violence is ever with us though and there are some highly unpleasant fire fights going on at the fringes of the great empires but largely, comparatively, the world is at peace.

So we won.

And that system, that set of philosophies, that trend in political and social thought, born in the 60s and refined in the decades since; that essentially peacenik vibe prevails. Job done. This largely explains the utter lack of interest that the bulk of the world's youth had (until Obama) in politics. What's the point? The imminent destruction of everything has been successfully averted; the great damaging ideologies of communism and facism have been defeated; our representatives are attempting to grapple with the state of the planet's ecology in a semi serious fashion. What's left to get upset about except a bit of small-scale genocide here and there, earthquakes, tsunamis, economic crashes and a famine or two? All the big issues are receiving various degrees of attention so why should we overly bother ourselves?

All those institutions that the flower children constructed: Amnesty International, Greenpeace, Friends of the Earth, Release, Shelter and their bastard offspring, Live Aid, Make Poverty History, Comic Relief, have in theory, on our behalves, been monitoring the politicos who on the whole have an aversion to being outed in the intense glare of publicity so as a consequence, in general, they behave themselves. The TV camera has become our instrument of inquisition. Politicians, much like show business celebrities, in fact rather too much like show business celebrities, live and die by it.

The 60s continue to cast a long shadow.

Pos/Neg: what was then a healthy mistrust of authority and organised religion has given rise to lack of respect for the police, teachers, A&E nurses and old people. Stroppy parents beget stroppy children and this anti-institution insolence, egged on by the media that could be said to have originated from a few disrespectful, over educated kids just being cheeky, is now endemic. As we sowed, so we have reaped.

The rampant pursuit of individualism just becomes selfishness. LSD was once used in a search for enlightment and meaning but today on the sink estates of London and Chicago, heroin, crack and binge drinking are used to seek oblivion.

We have a kind of Godless spirituality all around, the sort of wishy-washy New Age crackpot-ism, with its healing crystals and other bunkum that probably makes Richard Dawkins even angrier than God botherers.

It's the human condition to constantly quest for something to believe in and when people can't find it or even imagine what it might be then invariably they will find something else to fill the void; happy slapping, sex addiction or *Jerry Springer*. Could the real legacy be trashy media, Internet porn, drug addiction, drink abuse and selfishness all bequeathed by the 'do anything you wanna do' generation?

This is the task in a post-theistic society, to find some meaning above the pursuit of goods and the ownership of things. For many it is good causes and cleaning up the world, washing the face of Gaia before she washes us away. This is good and noble and keeps us off the street corners and if you can make a profit along the way so much the better. At least the monumental effort such a task entails is so exhausting and absorbing that it defers the moment when we have time to sit around and consider the awful possibility that our existences are pointless.

Yet there is tolerance and critical thinking and for many, the world is a better place.

Perhaps the most tangible legacy of it all is Silicon Valley, where the can-do T-shirt wearing non-conformist children of the hippies make money to live boho-chic, rock star lifestyles and drive low carbon impact cars while considering fresh ways to clean up our existence.

The very question, 'What is the legacy of the 60s?' only underlines its significance. We rarely ask the question what is the legacy of the 80s or 90s and any answer might well be brief. And even if you believe that the 60s provided nothing more than a crop of good music, then that at least is a legacy we can treasure.

WHO WAS WHO IN

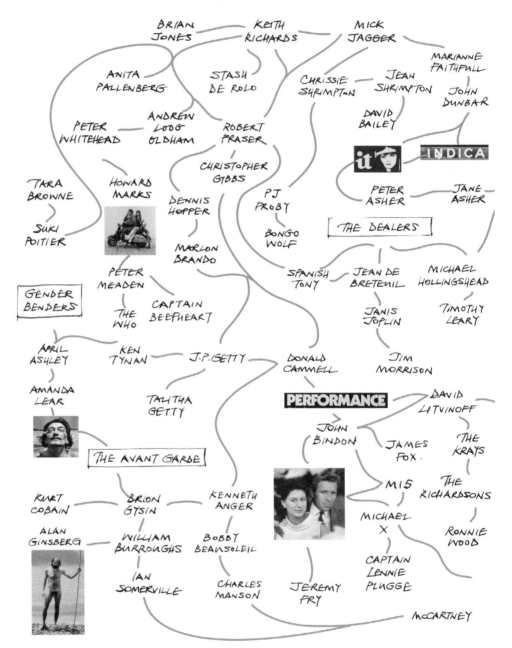

BRIAN JONES — KEITH RICHARDS — MICK JAGGER

MARIANNE FAITHFULL

ANITA PALLENBERG — STASH DE ROLO — CHRISSIE SHRIMPTON — JEAN SHRIMPTON — JOHN DUNBAR

DAVID BAILEY

PETER WHITEHEAD — ANDREW LOOG OLDHAM — ROBERT FRASER

it INDICA

CHRISTOPHER GIBBS

TARA BROWNE — HOWARD MARKS — DENNIS HOPPER — PJ PROBY — PETER ASHER — JANE ASHER

SUKI POITIER

THE DEALERS

MARLON BRANDO — BONGO WOLF

SPANISH TONY — JEAN DE BRETEUIL — MICHAEL HOLLINGSHEAD

PETER MEADEN

GENDER BENDERS

THE WHO — CAPTAIN BEEFHEART — JANIS JOPLIN — TIMOTHY LEARY

APRIL ASHLEY — KEN TYNAN — J.P. GETTY — DONALD CAMMELL — JIM MORRISON

AMANDA LEAR

PERFORMANCE — DAVID LITVINOFF

TALITHA GETTY

JOHN BINDON — JAMES FOX — THE KRAYS

THE AVANT GARDE

M15 — THE RICHARDSONS

KURT COBAIN — BRION GYSIN — KENNETH ANGER — MICHAEL X — RONNIE WOOD

ALAN GINSBERG — WILLIAM BURROUGHS — BOBBY BEAUSOLEIL

CAPTAIN LENNIE PLUGGE

IAN SOMERVILLE — CHARLES MANSON — JEREMY FRY — McCARTNEY

SWINGING LONDON

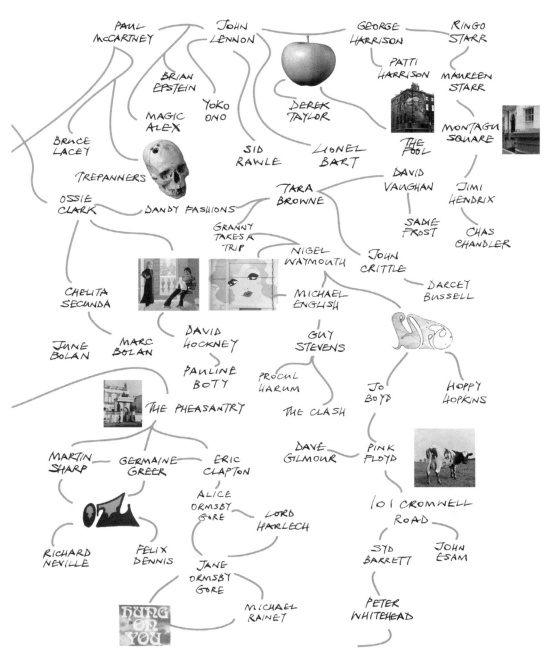

PAUL McCARTNEY

JOHN LENNON

GEORGE HARRISON

RINGO STARR

BRIAN EPSTEIN

PATTI HARRISON

MAUREEN STARR

MAGIC ALEX

YOKO ONO

DEREK TAYLOR

THE POOL

MONTAGU SQUARE

BRUCE LACEY

SID RAWLE

LIONEL BART

TREPANNERS

DAVID VAUGHAN

JIMI HENDRIX

OSSIE CLARK

DANDY FASHIONS

TARA BROWNE

SADIE FROST

CHAS CHANDLER

GRANNY TAKES A TRIP

NIGEL WAYMOUTH

JOHN CRITTLE

CHELITA SECUNDA

MICHAEL ENGLISH

DARCEY BUSSELL

JUNE BOLAN

MARC BOLAN

DAVID HOCKNEY

GUY STEVENS

PAULINE BOTY

PROCUL HARUM

JO BOYD

HOPPY HOPKINS

THE PHEASANTRY

THE CLASH

MARTIN SHARP

GERMAINE GREER

ERIC CLAPTON

DAVE GILMOUR

PINK FLOYD

ALICE ORMSBY GORE

101 CROMWELL ROAD

RICHARD NEVILLE

FELIX DENNIS

LORD HARLECH

SYD BARRETT

JOHN ESAM

JANE ORMSBY GORE

HUNG ON YOU

MICHAEL RAINEY

PETER WHITEHEAD

405

Guide to 60s London – Where was it at?

Crawdaddy Club, 1 Kew Road, Richmond

The Ship, Wardour Street, London WC2

The Ad Lib, 7 Leicester Place corner of Lisle Street

Cromwellian 3 Cromwell Road, SW7

Middle Earth 43 King Street Covent Garden WC2

Ricky Tick Thames Hotel, Barry Ave. Windsor

Bag o' Nails 8 - 9 Kingly Street, Soho W1

Kooks Kleek above the Railway Hotel 100 West End Lane NW6

The Flamingo 33-37 Wardour Street, W1

Blaises Imperial Hotel, 121 Queen's Gate, SW7

The Scene Ham Yard W1, 41 Great Windmill Street, WC2

The Scotch 13 Mason's Yard, SW1 now the Directors Lodge Club

The Speakeasy 48 Margaret Street W1

Marquee 90 Wardour Street W1

The Whisky 33-37 Wardour Street, W1

Happening 44 Gerrard Street, W1

Middle Earth 43 King Street, WC2

Hatchett's Playground 67 Piccadilly, W1

Revolution Club 14-16 Bruton Place

Tiles 79 Oxford Street, W1

UFO 31 Tottenham Court Road, W1

David Bowie's Arts lab - The Three Tuns pub (now The Rat and Parrot) in Beckenham High St.

100 Club, 100 Oxford Street, W1

Ronnie Scotts 47 Frith Street, W1

The Chelsea Set hangouts

The Pheasantry (now Pizza Express) 152 Kings Road SW3 4UT

Alvaro's (Mitre House) 124 Kings Road SW3 4TP (now Scribbler)

Club Dell'Aretusa (now Mamilanji members club) 107 Kings Road London SW3 4PA

Granny Takes a Trip - 488 Kings Road SW10 0LF

Hung On You (1st branch Cale Street, Chelsea Green) (2nd branch 430 Kings Road SW10 0LR)

Dandy Fashions (later Apple Tailoring) 161 Kings Road SW3 5TX now Paper Passions

Bazaar (Mary Quant) Markham House 138 Kings Road SW3 4UU

Chelsea Potter 119 Kings Road SW3 4PL

Markham Arms 138 Kings Road SW3 4XB now Abbey National

Chelsea Drug Store 49 Kings Road SW3 4ND

Chelsea Manor Studios Studio 4, 1-11 Flood Street – Sgt. Pepper sleeve photo

Eric Clapton's town pad 36a Old Church Street SW3 5BY

Sound Techniques Studio 46a Old Church Street

The Picasso 127 King's Road, London, SW3 4PW